# THE FIRST-TIME INVESTOR

### REVISED EDITION

# THE FIRST-TIME INVESTOR

REVISED EDITION

## BOB MADIGAN
## LAWRENCE KASOFF

**PRENTICE HALL PRESS**
New York    London    Toronto    Sydney    Tokyo

Copyright © 1986, 1987 by Prentice Hall Press
A Division of Simon & Schuster, Inc.
All rights reserved,
including the right of reproduction
in whole or in part in any form.

Published by Prentice Hall Press
A Division of Simon & Schuster, Inc.
Gulf + Western Building
One Gulf + Western Plaza
New York, NY 10023

PRENTICE HALL PRESS is a trademark of Simon & Schuster, Inc.

Library of Congress Cataloging-in-Publication Data

Madigan, Bob, 1949-
The first-time investor.

Bibliography: p.
Includes index.
1. Investments. I. Kasoff, Larry, 1949–
II. Title.
HG4521.M217   1987     332.6'78     87-14399
ISBN 0-13-942376-1

Manufactured in the United States of America

10 9 8 7 6 5 4 3

FROM BOB TO: *The Harmony in my life, she continues to be that!*

FROM LARRY TO: *My wife, Carmela; daughter, Melissa; parents, George and Isabel Kasoff; and my brother, Jan.*

# Acknowledgments

No one can write a book without help from numerous people, and this is no different. It would never had gotten off the ground without the introductions from Mike Schwager and the encouragement of our wonderful agent Anita Diamant and her staff, Robin, Al, and Robert.

First-time authors could not ask for better hand holding than we received from our original editor and project coordinator Robin Bartlett. He understood and allayed our fears.

Even though editor Paul Aron inherited this project, he treated it with the care he would show one of his own acquisitions and guided us over the remaining publishing hurdles. Thanks also to copyeditor Michael Moore.

We have a much better appreciation for visual and editorial presentation because of the hard work of Susan Tucker. Susan can sooth egos and smooth rough edges in a single bound.

Without the understanding of the NBC News and Operations divisions neither one of us would have been able to complete this book. We can't thank them all individually, but we do want to single out NBC News Vice-President Jim Farley; News Directors Shelley Lewis and Kevin Roche; Vice-President and General Manager, The Source, Willard Lochridge; and Vice-President and General Manager, NBC Radio Network, Craig Simon.

Our thanks also to Carrie Carmichael, Jeffrey Kestler, and Nick Sangiamo for their individual guidance.

—BOB MADIGAN
LARRY KASOFF

I would like to express my sincere appreciation to my wife Carmela for understanding the late nights without once checking my collar for lipstick. Her love and support helped me through some trying times. To my family and my mother-in-law Rosa Bonacia for their affection and direction. And, Bob, what can I say, but thanks for believing!

—LK

For my part there is one person who certainly deserves my deepest and most sincere gratitude, Richard R. Forster III, without whom I would still be wondering why you can't speak to a page and words don't simply appear. Rick taught me how to translate writing for the ear to writing for the eye! His dedication, constant guidance, and support made this book possible. And of course I can't forget both Ida Belle Mae, my faithful high-tech companion, and the real person behind it all, Robert J. Publicover, without whom there is no Bob Madigan.

—BM

# Contents

# Introduction

## THE RITES OF PASSAGE

We have all picked investment books off the shelf, thumbed through them, found one and thought, "Gee! that sounds like it has the answers"; fished into our pockets, found the cash, and carried the treasure home. That night with milk and cookies by the bed we started to read it, only to realize that we did not have the foggiest idea what the author was talking about. "Margin," "proxy" and "options" all appear without a second thought on the part of the financial expert or economics professor who penned the piece. Most of us think of convertibles as something made in Detroit and driven in warm weather, but not these investment authors. Their explanation makes them sound like something from NASA instead of Wall Street.

*The First-Time Investor* is directed to those who wish to do more than just get by, but who need a map to help them travel through the twisted maze of the financial and business world. Our purpose is not to educate university professors or to impress the wizards of Wall Street, but to help the novice become a successful initiate in the complex world of financial investment.

This book is aimed at you, the new investor, because you are beginning to realize that this is a world of limited resources and that if you hope to cash in later on you must begin to do something about it now. The main problem is that no one really takes a new investor seriously enough to help you get your foot in the door unless you have large sums of money to invest. If that is the case, doors will open suddenly, with smiling investment counselors and firms more than willing to help you spend the big bucks.

We will reveal just how the stock markets work; the reproductive cycles of stocks; and how you can help your investment family grow with Dividend Reinvestment Plans, Dollar Cost Averaging, and Leverage. These terms may sound strange right now, but like a foreign tongue it takes some understanding of the basics before you can carry on a decent conversation.

You will learn:

- How with only a few dollars to begin with you can actually get going and grow in a big way with different types of mutual and money market funds
- Why a retirement account is important even before you are old enough to drink booze and why IRA is more than the name of the deli owner
- What to look for in mortgages when buying that American Dream, your home, whether it is a house, a co-op or condo
- How to look at the financial page of the newspaper and untangle all those columns of figures
- The reasons why some people are enchanted with gold and silver and why others leave that to their dentists and jewelers to worry about

At the end of *The First-Time Investor* you will find a comprehensive glossary to help you deal with the wealth of terms, not only as you read this book, but also when you move on to more advanced publications and especially when you take on an active role in the world of investments.

We don't profess to know how to make anyone rich, but we can explain the tools needed and show how they are best used. Neither one of us is a registered broker; instead we are information brokers via a daily nationally broadcast radio program, "The Money Memo."

Bob Madigan is the financial and business correspondent for The Source, NBC's Young Adult Network. Larry Kasoff has been the Director of "The Money Memo" on The Source since its inception seven years ago. We decided to write this book after receiving cards and letters from listeners asking what books we might recommend for the beginner. They had come to us because through our broadcasts our audience realized that we not only know the principles we talk about every day but also have practiced them and know that they work. Both of us were once First-Time Investors, but we have learned a great deal through trial and error and hope you will benefit from our experiences.

*The First-Time Investor* is written for the individual who has little or no knowledge of investing. That person may be a doctor, lawyer, candlestick-maker, or student. Our job is to explain the fundamentals the other publications take for granted.

After reading this book, using its principles, and gaining some experience, you can dust off the others and understand their excellent expert advice. You will then have the tools necessary to join the rest of the world of investing.

## THE FIRST-TIME INVESTOR TEST

Get your pencils ready for a pop quiz. Don't worry if you didn't study; you should know the answers as well as you know yourself. That is because we are going to ask you about yourself. This is a test to see if you are indeed a First-Time Investor and to determine how much risk you can handle. Answer by circling the letter which does best describe you.

### Part One: Which Answer Best Describes You?

1. **A.** You have a $7,000,000 credit line with the same broker who, against his advice 15 years ago let you buy

McDonald's stock instead of just a burger and fries.

**B.** You joined Lee Iacocca in buying up depressed Chrysler stock before the turnaround and then sold when it had tripled.

**C.** Your idea of a stock exchange is asking the bartender to replace the celery in your Bloody Mary.

**D.** You think stock is something that belongs in a soup.

2. **A.** You spend the morning reading bank ads, searching for the best possible rate for your $25,000 Certificate of Deposit, which is about to mature.

**B.** You have just set up an electronic transfer from your Super-Now checking account to your money market fund.

**C.** To you a CD can be only one thing, a compact disc which provides the highest quality sound reproduction on earth.

**D.** You keep thousands of dollars in a regular checking account, so that you can get it right away in case of a rainy day.

3. **A.** Everyone at the bank knows your name, and even rushes to the door to offer you coffee and donuts as soon as you walk up.

**B.** You have run out of deposit slips for your MMDA.

**C.** You think a MMDA is a doctor who stutters.

**D.** You keep your money under your mattress.

4. **A.** The board of directors consults with you before deciding where to hold the annual meeting.

**B.** You bought a Blue Chip Stock three days before a three for one split was announced.

**C.** A split is something you keep trying to accomplish at aerobics class.

**D.** The only Blue Chips you have ever seen were the ones found in the bottom of the picnic basket this past winter.

5. **A.** The new wing for the Trust Department at the bank has been named after you.

**B.** Years ago you set up a Clifford Trust as a custodial account for your children.

**C.** The custodial account you deal with is for the janitor's Christmas gift.

**D.** When it comes to Savings and Loans, you have a better understanding of loans.

To score this quiz you get one point for each question you answered with an A or a B. Give yourself four points for each C answer and six points for each D. After you add them together if your score is 10 or under, you are a seasoned investor and certainly not a *First-Time Investor*; anything over that and you should certainly read on.

## Part Two: How Secure Are You in Handling Risk?

1. **A.** you can sleep alone without assuming the fetal position.
   **B.** You lock your doors at night.
   **C.** You lock doors, windows and your diary at night.
   **D.** You wake up in the middle of the night worried that your broker is living in Switzerland under an assumed name.
2. **A.** You keep your money in a stocking or sock in the top right-hand dresser drawer.
   **B.** You keep your money in a wall safe hidden behind a movable bookcase in the far corner of the attic.
   **C.** You have hired an armed guard to watch your house whenever you go to the store for a gallon of milk.
   **D.** You can't read mystery novels because you are afraid you might have done it.
3. **A.** You pack your bags as soon as you hear of a 3-week around-the-world trip on Kami-Kaze Airlines.
   **B.** You call another travel agent for a second opinion on the around-the-world trip.
   **C.** You worry all vacation that you left the iron on, and you don't own an iron.
   **D.** You use the in-flight telephone to reconfirm the reservations for the flight you are already aboard.
4. **A.** Your idea of fun is skydiving without carrying a backup parachute.
   **B.** You would put a portion of your life savings in a bank which is not federally insured.
   **C.** Just to make sure it is there, you look for the FDIC sticker on the bank window everytime you stop by to make a deposit.
   **D.** You look both ways before crossing the living room.

5. **A.** As a contestant on a TV game show your choice is to take $10,000 and run, or give it up and go for a super tough question and win $100,000. Without batting an eye you put it all on the line and try for the question.
**B.** On the same TV game show your choice is again to take the $10,000 and leave, or answer one more question to double your winnings. You go for the question.
**C.** You take the money and run without any more questions.
**D.** You don't even appear on the show, afraid you won't win anything.

6. **A.** The stock you bought 5 months ago has taken a nose dive. You buy more right away, figuring it looked good originally and the price is even better now.
**B.** You will wait another week before deciding if you want to buy more.
**C.** You sell right away, so you won't be bothered by any more losses.
**D.** You don't dare move without permission from a broker because you are afraid that if you sell now, it will go up next week.

7. **A.** Five months after you bought a stock, it doubles in price. You buy more because you have a gut feeling it is on a roll.
**B.** You sit tight, in the hope it will continue to climb.
**C.** You sell half and keep the original amount of the investment intact.
**D.** You sell it all, taking the profits now before it slips an inch.

8. **A.** You put your IRA in an aggressive speculative growth fund, hoping it will double every year.
**B.** You put your IRA in a Balanced Mutual Fund, realizing there might be a chance the fund could lose as well as gain.
**C.** You put your IRA in a conservative Bond Fund.
**D.** You put your IRA in ten-year CDs with a locked-in, guaranteed yield.

Now score yourself. For every A answer give yourself 1 point; for every B, 2 points; for every C, 3 points; and for every D, 4 points.

If you scored between 8 and 16 points, you can handle almost any kind of investment risk; you could be an aggressive investor. But don't be too cocky, because you could be blindsided by foolish risks.

A score of between 16 and 24 points shows that you would be willing to take calculated risks with your investments.

Finally, if you scored more than 24 points you are not a risk taker, but a conservative investor. If you plan to use a broker or investment counselor, find one who shares the same philosophy. This doesn't mean you will always be so conservative; once you have gained some knowledge and have some experience under your belt (and in your wallet) you may gain the confidence to take some risks. *The First-Time Investor* can certainly help you in that respect.

## THE FIRST-TIME INVESTOR FISCAL EXAM

Most of us have no idea how much we are really worth, and how much money there may be available for actual investing. In order to help you get a handle on your own fiscal condition, we have come up with a fill-in-the-blanks Fiscal Exam.

### INCOME

| | You | Spouse | Total |
|---|---|---|---|
| 1. Employment Income | | | |
| Take-Home Pay | ___ | ___ | ___ |
| Commissions | ___ | ___ | ___ |
| Other | ___ | ___ | ___ |
| Total Employment Income | ___ | ___ | ___ |
| 2. Investment Income | | | |
| Interest (taxable) | ___ | ___ | ___ |

| | | | |
|---|---|---|---|
| Interest (non-taxable) | _____ | _____ | _____ |
| Dividends | _____ | _____ | _____ |
| Trust Fund | _____ | _____ | _____ |
| Other | _____ | _____ | _____ |
| Total Investment Income | _____ | _____ | _____ |
| Total All Income | _____ | _____ | _____ |

Now that you know how much you have to spend, you are asking the musical question:

## WHERE DOES IT ALL GO?

Housing

    Mortgage or Rent        _____

    Property Taxes        _____

    Insurance        _____

    Utilities        _____

    Other Housing Costs        _____

Total Housing Costs        _____

Food        _____

Clothing        _____

Transportation

    Car Payments        _____

    Insurance        _____

    Gasoline        _____

    Repairs        _____

    Other Transportation        _____

Total Transportation Costs        _____

Phone        _____

Household Cleaning and Supplies        _____

Household repair and upgrade   _____

Personal Care (including health clubs)   _____

Health and Dental Insurance   _____

Life Insurance   _____

Other Insurance   _____

Credit Card Payments   _____

Charitable Contributions   _____

Other Lifestyle costs (yard work, etc.)   _____

TOTAL BASIC LIFESTYLE EXPENDITURES   _____

Divide by 12 for Average Monthly Costs   _____

Of course we all spend more than that, and that is why we also have another category:

## DISCRETIONARY SPENDING

Entertainment   _____

Eating Out   _____

Vacations   _____

Hobbies   _____

Personal Gifts   _____

Home Improvements (inside & out)   _____

Extra car, boat, or bike   _____

Personal Loan Payments   _____

IRA   _____

Keogh   _____

Pension (401-k)   _____

Other   _____

_____   _____

_____   _____

Total Discretionary Spending      _____

Divide by 12 for Average Monthly Spending    _____

*Now let's put all of that information together:*

Take-Home Income      _____

Spending

   Basic Lifestyle      _____

   Discretionary      _____

Total Spending      _____ subtract

What's Left . . . or What Isn't      _____

## What Are You Really Worth?

Now that you know how much money comes in and goes out, how much of it has stuck and can be counted as your net worth?

### WHAT YOU OWN

Liquid Assets

   Cash (checking, savings accounts)    _____

   Short Term Investments    _____

   Money Market Funds    _____

   Cash Value of Life Insurance    _____

      TOTAL Liquid Assets    _____

Investment Assets

   Treasury Bills    _____

   Certificates of Deposit    _____

   Marketable securities

     Stocks    _____

Bonds          _____

Real Estate (investment)     _____

Retirement funds        _____

     TOTAL Investment Assets        _____

Personal Assets

    Home (current market price)    _____

    Vacation Property      _____

    Furnishings         _____

    Art, Antiques        _____

    Cars, Trucks, Boats     _____

    Other           _____

     TOTAL Personal Assets        _____

     TOTAL Assets            _____

## WHAT YOU OWE TO OTHERS

Short Term Debts

    Credit Card Balances     _____

    Installment Loans      _____

    Personal Loans       _____

    Other Obligations

_____      _____

_____      _____

     TOTAL Short Term Debts      _____

Long Term Debts

    Car Loans          _____

    Home Mortgage      _____

    Investment Loans      _____

     TOTAL Long Term Debts        _____

TOTAL Liabilities                                    _____

TOTAL ASSETS                                         _____

TOTAL DEBTS          (subtract from Assets)          _____

YOUR NET WORTH                                       _____

Most people don't realize how much they are really worth, and are rather impressed with the figure, unless of course it is a negative net worth. If that is the case, you should spend your time trying to rebuild your fiscal fitness and worry about investing later.

# 1

# In the Beginning, Someone Created the MONEY

We all start off as virgins, in everything we do. It's a fact of life.

Another fact of life: you *never* forget your *first*; you may want to, but you never do. So, if you can avoid suffering, why not make your first-time investing a wonderful experience. The secret is to watch and then to learn from those who have the experience.

When it comes to *money*, the people to watch are the ones who have found ways to entice their little riches to procreate. Money isn't at all like rabbits; you have to do more than leave it alone for a few minutes to make it multiply. Money must be carefully caressed before it will respond.

The first step toward getting ahead financially is to acquire some money. How you get it can be just as titillating as your earliest fantasies. Don't let the acquisition of your fantasy become a chore; instead, anticipate the wonderful sensual feelings that come with the exhilaration of conquest and the excitement of fulfillment. But this is not *investus interruptus*; what you do with it later is also our concern.

Rule Number One is Take Care of Number One! Rule

1

Number Two is never forget that Rule Number One takes care of all the other rules. Before you can play around as a First-Time Investor, you must first make sure that you are sure of yourself. In other words, you must have enough money to live on, to take care of current expenses, and to pay off past bills. You should not consider making your first investment until you have assured your basic independence; it is the foundation of any really satisfying relationship.

Next, you need to determine your financial goals. Be sure to make those ultimate goals lofty, but create some easy intermediate goals so that you feel as if you are at least on the way to financial fulfillment and freedom. Even if you are only hoping to create enough of a nest egg to buy that first nest, you need to begin somewhere. It must be created, just as an initial investment in anything must be created. You could be thinking ahead to creating a college fund for your children, or you may want to create an impressive portfolio (the total of all of your investments) for your later years. If you have already started building toward any of these goals and have some money put aside, you may wish to skip a few chapters of our treasure map; otherwise, follow the clues so we can help you discover some rewards.

---

### Your Personal $$ Memo: Financial Goals

Financial goals should be set for three major areas:

1. Meeting and controlling regular expenditures such as food, clothing and housing.
2. Short term goals which include, among other things, cars, stereo gear and vacations.
3. Long term goals require early planning and constant attention so you will be prepared for college costs, retirement and, of course, investments.

---

No matter what your ambition may be, there must be a first bold move. Remember the nagging question that shadowed your first date, "Should we or should we not kiss?" Someone had to make the decision; someone had to make the first move or you would have ended up with nothing more than severe frustration. Investing, like love, needs a starting action, and, believe us, it's less frightening than the first kiss. It is simply forcing yourself to begin saving toward a goal. Preferably your first goal will be a special savings account which you will *not* touch for any reason other than to make it bigger.

## Your First Investment Is You!

Remember, we said you will never forget your "first"; well, why not make your "first" YOU! In other words, please yourself first by making yourself *number one*; pay *yourself* first every month. If you find such pleasure painful, consider having that payment taken out of your paycheck at work through a payroll savings plan. When you don't see the money, you are not tempted to spend it.

Another way to do it may seem easier said than done, until you have tried it for several months in a row. As you sit down to pay your bills each month, write the first check to yourself. Put that money into a savings vehicle of some sort. (Don't get too excited; we will unveil more about savings vehicles later.)

## Try It! You'll Like It!

After you have done this for several months, it will begin to feel so good you will wonder why you hadn't been doing it all along. Experience shows that if you try to pay all the other bills first, there won't be enough money left over to pay yourself. Just as you are committed to paying off a credit card balance, your financial future is also a commitment that you must honor. So, pay yourself first, even if it means you only make minimum payments to credit accounts. Of course you should avoid carrying credit balances whenever possible, but even if you do, don't put off paying yourself first. You need to develop the discipline right now, while you are getting your financial house in order. This is not being negatively selfish; it is being positively brilliant.

The plan now is to build that special savings fund to the point where it equals 3 or more months of take-home pay. It seems like a farfetched fantasy, but this can and must come true. When it does become a fiscal reality, you will tingle with excitement. This savings fund is your emergency stash of cash. It represents a commitment to yourself, a basis for financial freedom. You will feel more confident in those first vital moves when you finally get to the point of investing. This fund is sometimes called *sleep insurance* because it allows you to have pleasant dreams. This 3-month stash of cash (equal to 3 months' take home pay) is nothing more than a safety net that you know is available should anything happen. Because this money is for emergencies, it must be in some type of account that is *liquid* (i.e., where you can get at the money rapidly with very little hassle).

Warning: Using this money for anything other than a serious emergency can be hazardous to your financial health. In other words, you must promise yourself that this fund is to be used *only* in the case of serious financial strain and only when no other resources are available. "But wait!" you say, "I don't have a 3-month safety net and I want to start investing now!" Okay, that is simple, you just need to recognize that the money you are saving for the "rainy day" *is* an investment. You are protecting yourself while at the same time you are investing in yourself. You are investing in your dream castle. It is just like planting a tomato patch in the garden; you need the seeds first before you can expect anything to grow, and they need fertilizer to flourish. In your case, the fertilizer is your "will power" to accomplish this objective. By being patient you are also learning the disciplines necessary for putting money aside to invest.

It's nice to have that psychological and financial comfort

before you risk your hard-earned money by investing. "Risk? Did someone say *risk*?" That is correct; investing is a risk. However, there is little or no risk in a savings account, whether it be a passbook account or Money Market Deposit Account, as long as the bank or savings institution is insured through the Federal Deposit Insurance Corporation (FDIC) or the Federal Savings and Loan Insurance Corporation (FSLIC).

## Cutting Costs

Many experts suggest that if you want to make meaningful investments you should put aside 15 percent of your take home pay. "Fifteen per cent! Are you crazy?" Just bear with us for a minute.

There are ways to cut your spending so that your sacrifices won't hurt as much. You might take a look at your budget and realize that you eat up more than 15 percent of your take home pay just by eating at fast-food restaurants, buying clothes, and entertaining yourself.

Of course! There it is! That nasty hole in your pocket and it seems so easy to sew it up. Quick, grab the thread and you will not have lost the money that you intend to save. It's easy: Simply cut out new clothes, movies, records, burgers and fries. Right? Wrong! That would mean your life would be miserable and you would resent saving or investing. The idea is to cut out a little bit from each part of your living expenses. If it means one less movie or album every so often, so be it. Remember, you have a goal.

There is nothing that says you have to suffer to save. Just be a bit more prudent. Watch for sales, clip grocery coupons, buy in quantity and stash those savings. Of course a "40% Off Sale" doesn't save a penny if you don't need the item. If you really need something, then start looking for the sale. *Need* is of course a relative term. Many of us live in the "Need Generation." We need to impress everyone that we are a success. We need to have a fancy address, we need fancy designer clothes, and of course we need a fancy sports car in order to advertise our success.

Hey, you worked hard to get to where you are. You deserve those trappings of success. Right? Well, think about it. Consider that the word *trappings* includes the word *trap*. Are you trapped by your trappings? Have any of them given you great pleasure recently? Did you feel wonderful as you made out that huge rent or mortgage check? Did the name-brand jeans help you get the love you were looking for? Does your mechanic love you more than you love your car? Do the dollars you throw that way really make you feel good? If some of your answers are an unqualified "Yes!" maybe you need to find another area in which to trim your expenses in order to fatten your reserves.

Maybe you suffer from Gadget Disease. Symptoms include spending hundreds, even thousands of dollars on every new gadget, from watches that chime, calculate, and vibrate to an $80 electronic automatic nailpolish remover. We are sure each one of those gadgets gave moments of extreme pleasure, but nothing long term. Take a mental trip to your garage or closet; can you find more than three things that you bought in the past year that you used more than once or twice?

We must be aware that many of us have been turned into impulse buyers. We are turned on by flashy signs, beautiful displays and the nagging fear that we may be missing out on a great score.

Be strong, protect yourself. Don't carry more cash than you need in order to meet your already programmed expenses, leave your blank checks at home, and seriously consider plastic surgery (cutting up credit cards).

### Fight the "I Wants!"

A very effective way to avoid the meaningless instant gratification of impulse buying is to work from a list. When you feel you just *need* to have something, put it on your Wants and Needs list. Decide which items are most important and buy those first. We can almost guarantee that everytime you jot something down you will scratch off several earlier entries. That's because you will begin to realize your true needs as soon as you can visualize them. Wants and needs are not the same even though at times they seem that way, so this list will help you separate one from the other.

Of course the major benefit of the Wants and Needs list is an immediate saving of money. Remember that you are supposed to add each and every item to the list before you buy it. That can be a problem considering you may not be carrying the list with you. This is the key that makes this system work. If you can't add the item to the list until you get home, you may lose interest in it before it even makes the list. This little exercise helps you over the impulse hump. *Shoppus interruptus*.

You might want to keep track of all of your nickel and dime expenditures by jotting them down as they occur. A calendar notebook is perfect for this exercise. Soon you will realize how much you spend, and just as importantly it will help you recognize just how important any one purchase is.

Food? Shopping lists play a double money-saving role at the supermarket. First, you become a more organized shopper, and second, you know exactly what you will and will not buy. It saves you from having to depend on your "will power" by giving you "won't power." You *won't* buy anything unless it's on the list. The other cash-saving benefit of a list is that it reminds you which money-saving coupons you should clip and carry with you. For a number of years we have been the grocery-shopping partners in our respective families, and at first people laughed when we started clipping coupons. But in the end we laughed all the way to the bank. You can sometimes save 10 to 20 percent at the Super-Mark-Up checkout counter by saving and swapping coupons. It doesn't take long to clip them, and by keeping a shopping list you learn very fast which ones are good for you and which ones are good for swapping. Some grocery stores offer "Double Value" on coupons; others have coupon swap bins where you exchange the ones you don't need for some you can use. Other places to look for coupon swap bins are day care centers, community centers or the neighborhood library. If you save your grocery receipts, you will begin to notice the savings. Put that amount aside for your investments. It may not seem like much, but it only takes a little cut from each budget item before adding up to real money.

---

## Coupon Clipping

Like the rest of my family and friends, you may be chuckling under your breath about coupon clipping, saying, "Right! Sure! Ah-hah! This guy's had his hair clipped too short!"

Skepticism is healthy, but so is saving money. As soon as I realized how effective the system could be and had tried it for several weeks, it became second nature. Whenever I read the newspaper or magazines I always kept two things by my side. One was a pair of scissors, the other an envelope to hold the coupons. When I saw a coupon for something I would buy anyway, I clipped it and saved it. The next time I made out my shopping list I would match the coupons against the list.

My regular supermarket helped a great deal by offering "Double Coupon Days" when each of those seemingly worthless little pieces of paper took on a serious value. The checkout clerk helped next by adding the coupons together and subtracting the amount from the grocery total. That gave me instant evidence of how much I had saved. In the beginning it was only a few dollars, but as I became more adept at coupon shopping I could sometimes save up to $25 a week. All on items I would have bought anyway.

The most crucial step in this process was to remember to write 2 *checks* at the checkout register. The first of course to the supermarket for the groceries, the second to myself for my investment account. It didn't take long before the investment account was building and even my then 7-year-old daughter, Harmony, was keeping an eye out for coupons for me.

—Bob

Another savings vehicle is to shop smarter and buy your favorite products only when they are on sale. If you have the room, why not buy a 6-month supply. Of course you do have to be sure that the item has a longer than 6-month shelf life, but things like toilet paper and paper towels live forever. Depending on the size of your family, it's possible to save between $500 and $1,000 a year just by stocking up on such items as shampoo and cosmetics during sales and using those money-off coupons. You didn't have to give up anything, did you?

There is also no reason why you can't buy beer or wine by the case, fly on discount fares, burn no-name gasoline and ask your doctor to prescribe generic drugs.

You are not only saving money, but it's like earning it tax free. Think of it this way: It's easier to save a dollar than to replace one already spent. Remember, Uncle Sam always wants a piece of the action, so before you get to keep just one buck you may have to earn two new dollars.

Another way to fill your coffers is to empty your pockets. Why not save your loose change every night and every so often roll those pennies, nickels and quarters into greenbacks. When these new saving habits are added together, the money will add up faster than you might think.

## Green Thumbs

Before anything can grow and flourish, seeds must be planted. There are many fertile spots to leave your dollar seeds, among them:

Banks
Savings and Loans
Credit Unions
Money Market Mutual Funds
Mutual Funds
Stock Markets
Bond Markets
Real Estate

The list goes on. Just remember that there are pros and cons with each investment because each one is a risk. You need to know and understand those risks, and *The First-Time Investor* is designed to help you recognize and minimize them.

We will show you why researching and understanding each investment yourself is so very important, even when you have the help of an expert. It is amazing that each and every one of us might spend weeks or months researching the pros and cons of certain refrigerators before buying one, but when it comes to investing we hear a tip and often hand over our money to a broker without thinking twice, or even once. Remember, it is your money, something you worked very hard to earn, so don't just scatter it to the wind without checking the weather forecast first. Right now everything may seem foggy but it will begin to clear on the pages to come.

## Life and Death

Just wanted to get your attention! None of these decisions so far have been life or death ones, but this one is. Do you have your family protected? In a sense you are gambling not only with your own future, but with theirs as well. Please look into some sort of Term Life Insurance policy to cover them, should anything happen to you. It is important that you buy only straight life insurance. To be blunt, what you are buying is not Life Insurance, but Death Insurance. It pays only when you die; there are no retirement benefits or promises of future riches. Do not buy Whole Life, only Term. How much insurance you buy depends on how much income you estimate your family will need and for how long. Of course, if no one will need your financial support, you can easily get by with a simple burial policy that pays for all those expenses. One hopes it won't be your only chance to ride in a Cadillac.

# 2

# Where to Stash the Cash

Congratulations! You have finally made up your mind to put your money to work somewhere. This commitment to yourself is probably the biggest dividend you will ever receive. You are well on your way.

To start saving for your financial future there are two roads you can take on our financial map. Each has advantages and disadvantages. The road that you take should be comfortable and conform to your lifestyle.

If you take the first road, the first stop is probably only a short distance from home. It's your bank or savings and loan. Either institution offers a number of interesting places to stash your cash. They include those old standby passbook savings accounts, interest-bearing checking accounts (Now Accounts), Money Market Deposit Accounts (MMDAs), Certificates of Deposit (CDs) and Savings Bonds, all of which we'll discuss in this chapter.

The second road that you should consider is not at all like

11

a bank; there is no building to admire and no people to sit down with to discuss your financial picture. As a matter of fact, most transactions in it are done by mail or on the phone. We are talking about Money Market Mutual Funds. They are another type of savings vehicle, where you can park your money for however long you wish and still earn high interest rates. We will explain in the next chapter how to save in a money market fund after we first check out the more familiar banks and savings and loans.

### You Can Bank on It

Until recently banks were very predictable; they all offered the same savings services and paid the same amount of interest. The banks had no choice; the interest rates were set by law. Now that the institutions are being deregulated, about the only things that are consistent are deposits being insured up to $100,000 and passbook savings accounts that don't pay very much. Your traditional passbook account still pays only around 5½ percent.

It doesn't take a mathematical whiz to realize that you can't make a whole lot of money when you are earning slightly more than $5 a year for every $100 you have in the bank. The banks know you want to make more, and now they can give you that chance. Under deregulation they are offering a variety of savings devices which will pay you higher interest rates. Just how much higher depends on each institution's strategy and personality.

This is where the pressure is going to be on you. You will need to ask a number of important questions while you shop for the best deal. For instance, what is the interest rate? Followed by, how is the interest paid?

# The Power of Compounding

Of course interest is paid in spendable currency, but the way it is applied can make the difference between making a lot of money and only a few pennies. Many banks pay only *simple* interest on small accounts, which means they pay the interest only once and that is at the end of the term.

Other banks *compound* your interest, either daily, weekly, or monthly, adding to your account whatever interest is earned on the money, creating a new and larger principal which in turn can earn even more money.

Benjamin Franklin understood the concept of compounding when he said, "Money makes money and the money that money makes makes more money."

$1,000 deposited at 10 percent and left alone would look like this at the end of one year:

| Compounded Annually | Compounded Daily |
| :---: | :---: |
| $1,100 | $1,105.46 |

It may not seem like that much of a difference, but when added to and compounded over a period of years the gap between the two figures widens considerably.

You can get an idea of which kind of interest the institution pays by simply looking at its ads. These advertisements usually quote two interest figures, the effective yield and an annualized yield. The effective yield is the stated rate of interest, the annual yield is the maximum return that can be earned on deposits of more than one year. If both figures are the same it means the institution pays simple interest. If the annualized yield is higher than the effective yield, it probably means the interest is compounded.

## WHAT $1,000 DEPOSITED ANNUALLY WILL GROW TO IN A GIVEN NUMBER OF YEARS

### % INCREASE COMPOUNDED ANNUALLY

| Year | 5% | 6% | 7% | 8% | 9% | 10% | 11% | 12% |
|------|------|------|------|------|------|------|------|------|
| 1 | $ 1,050 | $ 1,060 | $ 1,070 | $ 1,080 | $ 1,090 | $ 1,100 | $ 1,110 | $ 1,120 |
| 2 | 2,153 | 2,183 | 2,215 | 2,246 | 2,278 | 2,310 | 2,342 | 2,374 |
| 3 | 3,310 | 3,374 | 3,440 | 3,506 | 3,573 | 3,641 | 3,710 | 3,779 |
| 4 | 4,526 | 4,637 | 4,751 | 4,867 | 4,985 | 5,105 | 5,228 | 5,353 |
| 5 | 5,802 | 5,975 | 6,153 | 6,336 | 6,523 | 6,716 | 6,913 | 7,115 |
| 6 | 7,142 | 7,394 | 7,654 | 7,923 | 8,200 | 8,487 | 8,783 | 9,089 |
| 7 | 8,549 | 8,897 | 9,260 | 9,637 | 10,028 | 10,436 | 10,859 | 11,300 |
| 8 | 10,027 | 10,491 | 10,978 | 11,488 | 12,021 | 12,579 | 13,164 | 13,776 |
| 9 | 11,578 | 12,181 | 12,816 | 13,487 | 14,193 | 14,937 | 15,722 | 16,549 |
| 10 | 13,207 | 13,972 | 14,784 | 15,645 | 16,560 | 17,531 | 18,561 | 19,655 |
| 11 | 14,917 | 15,870 | 16,888 | 17,977 | 19,141 | 20,384 | 21,713 | 23,133 |
| 12 | 16,713 | 17,882 | 19,141 | 20,495 | 21,953 | 23,523 | 25,212 | 27,029 |
| 13 | 18,599 | 20,015 | 21,550 | 23,215 | 25,019 | 26,975 | 29,095 | 31,393 |
| 14 | 20,579 | 22,276 | 24,129 | 26,152 | 28,361 | 30,772 | 33,405 | 36,280 |
| 15 | 22,657 | 24,673 | 26,888 | 29,324 | 32,003 | 34,950 | 38,190 | 41,753 |
| 16 | 24,840 | 27,213 | 29,840 | 32,750 | 35,974 | 39,545 | 43,501 | 47,884 |
| 17 | 27,132 | 29,906 | 32,999 | 36,450 | 40,301 | 44,599 | 49,396 | 54,750 |
| 18 | 29,539 | 32,760 | 36,379 | 40,446 | 45,018 | 50,159 | 55,939 | 62,440 |
| 19 | 32,066 | 35,786 | 39,995 | 44,762 | 50,160 | 56,275 | 63,203 | 71,052 |
| 20 | 34,719 | 38,993 | 43,865 | 49,423 | 55,765 | 63,002 | 71,265 | 80,699 |
| 21 | 37,505 | 42,392 | 48,006 | 54,457 | 61,873 | 70,403 | 80,214 | 91,503 |
| 22 | 40,430 | 45,996 | 52,436 | 59,893 | 68,532 | 78,543 | 90,148 | 103,603 |
| 23 | 43,502 | 49,816 | 57,177 | 65,765 | 75,790 | 87,497 | 101,174 | 117,155 |
| 24 | 46,727 | 53,865 | 62,149 | 72,106 | 83,701 | 97,347 | 113,413 | 132,334 |
| 25 | 50,113 | 58,156 | 67,676 | 78,954 | 92,324 | 108,182 | 126,999 | 149,334 |

| Year | 13% | 14% | 15% | 16% | 17% | 18% | 19% | 20% |
|---|---|---|---|---|---|---|---|---|
| 1 | $ 1,130 | $ 1,140 | $ 1,150 | $ 1,160 | $ 1,170 | $ 1,180 | $ 1,190 | $ 1,200 |
| 2 | 2,407 | 2,440 | 2,473 | 2,506 | 2,539 | 2,572 | 2,606 | 2,640 |
| 3 | 3,850 | 3,921 | 3,993 | 4,066 | 4,141 | 4,215 | 4,291 | 4,368 |
| 4 | 5,480 | 5,610 | 5,742 | 5,877 | 6,014 | 6,154 | 6,297 | 6,442 |
| 5 | 7,323 | 7,536 | 7,754 | 7,977 | 8,207 | 8,442 | 8,683 | 8,930 |
| 6 | 9,405 | 9,730 | 10,067 | 10,414 | 10,772 | 11,142 | 11,523 | 11,916 |
| 7 | 11,757 | 12,233 | 12,729 | 13,240 | 13,773 | 14,326 | 14,902 | 15,499 |
| 8 | 14,416 | 15,085 | 15,786 | 16,519 | 17,285 | 18,086 | 18,923 | 19,799 |
| 9 | 17,420 | 18,337 | 19,304 | 20,321 | 21,393 | 22,521 | 23,709 | 24,959 |
| 10 | 20,814 | 22,045 | 23,349 | 24,733 | 26,200 | 27,755 | 29,404 | 31,150 |
| 11 | 24,650 | 26,271 | 28,002 | 29,850 | 31,824 | 33,931 | 36,180 | 38,581 |
| 12 | 28,985 | 31,089 | 33,352 | 35,786 | 38,404 | 41,219 | 44,244 | 47,497 |
| 13 | 33,883 | 36,581 | 39,505 | 42,672 | 46,103 | 49,818 | 53,841 | 58,196 |
| 14 | 39,417 | 42,842 | 46,580 | 50,660 | 55,110 | 59,965 | 65,261 | 71,035 |
| 15 | 45,671 | 49,980 | 54,717 | 59,925 | 65,649 | 71,939 | 78,850 | 86,442 |
| 16 | 52,739 | 58,118 | 64,075 | 70,673 | 77,979 | 86,068 | 95,022 | 104,931 |
| 17 | 60,725 | 67,394 | 74,836 | 83,141 | 92,406 | 102,740 | 114,266 | 127,117 |
| 18 | 69,749 | 77,969 | 87,212 | 97,603 | 109,285 | 122,414 | 137,166 | 153,740 |
| 19 | 79,947 | 90,025 | 101,444 | 114,380 | 129,033 | 145,628 | 164,418 | 185,688 |
| 20 | 91,470 | 103,768 | 117,810 | 133,841 | 152,139 | 178,021 | 196,847 | 224,026 |
| 21 | 104,491 | 119,436 | 136,682 | 156,415 | 179,172 | 205,345 | 235,438 | 270,031 |
| 22 | 119,205 | 137,297 | 158,276 | 182,601 | 210,801 | 243,487 | 281,362 | 325,237 |
| 23 | 135,831 | 157,659 | 183,168 | 212,978 | 247,808 | 288,494 | 336,010 | 391,484 |
| 24 | 154,620 | 180,871 | 211,793 | 248,214 | 291,105 | 341,603 | 401,042 | 470,981 |
| 25 | 175,850 | 207,333 | 244,712 | 289,088 | 341,763 | 404,272 | 478,431 | 566,377 |

Source: No-Load Fund Investor, Inc., Hastings-on-Hudson, N.Y.

## WHAT $10,000 WILL BE WORTH IN A GIVEN NUMBER OF YEARS

### % INCREASE COMPOUNDED ANNUALLY

| Year | 5% | 6% | 7% | 8% | 9% | 10% | 11% | 12% |
|---|---|---|---|---|---|---|---|---|
| 1 | $ 10,500 | $ 10,600 | $ 10,700 | $ 10,800 | $ 10,900 | $ 11,000 | $ 11,100 | $ 11,200 |
| 2 | 11,025 | 11,236 | 11,449 | 11,664 | 11,881 | 12,100 | 12,321 | 12,544 |
| 3 | 11,576 | 11,910 | 12,250 | 12,597 | 12,950 | 13,310 | 13,676 | 14,049 |
| 4 | 12,155 | 12,625 | 13,108 | 13,605 | 14,116 | 14,641 | 15,181 | 15,735 |
| 5 | 12,763 | 13,382 | 14,026 | 14,693 | 15,586 | 16,105 | 16,851 | 17,623 |
| 6 | 13,401 | 14,185 | 15,007 | 15,869 | 16,771 | 17,716 | 18,704 | 19,738 |
| 7 | 14,071 | 15,036 | 16,058 | 17,138 | 18,280 | 19,487 | 20,762 | 22,107 |
| 8 | 14,775 | 15,938 | 17,182 | 18,509 | 19,926 | 21,436 | 23,046 | 24,760 |
| 9 | 15,513 | 16,895 | 18,385 | 19,990 | 21,719 | 23,579 | 25,580 | 27,731 |
| 10 | 16,289 | 17,908 | 19,672 | 21,589 | 23,674 | 25,937 | 28,394 | 31,058 |
| 11 | 17,103 | 18,983 | 21,049 | 23,316 | 25,804 | 29,531 | 31,518 | 34,785 |
| 12 | 17,959 | 20,122 | 22,522 | 25,182 | 28,127 | 31,384 | 34,984 | 38,960 |
| 13 | 18,856 | 21,329 | 24,098 | 27,196 | 30,658 | 34,523 | 38,833 | 43,635 |
| 14 | 19,799 | 22,609 | 25,785 | 29,372 | 33,417 | 37,974 | 43,104 | 48,871 |
| 15 | 20,789 | 23,966 | 27,590 | 31,722 | 36,425 | 41,772 | 47,846 | 54,736 |
| 16 | 21,829 | 25,404 | 29,522 | 34,259 | 39,703 | 45,950 | 53,109 | 61,304 |
| 17 | 22,920 | 26,928 | 31,589 | 37,000 | 43,276 | 50,545 | 58,951 | 68,660 |
| 18 | 24,066 | 28,543 | 32,799 | 39,960 | 47,171 | 55,599 | 65,436 | 76,900 |
| 19 | 25,270 | 30,256 | 36,165 | 43,157 | 51,416 | 61,159 | 72,633 | 86,128 |
| 20 | 26,533 | 32,071 | 28,697 | 46,609 | 56,044 | 67,274 | 80,623 | 96,463 |
| 21 | 27,860 | 33,996 | 41,406 | 50,338 | 61,088 | 74,002 | 89,492 | 108,038 |
| 22 | 29,253 | 36,035 | 44,304 | 54,365 | 66,586 | 81,403 | 99,336 | 121,003 |
| 23 | 30,715 | 38,197 | 47,405 | 58,714 | 72,579 | 89,543 | 110,263 | 135,523 |
| 24 | 32,251 | 40,489 | 50,724 | 63,412 | 79,111 | 98,497 | 122,392 | 151,786 |
| 25 | 33,864 | 42,919 | 54,274 | 68,484 | 86,231 | 108,347 | 135,855 | 170,001 |

| Year | 13% | 14% | 15% | 16% | 17% | 18% | 19% | 20% |
|---|---|---|---|---|---|---|---|---|
| 1 | $ 11,300 | $ 11,400 | $ 11,500 | $ 11,600 | $ 11,700 | $ 11,800 | $ 11,900 | $ 12,000 |
| 2 | 12,769 | 12,996 | 13,255 | 13,456 | 13,689 | 13,924 | 14,161 | 14,400 |
| 3 | 14,429 | 14,815 | 15,209 | 15,609 | 16,016 | 16,430 | 16,852 | 17,280 |
| 4 | 16,305 | 16,890 | 17,490 | 18,106 | 18,739 | 19,388 | 20,053 | 20,736 |
| 5 | 18,424 | 19,254 | 20,114 | 21,003 | 21,924 | 22,878 | 23,864 | 24,883 |
| 6 | 20,820 | 21,950 | 23,131 | 24,364 | 25,652 | 26,996 | 28,398 | 29,860 |
| 7 | 23,580 | 25,023 | 26,600 | 28,262 | 30,012 | 31,855 | 33,793 | 35,832 |
| 8 | 26,584 | 28,526 | 30,590 | 32,784 | 35,115 | 37,589 | 40,214 | 42,998 |
| 9 | 30,040 | 32,519 | 35,179 | 38,030 | 41,084 | 44,355 | 47,854 | 51,598 |
| 10 | 33,946 | 37,072 | 40,456 | 44,114 | 48,068 | 52,238 | 56,947 | 61,917 |
| 11 | 38,359 | 42,262 | 46,524 | 51,173 | 56,240 | 61,759 | 67,767 | 74,301 |
| 12 | 43,345 | 48,179 | 53,503 | 59,360 | 65,801 | 72,876 | 80,642 | 89,161 |
| 13 | 48,980 | 54,924 | 61,528 | 68,858 | 76,987 | 85,994 | 95,964 | 106,993 |
| 14 | 55,348 | 62,613 | 70,757 | 79,875 | 90,075 | 101,472 | 114,198 | 128,392 |
| 15 | 62,543 | 71,379 | 81,371 | 92,655 | 105,387 | 119,737 | 135,895 | 154,070 |
| 16 | 70,673 | 81,372 | 93,576 | 107,480 | 123,303 | 141,209 | 161,715 | 184,884 |
| 17 | 79,861 | 92,765 | 107,613 | 124,677 | 144,265 | 166,722 | 192,441 | 221,861 |
| 18 | 90,243 | 105,752 | 123,755 | 144,625 | 168,790 | 196,735 | 229,005 | 266,233 |
| 19 | 101,974 | 120,557 | 142,318 | 167,765 | 197,484 | 232,144 | 272,516 | 319,480 |
| 20 | 115,231 | 137,435 | 163,665 | 194,608 | 231,056 | 272,930 | 324,294 | 383,376 |
| 21 | 130,211 | 156,676 | 188,215 | 225,745 | 270,336 | 323,238 | 385,910 | 460,051 |
| 22 | 143,138 | 178,610 | 216,447 | 261,864 | 316,293 | 381,421 | 459,233 | 552,061 |
| 23 | 166,266 | 203,616 | 248,915 | 303,762 | 370,062 | 450,076 | 546,487 | 662,474 |
| 24 | 187,881 | 232,122 | 286,252 | 352,364 | 432,973 | 531,090 | 650,320 | 794,968 |
| 25 | 212,305 | 264,619 | 329,190 | 408,578 | 506,578 | 626,686 | 773,881 | 953,962 |

**Source:** No-Load Fund Investor, Inc., Hastings-on-Hudson, N.Y.

---

**Your Personal $$ Memo: Saver Beware!**

Just because the annualized yield is higher than the advertised effective yield doesn't necessarily mean that you will earn that much interest. The higher annualized yield is based on the assumption that at the end of the term (such as 6 months) you will create the compounding by reinvesting the entire amount in the account including the simple interest you have just earned.

The easiest way to comprehend interest rates is to ask the banker exactly how many dollars you will have at a certain point based on your current balance. With this figure in hand, it will be easier to compare how different compounding styles affect your money.

---

How often interest is paid and compounded is a very important factor and could make a very significant difference in the total return on your investment. As a simple example let's say that the advertised rate is 10 percent. If the money is compounded annually, by the end of a year your money would have earned only 10 percent. But, if the interest is compounded daily (reinvested each day to earn more money) at the end of a year you would have earned not just 10 percent but more than 10.52 percent. The fact is *the more often the interest compounds, the more money you earn.*

### Money Is Like Water—Liquid

Once you see how much interest you can earn, you must decide how long you can survive without that cash. If you put it into a low-interest–paying passbook account, your money is considered liquid, available to you just minutes after you walk into a bank. On the other hand, once you lock your cash into a CD (certificate of deposit) it is supposed to stay right there until the date that it matures. The bank is depending on your financial maturity as well. In order to help you grow in that direction, institutions offer some earn-while-you-learn programs.

There are many different types of accounts available which pay interest. These include: NOW accounts, Super-NOW accounts, and Money Market Deposit Accounts. Each type of account has its own particular degree of liquidity, so it is important to remember one rule of banking: *the more liquid your money, the less interest will be offered.*

---

### Your Personal $$ Memo: Double Minting

Double your money—double your funds, with double minting. Ever wonder how long it would take to double your money? The answer isn't all that difficult to figure out; all you need to do is to remember the Rule of 72, which is nothing more than dividing interest percentage into the number 72. If the interest rate is 7 percent, it would take 10.3 years to double. That's the result of dividing 7 into 72. Another example: If your money is earning 10 percent it will only take 7.2 years to double. If you can get 12 percent you get double your money back in six years. If your money is in a passbook savings account, it would take more than 13 years to double because the interest rate is only 5.5 percent.

---

### Is the Time NOW for NOW Accounts?

Chances are that by now you have heard of NOW accounts, which are interest-bearing checking accounts.

It sounds like a wonderful idea. As your money sits in a checking account waiting for you to spend it or waiting for checks to clear, it actually earns money. You won't get rich earning 5.25 percent (rates can vary), but in regular accounts your money is just sitting there doing nothing.

Of course, as with many of life's good things, there are some drawbacks to a NOW account. Despite banking deregulation you must keep a minimum balance in the account, though the amount will vary from bank to bank. No matter how much that minimum balance is, it is *not* to be touched. If you are forced to dip into that to pay bills or for a quick get-away vacation, you will lose the chance to earn any interest on the account. Another factor to consider is that there are service charges, and there might even be a monthly main-tenance fee. Those service charges, which are present no matter what your balance, could easily wipe out any interest you earn on your monthly checking account balance, espe-cially if you have to pay between 10 and 40 cents for each check you write or 10 cents to use the automatic teller ma-chine (ATM).

### Not So Super—Super-NOW

How super are Super-NOWs now? Not very super, even if you find them offered. Another result of deregulation is that banking institutions can now do away with separate NOW and Super-NOWs and replace them with a single type of in-terest-paying checking account. While it may seem as if that will make life less complicated, it is quite the opposite for the consumer because the rules are no longer uniform from in-stitution to institution. Where one may demand you keep a minimum daily balance of $1,000 or else you will no longer earn interest, another will allow your minimum daily bal-ance to drop to $100 before you stop earning interest and start having to pay fees.

You have to do some very important comparison shopping or else your account may pay less than expected in the end.

Why? Well, the banks are in the business to make money and processing a single check can cost as much as 40 cents. With regular (non–interest-earning) checking accounts those transactional expenses are covered by the money the bank earns off the balance in your account. When they have to pay out interest on the balance, someone has to pay for transactions. Guess who?

In order to get the most out of your checking account money, you need to employ some good consumer strategies such as:

1. Remember a banker's hand can be quicker than the eye. You might be drawn in by lower fees that can magically disappear. They are advertised to look cheap, but the institution still needs to make money and might do so by dramatically increasing the cost of each check you write or every time you use the ATM.
2. Figure out your lowest likely monthly checking account balance and look for a bank, savings and loan, or credit union that pays the most and charges the least for that amount of money.
3. Check to see if the institution will consider the amount in all of your accounts in that same institution before assessing charges based on a minimum daily balance. If that is the case, consider centralizing your accounts because it will allow you more financial flexibility. You also benefit from not having to deal with as many monthly statements and you might get a break on consumer loans rates.
4. Many institutions charge based on the total number of transactions. There are several ways to reduce the number of times you need to use the account and avoid being hit by those charges. For instance, use cash more often. When you drop by the bank to deposit your pay check, hold out enough cash to cover groceries and other shopping that you often do by check. Use only one credit card; that way you have only one credit card bill to pay each month, cutting down on the number of checks. And consider electronic bill paying. A number of banks will now let you pay regulars bills—such as loans, electric, phone, and credit card bills—through electronic fund transfers. These are much less expensive for the bank to handle, and that saving is passed on to you by not charging it against your maximum number of transactions each month.

## Emergency Cash

If there is one thing my family has learned, it is that a 3-month stash of emergency cash must be easy to get to in an emergency, but not so easy that you will be tempted to dip from it when the urge to buy strikes. For that reason, we have set up our emergency funds in bank Money Market Deposit Accounts that compound and credit interest on a daily basis. We use an MMDA instead of a regular Money Market Fund because the restrictions of the MMDA make it more suitable to holding emergency stashes of cash. You are limited to the number of checks you can write each month, and understanding that limitation makes me think twice before touching that money.

On the other hand, the money we are putting aside for eventual investments is deposited into a Money Market Fund. That way we can use that account for as many other investments a month as we wish without worrying about check writing restrictions. In addition we earn interest on the money until the check clears.

If you deposit money in an MMDA make sure that it is in an account which compounds and credits your interest daily. This protects you in case you must withdraw the money in an emergency. Many MMDAs compound daily but only once a month do they actually add that earned interest to your account. If you need that money before the crediting date, you will lose all the interest earned since the last time it was posted.

—Larry

## Splish Splash, Liquid Cash

A big splash in the liquid cash area is the Money Market Deposit Accounts (MMDA). They are so liquid that your money can flow in and out without much trouble. MMDAs pay much higher interest than passbook savings accounts, and they are also federally insured. The interest rate is set every week and many compound daily. But, exactly when that interest is credited to the account and actually available to you depends on the institution. Sometimes the interest is determined daily, but credited only monthly. The biggest single disadvantage of MMDAs is that, even though government regulations have relaxed, most require a rather substantial minimum deposit. The minimums can run between $1,000 and $2,500. Should your balance drop below that figure your high interest rate disappears and falls to the passbook figure (traditionally 5½ percent).

While we have said there is never a penalty for withdrawing the funds, there are some rules you must obey in order to get and keep the high interest rate.

1. To open the account the minimum initial deposit is between $1,000 and $2,500.
2. You must maintain that minimum balance.
3. There is no limit on the size or number of withdrawals as long as you go to the bank, send a messenger or use the mail.
4. If you don't want to handle the money personally you are only allowed up to six third-party transactions a month. (That's when you write a check or transfer money to your landlord or someone other than yourself.) Only three of those can be by check.

### Frozen Cold Cash

If money burns a hole in your pocket, why not freeze it? You can do that with a Certificate of Deposit (CD). A CD is great if you don't need immediate access to your money and are interested in higher interest rates. Once you put your money into a CD, it is supposed to stay there until the maturity date. That is the length of time on which you and the bank agree. The traditional maturity dates run from as short as one week to longer than 10 years.

If you want your money before the time is up, you are in effect breaking your contract with the bank. You make things difficult for them; therefore, they will make things difficult for you. You will be forced to pay a penalty before you can touch the money. Exactly what that penalty will be depends on each institution's rules and how long the money has been sitting in the account. The government has relaxed the rules on early withdrawal penalties, but some institutions are still charging a substantial fine which can cost you from 1 month's interest to more than 3 months. As if that's not punishment enough, if you withdraw a CD before it has earned enough interest to cover the penalty, you could lose some of your principal (original deposit). That can really hurt because you end up with less money than you put into the CD originally. The rule of thumb is that the longer you want to commit your money, the higher the interest rate, which is why you face a higher penalty for early withdrawal.

---

### Your Personal $$ Memo: Ask Your Banker

With all of this in mind, there are four very important questions to ask your friendly banker:
1. What is the interest rate?
2. How is the interest paid? (daily, quarterly, or annually)
3. What is the penalty for early withdrawal?
4. And *be sure to ask* exactly how many dollars you will have at the end of the term when the certificate of deposit matures.


When you are asking these questions, don't worry about sounding foolish. These are your hard-earned dollars and you should fully understand what you and the bank are doing with your money.

---

# Make Your Own CD

One of the greatest feelings of power is when you can dictate your own destiny. Very few of us have that chance except when we are allowed to make our own sundaes or create a feast at a salad bar, but that is changing. Now the big cheeses at the banks and savings and loans are letting us design our own Certificates of Deposit. Many are now offering flexible CDs so that you the customer have the power to pick the time limit, anywhere from 7 days to 10 years or longer. Some banks are not as generous as others, but who cares about the stingy ones. This has become a competitive business where you get to call more of the shots. You should take this new-found power to a bank or savings and loan which will let you decide exactly what day your money will be returned. Once that date is determined the banker will assign an interest rate for that maturity date. The rule: The longer the banker can use your money the more money it can earn with the help of higher interest rates. A simple example of making your own CD: If you have found your dream house and the money for the down payment is due in exactly 64 days, the institution will sell you a CD that comes due in 64 days.

There are many variations on this theme. A number of banks offer a "discounted" certificate of deposit. It has been called by at least one bank the Guaranteed Goal Certificate and is designed for those who want to have a specific amount of money by a specific date. If you need $10,000 for a child's college tuition in 3 years, this type of program will tell you how much you would have to put away right now to have that much money then. In effect you are buying a "discounted" $10,000 CD. For example, if a bank is offering 10 percent for 3 years, you would need to stash $7,375.46 in cash right now to have the full ten grand in 3 years.

# When RED, WHITE, and BLUE Make GREEN

If you feel even the slightest bit guilty about watching your money make even more money, one way to fight that feeling is with Patriotism. You can buy a piece of America and actually earn some intriguing interest rates.

U.S. Savings Bonds (Series EE) now pay market-based rates, which means that they are now an investment that offers both variable market-tied rates and a guaranteed minimum. "Variable" means Uncle Sam can increase or decrease the interest rate he pays depending on what other federal government (Treasury) securities are paying. The beauty of the new rules is that as long as you hold the bonds for 5 years you will never earn less than 6 percent. It makes them much more attractive than the old style Series E U.S. Savings Bonds which paid a very low interest rate.

The drawback to U.S. Savings Bonds is that you must keep your money tied up for a number of years in order to get the higher interest rates. The government's formula dictates that the interest paid on Series EE bonds be pegged at 85 percent of the yield on marketable Treasury securities with similar maturities. What that complicated language means is that since the new interest rules were introduced the bonds have paid several points higher than the guaranteed 6 percent.

If you find you need to get your money out before the bonds mature, you lose out on interest. You can't cash them in for 6 months, but after that you earn:

| | |
|---|---|
| 1st year | 4.27% |
| 2nd year | 4.64 |
| 3rd year | 5.01 |
| 4th year | 5.5 |
| 5th year | 6.0 |

The Treasury Department reviews the guaranteed minimum several times a year. If it is lowered, it will not affect previously purchased Series EE Savings Bonds.

So, Savings Bonds may not really be an answer if you plan to use that money for any other kind of investing within the next few years. But, they are a secure way to save for a mortgage down payment, college education or even retirement. They might also be the answer if you are the type who can't seem to save any money. Many companies offer payroll savings plans for savings bonds. It may not be the best way to put away money, but if you can't save on your own, give it a try.

As you talk to your friends, listen to their experiences and find out where they have stashed their cash; press for good solid information, plus any horror stories. Everyone has some sad tale about his or her early experiences. The old statement still holds true: "The only two certainties in this life, are Death and Taxes." There are no guarantees, but you can minimize your mistakes and maximize you profits by understanding where you are going and why. Stay with us because there is a lot to learn and money to be made.

Of course it is you who must decide in which direction and how far you will go in this newly discovered relationship with your money. But, to make it an increasingly stimulating and fulfilling relationship it must be carefully nurtured.

# 3

## Shopping in the Money Markets

What can be more exciting than having people owe you money? Well, in this financial supermarket there are IOUs everywhere, all shapes and sizes—some quite enticing. So grab a basket and follow us.

**Aisle 1:** As we travel down this aisle, it's easy to get turned-off by shelf after shelf stocked with high-priced IOUs because some of them play very hard to get and it may be a good idea not to worry about them for now. Though in the end *they* may be the safest money instrument you will ever see. These are government securities such as T-Bills that take a minimum of $10,000. Perhaps a bit too rich for The First-Time Investor's blood. Nonetheless, we have devoted a whole chapter to T-Bills and other government desserts.

**Aisle 2:** All of us need something delectable and nourishing, but not too rich. Even The First-Time Investor must watch his or her diet. So, let's check out Aisle 2. It's just the

28

thing for the person who likes to share wonderful experiences.

How about having some mutual fun with Money Market Mutual Funds?

Every shelf is stacked with different delights. Some more delectable than others, but they all have one thing in common—financial sex appeal. Somewhere on these shelves is a fund that will satisfy your particular desires, and there is more behind each fund than just an alluring face.

Money Market Mutual Funds are nothing more than pools of money filled by individual investors buying up short-term debt instruments otherwise known as loans. In short, these pools of money are often called Money Funds or Money Market Funds. The true beauty of these Money Funds is that you don't have to worry constantly about the relationship. The funds take care of themselves with professional management and diversified portfolios.

Wouldn't it be nice to let someone else do the day-to-day shopping for you? That's what happens. You simply buy shares in the fund, and your shares are combined with other people's money so the fund can buy bigger and better IOUs. Something that makes life even easier with a Money Market Fund is that the value of each share never fluctuates, always equaling $1, which means that you own 1 share for each dollar you invest.

Here is a case where size counts; a fund can do a lot better when it is more endowed. Funds can buy bigger IOUs than an individual, which means higher yields. And the fund can spread the risk over a large number of debt instruments.

Other exciting qualities of Money Market Funds include no or low initiation fees and service charges, easy accessibility to your money and an interest rate that is often paid to your account every day. Also, even though you have a professional team tracking your money as it makes even more money, the cost of that management is very low. You never really feel a Money Market Fund management fee because it is figured in before the interest is paid out.

Something very important to remember: Even though Money Market Mutual Funds pay you for the pleasure of using your money, the funds do not insure that money. But, wait, no need for the affair to be over before it starts. The risk is very slight. While Money Funds are not insured, most are considered very safe because by law no more than 25 percent of the assets of any fund can be tied up in the IOUs of any single bank or corporation. Beyond that, no more than 5 percent of the remaining 75 percent can be invested in any single institution with the notable noble exception of the government. That diversification is a kind of insurance in itself. If one of the fund's investments should happen to belly up, there are enough other investments to help keep the fund strong. If after that explanation you still want or need FDIC-type insurance, you can either go back to a bank for an insured fund account or check into special fund insurance policies.

As you look around, you will see hundreds of Money Funds, and they are all attractive for one reason or another. Some of their fiscal attributes are more visible than others so you need to decide what you want from a Money Fund. The beauty of a high interest rate is only one of its strong appeals, so what else attracts you?

## Is the Fund Easy?

How easy? Check to see if it has a toll-free 800 number so that you can easily question the people who will hold your money. Find out how professionally, courteously and fast they act. These factors are important from the time you make your first call asking for a prospectus and application form to the time when you may need to get your money right away.

There is comfort in knowing you can act immediately should something pop up unexpectedly.

## Any Money Up Front?

We are not talking about a minimum investment just yet. More important is whether the fund is going to charge you an application or initiation fee. Is there a load (a commission or sales charge) as you might find with some other types of mutual funds? These up-front fees mean that you have less money to put into the account, and that means you earn less money. Some funds have other charges such as monthly, quarterly, or annual service fees, while others sometimes charge a fee whenever you make a deposit or write a check for a withdrawal. If these services cost you money and it isn't reflected in a consistently higher interest rate, you might want to look elsewhere. How do you find out this information? The 800 number is one way, a prospectus is another, and there are some guides on the market such as Donoghue's *Mutual Funds Almanac*, which is periodically revised.

## Minimum Investment?

Only a few Money Funds have no minimum investment, and that convenience of being able to start off with any desired amount of money often means you earn a lower yield. The reason for a lower yield is understandable: Since the fund has less money to invest, it cannot command as high a yield. In addition, paperwork costs the same whether you have $50 or $50,000 coming in, and if a fund has to fill out the same form one thousand times instead of once, someone has to pay for that. There are trade-offs in investing just as there are in Love. But this also means that you don't have to let the fact that you don't have much money in the beginning stop you. When you have more money, you can always change to a Money Fund with a higher minimum investment in order to earn a higher yield.

See, there is no need to panic over that beginning balance, because you can find Money Funds that require almost no money down to those that require $250, $500, $1,000 and even more.

Future Deposits, also called Subsequent Investments, should also be considered since the minimum amounts vary and you need to decide what will be convenient for you. Some funds allow any amount to be deposited, while others demand a $500 minimum investment. One nice thing is that most subsequent investments or deposits can be lower than the initial amount.

---

**Your Personal $$ Memo: Money Fund Checklist**

1.  Check for a toll-free 800 number.
2.  Listen for professionalism and courtesy.
3.  Pay attention to how fast they send your application.
4.  Check for accuracy on the mailing label.
5.  Ask if there is an application or initiation fee.
6.  Ask about the monthly service charges for checks and deposits.
7.  Find out the minimum initial investment and minimum average balance required.
8.  Ask about the minimum subsequent deposit.
9.  Check the check-writing rules and see if there are minimum amounts for each check.
10. Inquire into what services are offered without charge.

---

## Depositing

Deposits are the aphrodisiac for Money Funds, so the fund will do anything it can to make depositing easy for you. Deposit by mail is the method most frequently used, but the money won't be earning interest until a day or two after the check arrives. So you want to make sure the money gets to the Money Fund as rapidly as possible. The amount of the deposit will determine the most cost-effective way of transferral. Speed is not always the best answer, financially speaking. Express mail or one of the private overnight delivery services may cost considerably more than the interest you lost because of the few extra days it takes the postal service to complete its appointed rounds.

---

### Your Personal $$ Memo: Prepaid Envelopes

You don't save a lick trying to save the price of a stamp by using prepaid postage envelopes. Yes, those envelopes are convenient, but you lose interest in the long run because they can take longer going through the mail than a first class stamp. Each prepaid postage envelope has to be counted by the post office for postage billing purposes. So, if you want to use that Money Market Fund postage-paid envelope, we suggest you cross out the portion that says prepaid and put your own stamp on it. It saves using one of your own envelopes, it is pre-addressed and, best of all, your money starts earning money that much faster.

---

Another method for fast deposits is electronic transfer from either your bank or boss. While it does mean the money will be credited to your account and earning interest within 24 hours, an electronic transfer from a bank could cost a fee and not be worth it for a deposit of less than $5,000. How can your employer do it for you? Well, you might want to have your paycheck automatically deposited into your Money Fund account. If your employer offers this convenience for bank accounts, a money fund is just as easy because it's the same electronic transfer procedure.

## How to Get Your Money Back

Check writing is the easiest way to get your money back, and many people treat their money fund just like a checking account. But again, it depends on the particular fund. Most do send you checks, but many say each check must be written for a minimum amount of $500. Again, there are exceptions: some say $250, and others say no problem, write as many checks as you wish for whatever amount. Check out the restrictions of each fund. And remember these are the same as bank checks drawn against your account. Most people receiving one of these checks won't be able to tell the difference between a Money Market check and a bank check. The critical difference is something *you* benefit from: Daily dividends are paid to your Money Market account until the check clears. This delay, known as the *float*, means you can earn another week to 10 days of interest depending on how fast the recipient cashes the check.

Another way to get your money back is through telephone redemption. This feature sets up a wire transfer back to your checking account at the bank designated on your application. Should you need a fast $500, a phone call to the Money Fund will transfer the money electronically. This can be a tremendous time saver as it clears faster than a check. However, telephone redemption is not offered by all Money Funds. And of course, high finance is going high tech and now the home computer is being used by some people to shift funds through their local banks.

## Your Money Counts

We keep talking about how much interest your money will earn in one of these Money Market Funds. That of course depends on how well the money managers of each fund perform. But it is nice to know that most funds pay dividends daily, which means compounding. The interest earned today earns its own interest tomorrow; it's a chance to earn a few more dollars.

For example: $100 earning 8½ percent, compounded daily yields on: Day (1) 0.023288, which is less than a penny.

(30) 0.700994—which is slightly more than 70 cents.

(60) 1.406903—all of a sudden more than $1.40.

(90) 2.117759—already it has earned $2.12.

(180) 4.280368—growing like a weed at $4.28.

(365) 8.870629— now that a year has passed that $100 is worth $108.87.

### How to Find Funds and Happiness

As you start your search for the perfect fund, don't expect to find an imposing building. Most Money Funds don't have their own building and definitely don't have branches. A single central office keeps overhead down and that means more money left over for you. The most recognizable monument to a money fund is that simple mailbox on the corner.

So that leaves us with the question: How to find a fund? If you have a broker ask, but it may cost you money if the broker sets you up in one of his or her firm's funds, or it could cost you your comfortable relationship with a broker who realizes that particular money you plan to invest elsewhere won't buy stocks and, therefore, won't pay him or her any commission. So, it's probably easier and less painful to check newspaper and magazine ads and check out weekly fund tables in the papers. When you see a name that catches your eye, check with toll-free 800 directory assistance, and if there is a toll-free number simply phone for an application and a prospectus.

## Good Bedtime Reading

If you are looking for something to cuddle up with late at night, something that could help you realize your dreams and help you sleep better, might we suggest a Money Market Fund *prospectus*. Sounds familiar, doesn't it? Well, a prospectus is a brochure required by the SEC (Securities and Exchange Commission) to provide all of the salient information relevant to the fund. A prospectus will tell you the management philosophy of the fund, which can help you decide if it's the fund for you. It can tell you where the fund likes to put its money; however, a prospectus can't be too detailed about its holdings because a portfolio changes daily. By combining this information with yield rates, which can be found in newspapers and financial magazines, you can see how the fund has performed over a period of time. All this research takes is a quick visit to your local library. Ask the librarian where the latest financial publications are kept and look for the latest listings for Money Market Mutual Funds; these will provide information on current yields and the average maturity date of the fund's investments. Just keep in mind that there is no guarantee the fund will continue to pay the kind of interest you found in your research. But, this little exercise does give you a feel for how well things have gone for that fund.

We have already mentioned Donoghue's *Mutual Fund Almanac* (current cost $23), which has basic information on every fund. Bill Donoghue also likes to make it easy to obtain by having an 800 number.

Looks can be deceiving and bigger isn't always better. This is your money and you need to be careful and do your homework when you get the prospectus. If you see a fund that is paying a suspiciously high yield (interest rate or dividend), it may be a danger signal. The highest yields may mean some risk; remember these funds are only as good as their investments. A high risk could be deposits in foreign branches of American banks where the host country might take over the branch and its assets, or it could be heavy investments in foreign securities. Another high risk could be the fund putting more money in low quality corporate IOUs. When the chances are greater that a corporation can't make good on its IOUs, the interest rate is much higher but so is the risk of the Money Fund losing on the gamble.

Not all high yields signal high risk; sometimes it's just a matter of a Money Fund investing heavily in long-term paper (debts which will be paid back in a year or more), which often pays more. The problem is that it reduces the overall liquidity of the fund, meaning that if too many people wanted their money right away, the fund might not be able to handle the rush.

## Risky Business

Liquidity and Risk do go hand in hand. So, we should take a moment to explore two types of risk—Liquidity and Maturity Risk.

In the investment world, maturity is the date that an investment pays off. The longer it takes for an investment to mature, the more risk of that fund's not being able to respond to the market. In other words, if the maturity is 90 days, the IOU can't be redeemed until 3 months from issue date. While that investment may offer an attractive yield, it may also tie up the fund's money too long, meaning that the fund may miss a chance to earn even higher yields. Of course if there is a dramatic shift in rates, the fund might be able to sell the paper, but it would almost guarantee a loss of income. For that reason, funds spread that maturity risk by investing in paper of differing due dates.

Liquidity, of course, means how easily your money flows back to you in the form of cash; in other words, how fast you can get your money. Securities and Exchange Commission rules say shareholders must be paid within 7 days if they demand their money back. Not only that, SEC rules state 7 days "max" even if it means the fund has to sell off securities at a loss. In order to minimize that risk, each fund holds a mixed portfolio of short- and long-term paper. Therefore, unless the fund is in very serious trouble, there should be no problem with demand payments.

---

### Your Personal $$ Memo: Donoghue's Money Fund Tables

If you are looking for a rule of thumb for finding a fund with the best liquidity, look for one with an average maturity date of 28 days or less. That information is easy to find, as many newspapers publish charts such as *Donoghue's Money Fund Tables* that with a quick glance can show you the average maturity in days for Money Funds with assets of $100 million dollars or more.

---

You want a fund that has shown some spunk and creativity, but not too much. There has to be some risk in the fund's investments or else the fund won't make much money. You want some risk, but not all risk. If you would like more detailed information on where the funds invest your money, we define the different commercial papers at the end of this chapter.

### Sleep-Ease

If you find yourself a bit uneasy with your money propping up corporations or banks, you might want to consider "sleep insurance" funds which deal only in government agency issues. The added comfort is that the fund probably won't go under unless the government goes belly up. The exception to that infallible rule is the fund failing because of mismanagement, though to date there has been no history of that.

You can save many tears by dealing with so-called Government Money Market Funds. (They aren't owned by the government but deal only in government securities.) You get the super security of Uncle Sam, but also much more liquidity than if you bought those bonds and T-Bills yourself. You don't have to wait for them to mature; that is the fund's worry, not yours. Government IOUs can tie up money from 30 to 180 days, but the fund takes that into consideration and will have enough mature, or short, paper so that you can get your money whenever you need it.

Government-type funds deal in more than just T-Bills; they also dabble in U.S. Government Agency Issues such as Ginnie Maes and Freddie Macs. These are not direct obligations of the U.S. Treasury, but they are backed by Uncle Sam's good name (which is one way of saying the full faith and credit of the federal government). The instruments include federal government loan guarantees and sponsorships, such as student, home, farm and small business loans.

Of course nothing is free. The added feeling of safety can mean giving up 1 percent of your yield. Remember: The lower the risk, the less your money is expected to earn. What you need to do is ask yourself, "Is this kind of comfort insurance worth the price?"

## Paper Training

One way to get an even higher interest yield and retain some safety is to find a fund that deals only in first-class *commercial paper*. Commercial paper is nothing more than IOUs floated by corporations. It's something much better than the old line "The check is in the mail" because each corporation's good name is on the line. Of course, just like an IOU you might get from a friend, there is no collateral. These loans are short term, usually 60 days or less, and they are designed to get a company over some financial humps such as inventory irregularities or the ups and downs of seasonal earnings.

If a Money Fund dabbles in commercial paper, it has to make sure that company's name isn't mud. That is easy to find out. Each company's paper is rated for quality by several rating services. The top-rated paper sells for a higher price, but pays a lower yield. As to be expected, high quality paper means there is less likelihood of the company's defaulting on the loan and less chance the Money Fund will lose money. Again, when there is little risk involved, the company doesn't need to pay as much interest in order to attract the money. Of course, Money Funds worry about such things, which is the beauty of professional management. They know where to look and how to find the best yield for the lowest risk.

### Anxiety Relievers

Money Funds, banks and brokers all subscribe to a number of rating services in order to keep track of the credit worthiness of corporations. By studying the management, business plans, financial dealings and public records of a corporation, these services can fairly accurately judge the fiscal fitness of the investment. The services make their money from those subscriptions and have no dealings at all with the companies they rate. Each service also has a different rating method and code, but the most important ones to remember when it comes to corporate paper for money funds are:

Standard and Poors top rating is A-1
Moody's is termed Prime-1
Fitch's is called F-1

Of course there are sub-categories within each rating, and each of these adds a certain degree of risk, again something assessed by the professional managers of each fund.

## Tired of Sharing?

If you are already giving too much of your income to Uncle Sam's tax collectors, and you want to increase your income, you might want to consider Tax-Free Money Market Funds. But, before you get too excited about legally avoiding paying taxes, you really do need to be in one of the highest income tax brackets to make the much lower, tax-free interest rates pay off. These are much like other Money Funds, except that they invest only in instruments that provide tax-free income. Tax-free funds invest in a combination of high grade, short-term and tax-exempt bonds and revenue notes from states and municipal governments. While the interest yield is usually lower, it is more than offset by being tax exempt.

## Check Out the Family

If you are the type who likes to play the field, there are some Mutual Fund Families that let you swap. It's a chance to dabble in Money Funds one day, gold the next and government securities the day after, all with a simple phone call, which is something to consider if you believe another type of investment will become more profitable than the ones in which your funds currently specialize. You can join many of these Mutual Fund Families through a Money Market Fund and then easily slip into and out of the different types of funds the groups offer.

There is often more to a family of funds than meets the eye. Just as there are family feuds, a fund relationship is not always easy, so you need to do some more homework and find out if its members get along. If they do, it can be a fun experience switching and swinging with the interest or market rates. There are no guarantees that any relationship will last forever and these switch and swap funds simply help make it better.

Many types of mutual funds are like seesaws; they have their ups and downs, and the value of each share can change daily. Keep in mind that the one rock-hard and steady thing about a Money Fund is the dollar per share value. Each share costs $1, and while the interest the fund pays may fluctuate and the number of shares you own may fluctuate, the cost of each share remains the same.

But, hold on to your pants; we are getting ahead of ourselves a bit. We will initiate you fully into Mutual Funds later.

## Where Your Money Goes

It is no mystery where your money goes once it's in a Money Fund's coffers; the prospectus will explain the general direction of the fund's investment philosophy. In general, Money Funds spread their money around by investing in a number of areas ranging from certificates of deposit to government securities, U.S. government agency issues, corporate paper, bankers' acceptance notes, repos, Yankee dollars, and Eurodollars. Each individual fund is a sort of mix and match, unless it's a tax-free government fund. For those who don't like blind dates with their funds, let us review the individual personality of the different investments Money Market Funds consider.

**Certificates of Deposit**—A receipt for money loaned to a bank by the Money Fund. They are negotiable for the fund, so the fund can sell them if the need or desire arises. These CDs represent huge loans of $100,000 + with terms of 14 days to 5 years. These are not to be confused with the smaller CDs you can buy at a bank or savings institution but can not cash before maturity. Remember, that's a big difference; while you can't sell your CDs before maturity without a penalty, the fund can sell its CDs anytime, making them a more liquid investment.

**Government Securities**—These are Treasury Notes, Bonds and Bills. They represent Uncle Sam's IOUs; he has to borrow to cover the federal budget deficits and national debt. Treasury Bills are less than 1 year, and almost as liquid as cash. Treasury Notes are from 1 to 10 years. Treasury Bonds have a maturity of from 10 to 30 years.

**U.S. Government Agency Issues**—While not direct obligations of the U.S. Treasury, they are backed by the full faith and credit of the government. So, they are quite solid federal government loan guarantees and sponsorships. Fun little items such as Ginnie Maes, where the fund shares in the pool of government-backed home mortgages; its official name is the Government National Mortgage Association. Another is Freddie Mac which is the Federal Home Loan Mortgage Corporation. Other government agency issues include those from the Federal Home Loan Bank, Farm Credit Bank and the Small Business Administration.

**Commercial Paper**—Short-term IOUs issued by large corporations, banks and other borrowers with excellent credit ratings. Most often commercial paper is backed only by the good name of the borrower; in other words, there is no collateral. Money Funds often deal in commercial paper because it can yield a reasonably safe and profitable return.

**Banker's Acceptance Notes**—A promissory note, a fancy name for a private loan guarantee to cover transactions in the import/export business. These obligations are backed by large banks and usually are also backed by goods in international trade.

**Repos**—Repurchase agreements. Most often it's when a fund loans a bank money overnight. Even though it's short term it's usually for $1 million or more, so the loan is usually backed with government securities. Repos are so short term, the bank agrees to buy the loan back the next business day.

**Yankee Dollars**—CDs held in a foreign bank, even though they are purchased through that bank's branches in the United States.

**Eurodollars**—Deposits in branches of American banks located outside the United States. (There is risk in having money overseas because the host country may refuse to let the money back out of the country.)

# 4

## It's Interest(ing) that Many People Like It Both Ways

Interest rates are out of the closet: they go both ways, up and down. In this changing world, you cannot survive by ignoring either way.

Those who have money love it when the interest rates are high. They have very little to lose. Consider the fact: High interest rates mean their money earns even more money faster. The best example is how much their cash can earn in Money Market Funds. When interest rates in general are high, a Money Fund must pay out more in order to attract money to lend out. The same goes for a bank and certificates of deposit. The bank will lose your money to another investment instrument if the interest rate a CD earns is not comparable. Another wonderful example of how the rich get richer is through corporate bonds. When money is tight and interest rates are high, bonds offer bigger yields. The higher a bond yields, the more liquid the instrument becomes by being more resalable.

People who don't have money love it when interest rates are down. Lower interest rates mean that it costs less to borrow money, giving those who don't have a lot of money a chance at enjoying life a bit more. Another major advantage is that lower interest rates make it easier to get a mortgage. That in turn makes it easier for someone to sell a home, to buy a more expensive place or to cash in on the money they have tied up in the house. Tapping that equity is one way to set up an investment nest egg; not the best way, but one way. Also, as the market drives down interest rates, more people can drive new cars because of more affordable auto loans.

Emotional highs are a benefit of lower interest rates, because job security is higher. You have a better chance of keeping your job if your company can afford to borrow money to keep growing and expanding. Instead of being burdened with huge interest payments when rates are high, many companies simply put projects and jobs on the back burner. So your paycheck can be affected by interest rates.

## The Great Equalizer

The rich, the famous, the poor and the rest of us can find excellent benefits in low interest rates as well. Remember the people who bought bonds when interest rates were high, locking in those high rates? They win that gamble whenever other rates take a nose dive. While everyone else is scrambling just to earn a decent interest rate, they smugly enjoy owning bonds which earn a fixed higher yield.

Even those of us just starting out can win when rates head upwards. As interest starts to skyrocket, the stock market can falter because companies find it too expensive to borrow money in order to expand. Added to that the higher cost of credit can soften the consumer market, leading to lower sales and profits for many companies. So people, especially those with money, often run from Wall Street. They want to put their money into interest-bearing instruments to get higher returns. This greed on their part provides the perfect opportunity for those of us who previously had been praying only for low interest rates because it gives us depressed stock prices. You see, when these people flee the market in order to grab the high interest rates, they sell stocks, which most often leads to lower stock prices. That's our chance to get in on the ground floor. High interest rates may be the only chance to buy low so that later you can possibly sell high.

## The Facts of Life

Where do interest rates come from? Certainly not from the stork or a cabbage patch; they are born of the "Fed." Some people find it difficult talking about the facts of life, but understanding how money procreates is very important to a meaningful investing relationship.

The Fed, as it is "lovingly" called, is the Federal Reserve Board. It's the seven-member board of governors for the central bank of the United States appropriately known as the Federal Reserve System. It's also the chief regulator for the nation's banking system. But its biggest and most important job is controlling the supply of money. Too little money can slow down expansion, too much can create inflation. The old story of too much money going after too few goods is, of course, the capitalistic dream of more demand than supply, giving the seller the opportunity to charge as high a price as the market will bear.

The Fed has indirect control over thousands of banks by requiring that each maintain reserves in proportion to the loans each bank makes. In other words, if the Fed says the reserve requirement is 12 percent, that means the bank must keep 12 percent of all deposits on hand. For example, if you deposit $2,000 the bank can loan out $1,760 of it, but must keep $240 in the vault, so to speak. If a bank runs low on those reserves, which can happen, the bank must then borrow more reserves. That's when your friendly banker goes next door to another bank to borrow the money at a 1-day rate known as the Federal Funds Rate. If too many banks are borrowing from each other the Federal Funds Rate can go up, which then affects other rates including the Prime Interest Rate. The "Prime" is the most widely reported interest rate. That may seem strange because the Prime is the short term rate available only to the banks' best commercial customers and therefore has only an indirect bearing on consumer interest rates. Still the Prime is something to watch because it will indicate the general direction of other interest rates.

If, for some reason, your banker doesn't want to borrow from another banker, he or she can always go to the Fed and borrow at the discount rate. This is lower than the Federal Funds Rate, but it's also more difficult to get because the Fed doesn't like banks filling up money bags at the discount window.

## M&Ms Melt in Your Mind

The power of the Fed is being able to control the money supply and control interest rates. This is done by raising or lowering the discount rate, or if the situation is serious enough, by actually changing reserve requirements. Of course, before doing that the Fed has to know how much money is out there. So every week the Fed totals various types of deposits held by banks, and these totals are the actual measures of the money supply. They have fancy labels such as M-O, M-1, M-2 and M-3.

M-O is the amount of all US currencies in every American's possession including all the bills and coins.

M-1 is the total of all US currency in circulation plus demand deposits (personal and business) at commercial banks. (Demand deposits are checking accounts and passbook savings.)

M-2 is M-1 plus timed deposits at commercial banks such as certificates of deposit but not the biggest CDs.

M-3 is M-2 plus deposits in savings and loans, mutual savings banks and credit unions.

Economists seem to be turned on by the M-1 because it measures cash in circulation plus checking and passbook accounts, which gives them the best single indicator of money supply trends.

## Follow the Bouncing Dollar

The Fed controls the money supplies and, in effect, the interest rates by buying and selling government securities. If it feels there is too much money in circulation, which could cause inflation, the Fed simply sells off more T-Bills and other securities. That pulls cash out of the marketplace, forcing the banks to scramble for reserves. The old law of supply and demand means that the banks bid up the Federal Funds Rate which in turn pushes up interest rates all around.

While gravity is a law of science, it is only a rule of thumb in the world of money; still, what goes up often comes down. In this case the Fed can, in effect, lower the interest rates by simply reversing itself and buying back some government securities. That releases more cash into the monetary system and, like dominoes, all the rates fall. First the Federal Funds Rate drops, then the Prime, and eventually, way down the line, consumer interest rates.

## Knowledge Is Money

What good is knowing this if you don't know how to cash in and follow interest rates? Each Thursday afternoon the Fed releases the money supply figures, and these can help you. Watching how Wall Street and the banking industry react in the days that follow can give you a clue as to how to use the news. If the money supply is allowed to grow, it means more cash available for loans, which in turn means interest rates will probably fall. The stock market loves falling interest rates and often closes higher with such good news. On the other hand, if the Fed *tightens* its reins on the money supply, it means interest rates may be going up and the reaction on Wall Street may be to sell now and put that money in bonds.

Of course, you can use this information even if you don't yet dabble in stocks or bonds. A perfect example is when shopping for CDs. If you notice the Fed clamping down, then you may soon notice CD rates going up.

---

### Your Personal $$ Memo: Shopping for a CD

Shopping for a CD is like shopping for anything else: Check the ads. See which institution is offering the highest annualized yield. Just keep in mind that rates can change between the time you see the ad and the time you act. But these ads can be most useful in comparing rates offered by competing banks as well as in tracking the *ups* and *downs* of interest rates as a whole. *Interest rates change but not every institution changes on the same day, and just understanding that can put money in your pocket.*

As soon as you find a rate at a bank or savings and loan that you like, keep an eye on a different institution—one which changes its rate earlier in the week. For the sake of clarity let's call that your indicator bank because it will give you an indication of which way the rates are going. If the rates drop at that bank (the indicator bank), you still have time to act on the older higher rate you liked. Another plus: If the rates are going up at the bank you are watching, you might want to wait because your institution may follow suit and raise rates in a few days. If yours doesn't, you may want to do more with your indicator bank than just watch it. It's not foolproof, but it can give you an idea without having to make love to the M-1.

You should keep your money liquid while you are looking for the best CD rate, and the easiest way to do this is, once again, Money Funds. Recognizing a good rate is a trick in itself, but a good way to avoid a pregnant pause in the action is to act when the interest rates start to mature. Anything yielding 8 percent or more is worth considering for tying up your money for at least six months. If interest rates break into the double digits, especially the teens, start thinking along the line of 12 months or more. There is nothing wrong with tying up your money for a period of 12 months or more if you are able to secure an interest rate that is interesting.

If you are not satisfied by what you can find close to home, sometimes you can find more exciting or satisfying interest rates with different banks around the country. Of course, there can be some serious pitfalls with long-distance affairs, such as lack of convenience. If you get a call from a long-lost loved one in another state who is going on and on about the wonderful interest rate that he or she is earning, check before you enter this long-distance relationship. Some institutions offer those high rates only to state residents or current depositors, and some are not protected by either the FDIC or FSLIC. There is the added problem of trying to keep track of an unfamiliar bank. Unless you have done your homework, you may find yourself putting money into a bank that is having its own problems. Whatever you do, never invest in an institution that is not insured by the FDIC or the FSLIC. There are many people in Maryland and Ohio who found out too late that their savings institutions were not members of either federal insurance plan. While state banking officials and governors worked with both the FDIC and FSLIC to protect those depositors, many of them could not get to any of their money for quite some time. Those hardships can be avoided by being specific when asking if the institution is insured by either the FDIC or the FSLIC.

Sometimes out-of-town and out-of-state banks offer higher yields to attract more money into that area. There might not

## Your Personal $$ Memo: 100 Highest Yields

Over the past few years, I have spent countless dollars on phone calls searching for the best interest rates or yields for CDs. Until one day I realized I was making the phone company rich and not myself. That was the day I received a copy of a great consumer investment publication called *100 Highest Yields* published out of West Palm Beach, Florida. This newsletter is published weekly and lists the highest yields paid by FDIC and FSLIC insured banking institutions around the country as well as the minimums needed to open the account. Included are the highest Money Market Deposit Accounts, 6-month CDs, 1-year CDs, and 5-year CDs as well as Jumbo CDs for people with $100,000 or more to invest.

The newsletter also includes interesting articles on banking and explains in easy layman's language some of the complex ways bankers figure your interest rate. For subscription information write to:

100 Highest Yields
Box 088888
North Palm Beach, FL 33408-8888
phone: (305) 627-7330

—Larry

be enough depositors to satisfy the demand for loans, so the higher interest rate carrot draws the cash rabbit into the bank. There are examples of banks offering interest up to 4 points higher than the national average, but to get those super-high rates you have to act fast.

During the summer of 1985 two banks on an island off the coast of Massachusetts, Martha's Vineyard National Bank and Edgartown National Bank of Martha's Vineyard, tried to attract money to loan to island residents by offering the highest yields in the nation on 6-month and 1-year CDs. As soon as the word got out to the rest of the nation, the two institutions were inundated with millions of dollars' worth of deposits. This was more money than the banks could handle, so they were forced to close their windows to off-island depositors and lower the rates somewhat. It was only a 2-day gold rush but an example of how investors need good up-to-date information in order to act fast.

Of course, haste can make waste if you don't first make sure that the institution will accept out-of-state deposits and that the accounts are insured by either the FDIC or FSLIC.

# 5

# Why Give It All to
# Uncle Sam?
# Consider Cousin IRA

Would you consider putting a match to a $500 bill or even a $100 bill? Of course not! Then why do so many of us do something that amounts to just that? Why don't people who qualify for an IRA tax deduction take it?

Uncle Sam has a gift for each person who opens an IRA. Remember, IRA is not the man behind the counter at your local deli; IRA stands for Individual Retirement Account. The size of the gift depends on whether or not you are covered by another retirement plan. If you are not part of another plan then your yearly contribution may qualify as a wonderful tax deduction. For instance if you are in the 28 percent tax bracket and you put $2,000 into an IRA, you realize a tax benefit, much as if Uncle Sam had given you an immediate gift of $560. Without an IRA, that $560 would simply be paid to Uncle Sam in taxes. If you are in the 15 percent tax bracket the tax savings would run $300.

If you are covered by another retirement plan, you can still

invest in an IRA; you just won't get the deduction on the contribution. But, you will be able to enjoy the benefits of tax-deferred compounding and growth.

No matter which category you fall into, an IRA remains an excellent investment. It is probably one of the most important investments you will make, because you are investing in yourself, your future, and your family's future. And, as we will keep stressing, you don't have to wait until you retire to see the benefits. The immediate result for those who qualify is that your tax load is cut; and for everyone, even if you don't qualify for the contribution deduction, there is the continuing benefit of not having to pay taxes on the IRA's growth until the money is withdrawn. That means more money is in the account and through uninterrupted compounding it can and will grow faster and bigger.

An IRA is a great way to get your first taste of investing, and you can do it with as much or as little risk as you wish. After your first taste of money earning money, you may lust for ways to make it work even harder. What an exciting way to earn money while not letting Uncle Sam stick his money magnet into your pocket.

Even if you are not legally old enough to buy booze, individual retirement accounts are an excellent tax shelter that can start you on the road to riches. Imagine being a millionaire and enjoying all the luxuries of that status! This is one dream that you can make come true.

This is not a Las Vegas or Atlantic City craps shoot, nor is it like a state lottery or some magazine sweepstakes. Everyone can be a winner. For example, if someone invests the maximum $2,000 each year starting at age 25 and it continuously earns 12 percent, it will be worth $1,106,431 when that investor is old enough to withdraw it at 59½-years of age. (This assumes that the yield stays the same and the principal doesn't fluctuate.) If you saved the same $2,000 a year for 35 years without the tax benefits of an IRA, it would only be worth $304,477. Yes, that is less than a third of a million dollars!

Gee! That sounds wonderful! But, wait a minute. You may have noticed that in order to make you a millionaire we used a rather high rate of interest (12 percent). While banks and money market funds have been known to pay that much, there have also been a number of years that the rates were far below that. The lower the rate the lower the chance of you having a million dollars by the time you retire. For instance if you average 8 percent return per year, after 30 years of $2,000 contributions you would have about $240,000. Now, before you get upset, there is something that you must consider: Becoming a millionaire via high rates is not all it's cracked up to be. When banks and Money Market Mutual

Funds are paying the higher rate, you are also losing a large percentage to the ravages of inflation. Meaning that while with higher rates you might retire a millionaire, a million dollars would not buy you very much if a cheeseburger and fries costs $75 and a car more than $100,000. You should be more concerned that your rate of return outstrips inflation than the idea of becoming a millionaire the easy way. Though, as you will learn, with a little work and some risk taking it might be possible to actually beat both low interest rates and inflation.

An IRA is your own personally managed retirement account; it is over and above any retirement program you may have with your employer and most certainly more reliable than Social Security. It's available to anyone with an earned income of more than $2,000 a year. The only catch is that the income must come from a job, not from stocks or bonds.

## Love and Money

A husband and wife can love each other and do many things in life together with at least one notable exception: They cannot have a joint IRA. The IRS rules say that married couples must maintain separate accounts, although the couple is allowed to decide how much will be deposited in each account. Married couples with two incomes get to put away $4,000 as long as the second income equals the $2,000 contribution. Uncle Sam is even giving married couples with one income a bit of a break, allowing a total contribution of $2,250 (but not all in one account).

Take, for example, the case of the single income couple: The bulk of the money could go into the account of the non-working spouse as long as there is no more than $2,000 put into either account each year. In order to protect family interests, the husband and wife may name each other beneficiary. Of course not all marriages are made in heaven, and Uncle Sam wants to be fair so that if there is a divorce each person keeps individual control of the separate account.

# Why an IRA?

An IRA is one of the few things on this earth that not only feels good but is without a doubt legal. As we have mentioned, you may be able to qualify for immediate tax benefits: but, everyone qualifies for tax-free compounding and the principal not being taxed until it is withdrawn. The master plan is that you will not remove any money from your IRA until you retire. At that point you will presumably be in a lower tax bracket when the tax bite is less painful. If you are not yet enticed by the fact that you stand a very good chance of eventually having millionaire status, how about the argument that nearly everyone else is doing it? Peer pressure can have some positive side effects. Finally, we could appeal to your patriotic duty. IRA investments help prop up the economy.

## Never Too Young?

The key to becoming filthy rich with an IRA is to make yearly contributions as soon as you start earning money. Take the case of Jill Kasoff, my niece, who at the tender age of 2 years was a hardworking actress. Playing a baby on a soap opera can be lucrative. Her parents opened an IRA right away; now, whenever she works she is able to contribute to it. You don't have to put aside a full $2,000. Any amount helps. The rule is that you can only put aside as much as you earn up to $2,000. In other words, if you are just working part-time and you earn only $1,500 you can put all of that or a portion of it into an IRA. But, you cannot take another $500 from somewhere else to reach the maximum contribution. That would be cheating, because you didn't earn a full $2,000.

*Warning! There are those who say it is silly for a student to open an IRA until his or her income exceeds $10,000 because there is no tax benefit. Those who say that may be tax-shelter shortsighted and not realize the overall long-term benefits of compounding. The earlier you put money into an IRA, the more tax-free interest it earns, so it builds even faster.*

**—Larry**

## $2,000 IRA ACCUMULATIONS AND DISTRIBUTIONS AT AGE 65

| Starting Age | 5% RETURN | | 10% RETURN | | 15% RETURN | |
|---|---|---|---|---|---|---|
| | Capital Accumulation | Monthly Income | Capital Accumulation | Monthly Income | Capital Accumulation | Monthly Income |
| 25 | $242,000 | $1,899 | $885,000 | $9,278 | $3,558,000 | $47,508 |
| 35 | 133,000 | 1,044 | 329,000 | 3,449 | 869,000 | 11,603 |
| 45 | 66,000 | 518 | 115,000 | 1,206 | 205,000 | 2,737 |
| 55 | 25,000 | 196 | 32,000 | 335 | 41,000 | 547 |

**Note:** Returns are based on the conservative assumption that deposits are made at the *end* of each year.

**Source:** No-Load Fund Investor, Inc., Hasting-on-Hudson, N.Y.

## When?

Immediately, if not sooner! For some reason, most people wait until tax-filing time to open their IRA or to contribute to their already open account. But it's not a prudent move. You not only lose all that tax-free interest which you could have earned throughout the year, you also lose the effect of tax-free compounding. The idea is to open a new account, or add to already existing accounts, as early in the new tax year as possible.

If this isn't clear, take the case of Procrastinating Peter, who would not stick money into his IRA until the IRS deadline of April 15th. He may be a bit late, but every year Peter makes his full contribution of $2,000 and if he follows the same pattern for 20 years, with an annual yield of 10 percent the Procrastinating Peter Principle will pay a paltry $110,000. Sure, you would like to have that much, but how about having another $16,000? Well, that could have been accomplished simply by putting Procrastinating Peter's principal into the IRA *at the beginning of each new tax year*. After 30 years the difference of the early contributions would work out to be an extra $42,000. Remember, an IRA is not just a tax shelter; it's designed to build and build and build into big bucks.

## How and How Much?

An IRA can be a cheap date, one that keeps on giving constant excitement and fulfillment. For as little as $38.46 a week, you can contribute and meet the maximum contribution. It's not really very much money when you consider a few pennies less than $39 a week can grow into a million bucks if given the time. The key is to put in as much as you can afford up to the limit. Anything contributed over the limit can be penalized 6 percent for each year it's in the account.

The how is easy, because you follow the same guidelines as you would when you open any investment account. Check out the risks and the benefits. Once you have done that, it's as simple as filling out a form and handing over the money. But remember to shop around for the best return that your heart can handle. The higher the yield your money earns, the more that money is at risk. Making that choice is both difficult and important. You need to realize that the earning power of the money will be reflected in your buying power later on down the line. It's amazing how much of a difference just a few "silly little" interest points can make. A good example of this would be if you put $1,000 dollars into an IRA each year and it earned 9 percent, you would have $55,000 dollars after 20 years. But, if your IRA (with the same contributions) was earning 13 percent, your pot of gold would have more shine—$91,470. A 4 percent difference is worth more than $35,000!

## Where?

You can invest your IRA almost anywhere from buying stocks to CDs and anything in between, including bonds, Mutual Funds, government securities and annuities. About the only places you can't put your IRA money are collectibles and direct ownership of investment real estate. (Income-oriented

**Your Personal $$ Memo: Beg or Borrow?**

One of the most often-asked questions about an IRA is "Does it pay to borrow the money to open an account?" The answer is *yes*, as long as you earn enough to qualify for the tax deduction. Of course, you do have to pay back the loan. On the other hand, you do get the ball rolling.

If you don't want to borrow and you can't save, don't give up. Your saving grace might well be payroll deductions. More and more companies are setting up automatic IRA deductions from employee paychecks. The plus is that the money comes out in small, almost painless amounts before you see it. That takes care of the embarrassing problem—lack of self-discipline. The opposite side of the coin is that periodic deductions don't give you a full year's tax shelter on the IRA earnings because compounding is not working in your favor. But it's still better than waiting until the next April to put it in all at once.

limited partnerships in real estate are sometimes acceptable.) The IRS defines collectibles as artworks, rugs, antiques, stamps, wines and certain other tangible properties.

Also avoid tax-free investments. Not only do they pay lower yields than taxable investments but you also have to pay taxes on the earnings anyway when you withdraw. IRS rules say everything taken out of an IRA is taxable. So tax-free instruments are a waste of time and money in an IRA or Keogh. (A Keogh is a super-IRA for people who are self-employed.)

The safest way to avoid making a costly mistake is to put your initial IRA money into a designated IRA Money Market Fund so that it is earning interest immediately while you are making your long-term decisions. Money Funds are helpful because you don't need the full IRA amount to open the account or keep it open. Even if you wait a while before you make the long-term decision, you have at least started the process and started making money.

You can open as many IRAs as your heart desires, just so long as your total annual contribution does not exceed your earnings, does not exceed the single-income-couple rule, or does not exceed the $2,000 maximum per working individual. For example, if you like diversification you could (though it might lose some of the compounding benefits) put $1,000 into a Mutual Fund, $500 into stocks and $500 into a CD.

### Fancy Moves

You can even move that money around as much as you wish, so long as you do nothing more than finger it. Those transfers must be handled by the investment trustees (the bank, fund or broker), although once a year you can actually withdraw your money for sixty days. You can do anything you wish with the money during those sixty days. It can be a quick and clean loan to yourself to cover an emergency or cash short fall. But don't get used to holding on to that money because at the end of those two months you must let go. If you don't put it back into an IRA, you face the penalties and taxes. Off the top the IRS will charge you 10 percent for what is known as early distribution. Then all the money you take out, no matter how little, is taxed as ordinary income—taxed just as if you had earned it over and above your regular salary. Remember, neither the principal nor the money the IRA has earned has ever been taxed before. And, yes, over and above all of that, you did lose all that tax-free interest it could have been earning while you were playing with it.

Remember all of that talk about RISK and TOLERANCE? Well, an IRA needs to include some sleep insurance in the beginning. If you already sleep well and you have other forms of wealth, maybe you can afford to be speculative. In any case, comparison shop and watch out for fees. Currently the most popular resting place for IRAs seems to be savings institutions. Banks, thrifts and credit unions also fill the bill because they charge little or no fee. There are sometimes penalties for early withdrawal of funds from these institutions.

The very popular fixed-rate CDs have security and stability of principal with the added sleep insurance of being insured by the FDIC or the FSLIC (up to $100,00). The stability of income is another important factor. The drawback to an IRA full of CDs is that you have only moderate liquidity in case of an emergency.

If forced to cash-in IRA CDs, you could face a case of double jeopardy, paying a severe penalty for early withdrawal on top of the IRS rule that you forfeit 10 percent of anything withdrawn before retirement, not to mention that the money is immediately taxable as income. As you will learn, each place you can stick an IRA has its drawbacks; you just have to understand them so that you won't be blind-sided.

---

### Your Personal $$ Memo: A Gift That Keeps on Taxing

**Warning**: *Accepting gifts can be hazardous to your wealth.* In order to attract new IRAs, some financial institutions have been known to offer bonuses. If they offer a toaster oven, your tax goose could end up cooked. If the bonus violates the IRS guidelines, the whole account could lose its tax-deferred status. The IRS says you are being greedy if you accept a bonus or gift valued at more than $10 for a deposit of $5,000 or less. Uncle Sam is only a tad more generous. When the deposit is over $5,000, your gift or bonus can then be worth only $20. Rule of thumb: A potholder may be fine, but a toaster oven is out.

Also be wary of an IRA tie-in account, a combination of an IRA and a low-interest taxable account at the same institution. The institution may offer a higher interest rate on the IRA, but this reward will raise a few IRS eyebrows.

## What to Watch For

Be sure to check both the listed interest rate and the effective yield. That's what makes your IRA swell with pride. The effective annual yield is the best indicator of whose CD is bigger. But, be careful; simply because it has already been factored in, that rate doesn't tell you when and how often interest is compounded.

As we have discussed earlier, the difference between 12 percent compounded annually and 12 percent compounded daily can make a huge difference over the life of an IRA. Daily compounding is by far the best way to have your money earning even more money.

The longer the maturity date, usually the bigger the yield. But, as in all things in life, bigger isn't necessarily better. A long maturity rate means you are locked into that investment. And if you want out, as we have mentioned several times, you pay an interest penalty. This simply means that you might have to forego an even better CD interest rate if it comes along at the wrong time. We are not talking small potatoes here. The penalty for early withdrawal could cost as much as 3 months' interest, and if you haven't earned that much it could cut into your principal.

## Up and Add' Em

Some people feel the solution to missing out on rising interest rates is to buy something that has a flexible interest rate. Variable-rate CDs have the security and stability of principal, but there is much less stability of income. They are a moderate gamble because rates can go down instead of up. Though if you feel interest rates will go up in the future, it might be a better bet than a fixed-rate CD. Unfortunately, no one has invented the interest rate crystal ball.

## A Big Zero

This is one time in your life where a Zero might add up to something. Consider Zero Coupon CDs which are designed not to pay any interest until maturity. The compounding factor is built into the advertised rate. The advantage here is that you don't have to worry about dealing with and reinvesting the interest payments as often. The biggest risk is being locked into a lower than desired interest rate. You won't find Zero Coupon CDs at banks very often (if ever) because they are mostly sold by brokerage firms.

**Whenever a brokerage house in involved, flashing red lights and sirens should go off in your head because it may mean an extra fee or commission, depending on the firm.**

## Mutual Aspirations

Mutual Funds are a wonderful place for IRAs. They can provide you with some of the thrill and excitement of slight speculation. There are Mutual Funds designed for aggressive growth; others are income funds looking to maximize income but not price appreciation; while still others combine the two concepts: growth and income. The field is so large that there is definitely something out there to meet your mood and temperament. Some are Stock Funds; others are Bond Funds. (Others deal in tax-exempt bonds, which you don't want for an IRA.)

One of the most important things you should look for is a No-Load Mutual Fund. A *load* is a commission or sales charge that comes right off the top of your investment. It varies from 3 percent to 8½ percent, depending on the fund. With a No-Load Fund, the $2,000 put into an IRA is exactly how much you have invested. With a loaded fund, your two grand could instantly become worth only $1,830. The $170 (or

8½ percent) difference is in someone else's pocket, and your money has to work twice as hard to recover that loss. The chances of a Load Fund catching up are between slim and anorexic. But we are not going to get into the bare facts of life about Mutual Funds right now because we have a whole chapter on those coming up after this one.

As a matter of fact, most every other instrument in which you can legally invest your IRA will be covered in future chapters.

---

### Almost as Good as a Free Lunch

There really is no such thing as a free lunch, but you can have a very enjoyable feast that costs you very little in the long run. In other words, almost all IRA programs have some sort of fee system. This includes No-Load Mutual Funds. You are not paying a sales charge or commission, instead, an administrative fee. The $10 to $50 a year is cheap when you consider it pays for all of the tedious bookkeeping you would have had to take care of yourself. Just realize that when you pay this fee every year.

---

### Taking Stock for Your Future

If you want your IRA to be full of stock, you need to consider several things. Are you going to have the time to constantly analyze your portfolio? Chances are the answer is no. An individual retirement account is different from a normal investment portfolio because you are gambling with the money you hope will feed you when you retire. While stocks can give you wonderful growth, you can also lose your shirt. So, until you have lost some of your investing virginity, we would advise you to be conservative and avoid stocks.

If you insist, there are a few things you should understand

about an IRA stocked with stocks. When you set up a self-directed IRA, you must set it up through a brokerage firm. That often means a $30 set-up fee, and another $50 a year for an account that allows you to be highly flexible. As we mentioned, you have to expect some fees, but on top of these brokerage fees you also pay commission for all trades, buy or sell. Many times these commissions will be higher because you will be trading smaller blocks of stocks; however, you can go through discount houses which are not as expensive. Still, until your portfolio (or the amount in your account) has built to more than $10,000, those commissions could eat up much of your profit, even if you trade infrequently. As with Mutual Funds, there is a complete stock market chapter coming up that will explain more about stock trading. One other important point about a self-directed IRA: You cannot just transfer stocks or bonds into an IRA. Stocks and bonds must be bought with cash specifically for your Individual Retirement Account. Also, while you are allowed to buy new issues, penny stocks or even options, they are much too much of a gamble for an IRA.

### Another Zero that Could Add Up!

Zero Coupon Bonds are sold by brokers and seem to be perfect for some people's IRAs. Like the Zero Coupon CD, you don't earn interest until it matures. So you buy the bond at a price far below the final face value. That means all of your return comes at maturity. For instance, you might pay $330 today for a bond that in 10 years will be worth $1,000. Consider how many bonds you can pick up and still be within your $2,000 a year limit. The answer to this pop quiz is 6. That means you can triple your money in ten years. Of course that also means your money is tied up that long and not very liquid.

## Annuities

While you cannot put your IRA money into life insurance, insurance companies do offer opportunities such as Mutual Funds and Fixed-Rate IRA Annuities. A Fixed-Rate Annuity is a great deal like a bank savings account. You earn a fixed rate of return, which can be adjusted periodically, usually once a year. The difference is that an annuity promises to pay periodically a fixed amount for a certain number of years when you retire. And it can look rather sexy at times, with some of them boasting guaranteed returns as high as 14 percent.

Sounds lovely doesn't it? Well, that beauty is only skin deep. Annuities are often more complex and costly than you might be led to believe by the brochures and sales pitches. True, with an annuity, the insurance company promises you a certain income each year after retirement no matter how long you live. But, once you make that annuity withdrawal commitment you are stuck with it. With any other kind of IRA, you constantly control the distribution when you retire. You could even change your mind and pull it all out at once if you needed it for an emergency or to buy a dream retirement home. (Of course, the income taxes on the whole thing could be a nightmare.) This is not so with an annuity because the distribution is written in stone in a contract between you and the insurance company. Some annuities don't care about your heirs even if you haven't spent all that you contributed. After you die, the annuity checks STOP! It's just as if the annuity, or even you, had never existed in the first place. You had a bet with the insurance company that you would outlive the amount of money you contributed; well, you could lose that bet. Also, many annuities have an initiation fee of up to 8¾ percent. That means that out of each of your dollars only 91¼ cents is working for you. If you want to shift your IRA out of an insurance company, an otherwise normal and simple rollover can cost you between 6 percent and 10 percent of the money you have invested. Something else to watch is the small print. A guaranteed high interest rate may be guaranteed for only the first year.

## Land

We have already mentioned that you cannot put your IRA money directly into real estate. Well, that doesn't mean all real-estate deals are out. You can enter into income-oriented limited partnerships that pool investors' money in real estate such as rental property. The investors collect the rental income, and after the property appreciates and is sold, the investors get the profit, otherwise known as the capital gains. Of course, rental property can be a gamble and your money is anything but liquid.

One more thing to remember: You want an income-oriented partnership, not one that is tax-shelter oriented. Since an IRA is already a tax shelter, what good is a tax shelter on top of a tax shelter?

## Running with the Money

The law now says that you can start withdrawing your money without penalty once you turn 59½. You don't have to take anything out until you turn 70½, but you must begin withdrawals by then. Remember, the longer it stays in the IRA, the bigger it gets. As soon as you withdraw, it starts to shrink. Life is just that way. You could take the lump sum out as soon as you hit 59½, but who would want to. Keep in mind that you would pay taxes on the full amount and it could no longer earn more tax-free money.

**INVESTMENT PYRAMID**

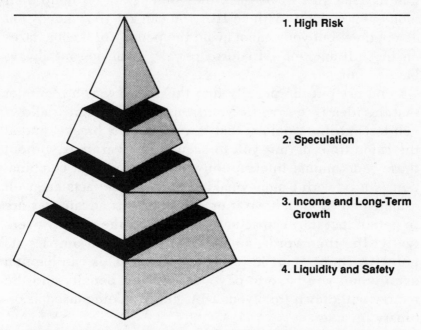

1. High Risk

2. Speculation

3. Income and Long-Term Growth

4. Liquidity and Safety

**1 High Risk**
Options, Futures
Tax Investments, Raw Land

**2 Speculation**
Lower Quality Stocks
Lower Quality Municipal Bonds
Lower Quality Corporate Bonds

**3 Income and/or Long -Term Growth**
Highest Quality Stocks
High Grade Corporate Bonds
High Grade Municipal Bonds
Writing Covered Options
Variable Annuities
Investment Real Estate

**4 Liquidity and Safety**
Cash
Money Market Deposit Accounts
Money Market Funds
Insured CDs
U.S. Treasury Bills and Bonds
Fixed Annuities
Life Insurance (Cash Value)
Equity in Your Home

**Source:** Courtesy Merrill Lynch

## Withdrawal Symptoms

This is where we say forget everything we told you about early withdrawal, for just a moment. Some people are reluctant to open an IRA because they don't want to tie-up their money for so long. With an IRA you can get your money out at any time, but you cannot avoid the penalty or income taxes on the full amount. Of course penalty pain doesn't always have to hurt.

Congress put the penalty into the IRA law as a reminder that the idea is to save for your retirement. Congress allows you to contribute dollars that lower your tax bracket and at the same time permit you to accumulate earnings without those rude annual interruptions by the IRS. That combination is a powerful moneymaking tool. These facts are well established. But, believe it or not, these tax advantages are so potent that they can actually overpower the penalty eventually. In other words, an IRA investment can outpace its non-IRA counterpart in just a few years. This can happen even when you have to pay a 10 percent penalty and the money withdrawn from your IRA ends up being taxed as ordinary income.

Some people may successfully beat the odds by accumulating money in an IRA for a faster down payment on a house or a child's college education. The higher your tax bracket, the less painful the penalty. Someone in the 28 percent bracket whose IRA earns 10 percent would hit the break even point in seven years. Someone else in the same tax bracket but earning 12 percent would break even after only 6 years.

**To Repeat:** You should never be reluctant to open an IRA even if you are planning a major expense in the future. *No Excuses! The only one who loses is you!*

## Getting Some on the Side

Uncle Sam has been called Uncle Sugar by some people because he can be very sweet at times. For instance, he has an extra gift for those who are self-employed or happen to have an income-producing business on the side. It is a chance to write your own ticket to retirement without having to worry about an employer's pension plan. Not only that, it is a first-class tax shelter retirement program that makes an IRA look like small potatoes. It is called a Keogh Plan, named after the congressman who introduced it more than twenty years ago.

It gives a qualified individual the chance to set aside up to $30,000 a year or 25 percent of his net self-employment income, whichever is smaller. Like an IRA, this contribution is deducted right off the top of your income for tax reporting purposes. Also, like an IRA, everything your Keogh earns is tax free until you start withdrawing. Even if you have a Keogh, you can still contribute $2,000 to an IRA.

Keoghs can start larger, be filled with more money and thus earn a lot more money faster, so you will need to give more consideration to risk, especially considering that having a Keogh often means not having any other kind of retirement program other than an IRA and Social Security. Because of its size, a Keogh will need more loving care and time on your part. Also, it will need a babysitter. You really do need to find an accountant well versed in Keoghs to help you keep from hurting yourself financially and with the IRS.

If you are excited by a Keogh, make sure you are qualified to open one and to keep feeding it. You must be self-employed, receiving income for personal services rendered, not a salary as would be paid to a regular employee. Doctors and lawyers often set up professional corporations and find they are eligible for a Keogh. The profession which may have the largest per capita number of Keoghs is plumbing. Plumbers not only know how to fix a leaky sink, but they often know how to plug a tax leak, too.

You say you are a full-time employee with a company? Well, you might qualify for a Keogh because of some outside freelance income. If you are not sure, simply contact your accountant, or look in the Yellow Pages to find one who specializes in Keogh plans or tax planning.

## Did You Take Your 401(k) Today?

Probably the best tax shelter going is the best kept secret in the world, though it is perfectly legal. It's called a 401(k), which more accurately describes where you can find it in the IRS code than what it is. A 401(k) is a company-sponsored savings plan offered by thousands of firms. Its special advantage is that all employee as well as employer contributions are not reported as income and grow untaxed until you withdraw them. You are allowed an annual contribution of $7,000.

You may have noticed that we said employer contributions. That's one of the most exciting aspects of a 401(k) because companies often match all or part of an employee's contributions. The 401(k) differs from an IRA or Keogh in that your investment opportunities are somewhat limited to what the sponsor offers.

Worried you may not spend the rest of your career with the same company? No problem! When you leave the company you can rollover your 401(k) into an IRA or another company's saving plan without having to worry about taxes. This is one of the few times you would be allowed to put more than $2,000 dollars into an IRA in one year, all because you are consolidating two tax-deferred retirement programs.

Also, you can get to your 401(k) money if you have a personal hardship. Currently the definition of personal hardship is up for debate, but it's rather liberal and the withdrawal can be made without the added imposition of a penalty over and above all the normal income taxes.

The real winner is someone who has a 401(k) through work *and* has a part-time, freelance job in another field, permitting both a Keogh and an IRA. Oh yes, if you are considering all of that for yourself, please consider one more thing other than sheltering income for retirment: At that pace will you live long enough to retire?

One final point about retirement accounts, these are all gifts from Congress and whatever Congress giveth Congress can taketh away at anytime.

# 6

# Mutual Delight

First-Time Investors have an overwhelming desire to make it on their first date with investments, but they must control their urges for only a short period. An important part of the foreplay will be Mutual Funds.

Mutual Funds are like the old saying "many hands make light work"; it's a way for people to do together things they couldn't do alone. Wouldn't it be wonderful to have a professional who spends all day worrying about and managing your investments, a Pro who is constantly watching the markets and moving your money around to your benefit while not getting rich off commissions. No, it's not a fairy tale. That's what Mutual Funds are all about. Like the Scouts, there is adult leadership through professional management. The *cost* of this professional advice and in-depth research is shared by the thousands of investors in each Mutual Fund. A Mutual Fund is a pool of money from many people that allows an individual to invest in a greater number of different stocks, bonds or even loans, thus providing protection through diversity. Also, larger transactions mean the mutual fund can get bulk discounts on commissions, thereby saving investors even more money.

Many different people are attracted by Mutual Funds ranging from individual investors to institutional investors who take care of pension funds, union funds, trust departments, foundations, business accounts and even other mutual funds.

One very big reason for the mutual satisfaction is the liquidity of mutual funds. Your money is often only a phone call or a letter away. Many funds make it even easier by providing check-writing privileges.

If a fund allows phone transactions, you can reach out and touch the right buttons. No phony baloney here because you get instantaneous confirmation that your order has been received and transacted. You also get the going market rate at the time the fund receives that buy or sell order.

### Getting Loaded

There are several types of mutual funds; the two most common labels are *load* and *no-load*. Remember that a load is a sales charge or commission ranging from 1 percent to 8½ percent. It comes right off the top, and that means your investment already has a bad start. For example, if the load is 8½ percent, it might take several years just to recover the load, not to mention the yield you lost had that money been working somewhere else, for example, in a money market fund or even a savings account.

An excellent example is a simple $1,000 investment which in a fund with an 8½ load would instantly be worth only $915. That means you would need to make an $85 profit just to get back to where you started.

If you are one who feels you get what you pay for and if you pay more you get more, this is one situation that is not the case. Study after study by Wall Street analysts have found that funds with loads do no better than no-load funds. As a matter of fact because of the start from behind position, investors often do not do as well in a loaded fund.

We are not saying anything about the funds themselves; load or no-load, they are run by honest professionals whose goals are the same as yours: to make BIG bucks! It is just a question of whether you want to pay a commission or sales charge when you don't need to.

If you would rather buy a Mutual Fund through a broker or salesman, make sure your commission-earning individual understands your particular needs. If the fund recommendation doesn't feel good, don't do it, and don't let a salesman force you into anything. Despite what your physical education instructor probably said, you *can* have gain without that pain.

### Go for No!

If a Loaded fund means a sales charge, then a No-Load means just the opposite. And with no commission to pay, you have instant full earning power. It is important to remember that No-Loads perform as well as Loads according to all statistics, and they potentially offer greater profits without those little money-eating Loads. An added benefit for future fun with No-Load funds is the greater flexibility in switching when you don't have to worry about those prickly loads or fees.

Of course, there are other charges you need to look for, as some funds have what is known as a Back Load. These funds charge nothing up front, but slap you in the back with a fee of up to 5 percent if you cash-in the fund in less than 5 years. *Read the fine print of the prospectus.*

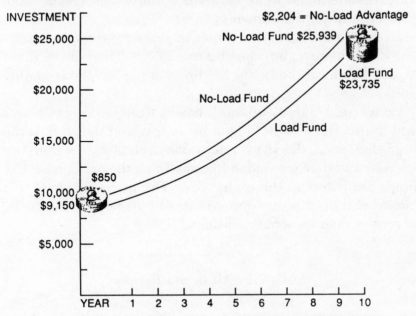

**COMPARISON OF $10,000 INVESTMENT IN TWO MUTUAL FUNDS EACH GROWING 10% PER YEAR, COMPOUNDED ANNUALLY**

INVESTMENT

$2,204 = No-Load Advantage

No-Load Fund $25,939

$25,000

Load Fund $23,735

$20,000

No-Load Fund

$15,000

Load Fund

$850

$10,000
$9,150

$5,000

YEAR  1  2  3  4  5  6  7  8  9  10

**Source:** Courtesy No-Load Fund Investor, Inc., Hastings-on-Hudson, N.Y.

## Not Just Open and Shut

Mutual Funds can also be *open-end* or *closed-end*. The open-end funds have a seemingly unlimited amount of shares for sale. New shares are issued for each deposit. Each share's value is dependent upon the success of the fund's investments (portfolio). The value changes on a day-to-day basis and is calculated by each fund through a simple formula of dividing the total daily value of the portfolio plus its cash reserves by the total number of outstanding shares. So, if the fund's securities do well, the price of each share goes up, and of course, the opposite is also true. If the fund makes poor picks, the value of each share decreases.

When a fund is successful, it obviously attracts more people and a larger asset pool. This is turn means more money for investment and more diversification, which means more protection from wild down-swings.

Of course the open-end hopes to sell new shares to some-one else whenever anyone else cashes out. This way the fund avoids having to liquidate holdings to pay off those getting out.

Conversely closed-end funds have a fixed number of shares and their value is determined by supply and demand. If the fund does well, the share prices rise as demand for them in-creases, and they are traded like stocks on the exchange. (The funds are listed on the exchanges.) The price per share of a closed-end fund is determined more by its popularity among investors than its actual holdings.

## Let's Play All in the Family

There is a population explosion in Family Funds, possibly a perfect proposal for First-Time Investors because they give you an inexpensive chance to sample many different types of Mutual Funds. Under the parent fund in these families there are many brothers and sisters, and you can switch among them as your investment strategies shift. It seems like the perfect answer for someone who likes the feel of a stick-shift but the comfort of an automatic transmission. You still have the power to change gears easily if you wish. In most families there will be a Money Market Mutual Fund, a Bond Fund, Income Funds, Growth Funds, and Growth and In-come funds (a balanced fund).

Each fund within the family has its own avenues to travel to reach its goal. The big advantage is that these families al-low switching, though they sometimes assess a nominal fee of $5 to cover some of the bookkeeping costs. This is not to be confused with a load or commission; instead it is a switching fee and it's cheap.

Next we are going to take some time to run through the different types of Mutual Funds and their philosophies. There are funds which deal with only one category and others, such as families, that include a number of categories. But to shop effectively you need at least a minimal amount of understanding about each major type. Skim these descriptions and come back to them later when you are ready to make a choice.

**Bond Funds** invest only in bonds. Bonds are nothing more than certified loans from you the bond holder to a corporation. They are known for producing relatively high yields with relatively low risks. The Bond Fund often tries to buy them at discount, below face value, so the fund can realize further capital gains as well as incomes. All bonds pay out interest to the fund, which in turn is paid to fund holders as income. Despite their conservative nature there is some risk that a bond-issuing corporation might call back the bonds early (paying them off, which in turn means less interest earned) or, on the other hand, the corporation could default. Whether either possibility seriously affects the net asset value of the fund depends on how the portfolio is diversified.

A Bond Fund is also much more liquid than holding bonds yourself. While you can redeem your fund shares at the net asset value, as a bond holder you might have to sell off those bonds at deep discount. This means you will get less than the price you paid for that bond in the first place.

Be careful; not all Bond Funds are the same. Some funds deal only in high-grade bonds with modest return, while others dabble in low-quality, high-risk, high-return bonds. The prospectus sent by the fund will give you an idea which way it swings.

**Municipal Bond Funds** are for the person who is looking for tax-free income, usually someone in a high income-tax bracket. These funds buy the bonds issued by municipalities. When a city, town or state wants to build a highway, school or city hall, it raises money by selling bonds that are exempt from federal taxes. That's not all; these bonds are sometimes exempt from state and local taxes as well. With a Municipal Bond Fund you definitely get that same federal advantage, and a number of funds will break it down further so you can enjoy the state and local tax advantages.

There is really very little risk with these funds because governments seldom default. If the worst should happen with one, you do get some risk insurance because of diversification. Another advantage of diversification is that you are somewhat protected from interest rate fluctuations.

Keep in mind, as with other types of Mutual Funds, interest rates play an important part in the increasing and decreasing value of the shares in these funds.

**Ginnie Mae Funds** deal in securities purchased from the Government National Mortgage Association, known as Ginnie Mae. These securities represent mortgages that are insured by the Federal Housing Administration (FHA) or the Veterans Administration (VA) and that gives the fund added security because it means they are backed by Uncle Sam. Often the advertised yield is several points higher than Money Market Mutual Funds and a few points below regular mortgage rates. The combination of government backing and diversification reduce the appearance of risk, though there is always the possibility that market conditions could affect the price per share so that the value of your initial investment could decrease.

**Junk Bond Funds** are not at all for queasy tummies: they invest in high-risk corporate bonds that pay high interest because there is more chance they could go under. Even with diversification, these funds are subject to wild swings in net asset value. Junk Bond Funds are super speculative.

**Income Funds** pay out income for those who need cash instead of growth. While young investors are interested in increasing the size of their portfolio, some people, as they get older, are more interested in a constant flow of income to meet day-to-day living expenses. An Income Fund accomplishes this feat by investing in high-yielding stocks, bonds and utilities. The Income Funds take a conservative approach to protect capital and to increase income.

**Growth Funds** instead of producing immediate income, do as their name implies—go for growth. They are riskier than Income Funds because they concentrate on more volatile growth stocks. Within this category there are a number of different types of Growth Funds.

**Long-term Growth Funds** are considered a middle-of-the-road risk, emphasizing stocks in companies that have potential for long-term growth and a good track record. These funds should show an average 10 percent growth over a 5-year period or they are not worth the risk. Past performance is only an indicator of history and not a promise for the future.

**Performance Funds** have the name because they constantly perform with an aim toward rapid growth. Of course, as in acting, not all performances are worthy of note. For that reason they are considered speculative and have been called "go-go funds." These funds can either go wild or your money can go bye-bye. But the risk is for maximum capital gains and growth. The beauty here is that these give semisophisticated investors the rush of high potential investments and at the same time much more security than someone simply buying stocks in the same companies. Again, the security comes from the principle of diversification. That way, if one or two of the higher risk ventures go south or even belly up, it is not a total tragedy. If the market is good, Performance Funds are usually very good; but when the market is bad, these funds can be very sad.

So, Performance Funds take some homework. If you feel a Bear (down) Market coming on, you might seriously consider selling out of your Performance Funds and moving into a Money Market Mutual Fund, which is done easily if both are part of the same fund family.

**Hedge Funds** are for those who like to hedge their bets a bit but who like even more excitement than performance Funds. Hedge Funds take a strong constitution because these funds do things you wouldn't expect from a Mutual Fund. They really do play the market, and if there isn't enough cash flow in the portfolio, Hedge Funds will borrow against their own stocks in order to buy more shares (leverage). Beyond that, these funds not only go for winners, but also try for losers, by betting those stocks will lose even more. This neat little trick is called *selling short,* a sophisticated system whereby the fund sells shares it doesn't own. If everything goes right, a fund will sell those shares at a higher price than it eventually pays for them. How do you sell something you don't have? Well, the fund still must deliver the shares to the buyer, so it borrows the stock from a broker and then prays. The idea is that when the price comes down the fund buys shares from the broker at the lower price to cover those shares already sold at a profit. It's enough to send your head spinning, so we will tell you more about that in the Stock Market chapter. But, believe us when we say that while it sounds like fun, it can be very expensive if the price of the stock goes the wrong way.

**Options Funds** spend their time and money buying and selling options. That would make sense, wouldn't it? But options such as *calls* are a complicated market maneuver: You pay a premium to bet that a stock will sell for more than you will pay for it. It's the right to buy or sell stock at a set price by a certain date. The fund hopes that the stock will increase beyond the set price which it promised to pay, plus the cost of premium, to create a profit. This is accomplished by exercising the option, buying the stock at the lower set price and selling it at the higher quoted price. And if that's got your head spinning, wait until we talk about *puts*. Actually, while investing in options is a complex maneuver, it's definitely fascinating and we will explain options completely in a future chapter. But it is safe to say these funds are not for the beginner because there is a real chance for a loss.

**Commodities Funds,** instead of being in stocks and bonds, play the commodities market, and "play" is the right word because it can be a craps shoot. The commodities market provides the chance to gamble on the future prices and supplies of such commodities as coffee, sugar and soybeans. A fund buys contracts that may hold promise of a certain delivery price by a specified date, but the future is hard to see and with commodities on the line it's even tougher. The price of hog bellies (bacon), corn, coffee, wheat or precious metals can jump or fall due to circumstances beyond anyone's real control, and that's where the gamble is. The contract sets the delivery price and date of delivery. If the market price of the commodity goes up by the desperation date (expiration date), a profit can be made.

If, because of too much supply or too little demand, the price goes down, then everything bought on margin can be lost. (Buying on margin is the use of a small down payment and of someone else's money to increase the yield when compared with the total amount of personal money on the line.) The real gamble is that if for some reason delivery isn't made by contract date, someone playing that game can lose not only what was leveraged but also the total difference between the contract price and what the market would bear and pay. Several hundred percent sometimes!

It is a system that has made many a rich investor poor very fast. Of course it can work the other way, too, depending on which side of the deal you find yourself. In commodities there are either big winners or big losers; there is no middle ground (though in a Commodities Fund an investor cannot lose more than the original investment because of a more conservative portfolio and the diversification that comes with size). But the risk of losing that original investment is still high. This is not for someone who ever really needs to see that money again.

**Multi-Funds** may be for the truly uncourageous. This type of a fund buys shares in other mutual funds, thus offering the greatest possible form of diversification. The theory is that covering many bases is a solid form of security. Needless to say, you pay for that with an often lower yield.

**Index Funds** are for those in love with the evening stock market report; these funds pick a certain stock market and buy some of all the stocks listed on a certain index in that exchange (for instance, the Dow Jones 30 industrials, the Dow Transportation or Dow Utilities index stocks or even Standard and Poors 500). There are several funds that own stock in all 500 companies on the S&P 500. Effectively this type of fund matches the performance of the stock market as a whole.

**Venture Capital Funds** may be for you if you like high risk, because they invest in smaller, little-known companies often not yet registered with the Securities and Exchange Commission. Venture Capital Funds provide seed money for companies who are depending on new untested management to succeed in a fast-growing field. The philosophy is to find a potential winner and get in on the ground floor. This means both the company and the fund can either take off like a rocket or misfire.

## Specialty

**Specialty** or **Sector Funds** specialize in only a particular sector of industry. For instance, Technology Funds go after high-tech industry companies that range from computers to components, electronics, software, microchips and products for space and defense. Bio-tech funds invest in medical advances such as genetic engineering and other medical research. Bio-tech may be one of the riskiest specialty funds because many of the companies have a very short financial history, if any at all. Health services funds invest in hospital management companies, medical equipment, drug companies, nursing services and medical suppliers.

Energy funds put money into utilities, oil, gas and exploration companies. You get the idea. There are many Specialty Funds investing in nearly every field from aerospace and defense to financial services, entertainment, forestry, mining and chemicals, just for starters.

One good example of a Specialty Fund also being a nice inflation insurance policy is a gold fund. A gold fund invests in gold mining stock that actually represents the precious metal. This kind of a fund is safer than the stock itself because there is some diversification within the industry. Gold funds are certainly better than bullion itself for at least two reasons: One, it is more liquid; two, there is no storage fee. One more plus with a Specialty Fund: Unlike investing in actual gold, you have a chance to earn cash dividends. While gold has had some scary roller-coaster rides over the years, it has always been considered a good hedge against inflation. So if inflation starts to take off, you might want to take a look at precious metal funds.

Although these Specialty or Sector Funds may be volatile, you can still protect yourself because it's easier for you to monitor one area of interest than a full and varied portfolio as is held by most funds.

One form of risk insurance is protecting yourself with timing, a system where you leave your "funds" in a fund until you smell danger. At the first sign, you shift over to a Money Fund. The danger might not be reflected in the Specialty or Sector Fund's net asset value right away, but your familiarity with the sector may give you some nice profitable insight.

If you don't have the time or insight, you can always dollar cost average. We will discuss this strategy in just a few pages as it works for all kinds of funds and many stocks as well.

**Geographic Funds** are another choice. If you want to invest in companies that you can see, why not look in your backyard? There might be a fund that specializes in industries in your part of the country. Just a few are the USAA Sunbelt Era Fund, the Sunbelt Growth Fund, North Star Regional Fund, and Fund of the Southwest, which were the trendsetters. They invest in a number of different high-powered industries that are either based, or spend a great deal of their resources, in their areas.

Of course definitions of geography do vary from fund to fund. USAA seems to feel that the Sunbelt includes twenty-seven states plus the District of Columbia. Some people might also argue with the fund that Idaho and Washington State don't really fit into the Confederacy. USAA is not alone; Sunbelt Growth stretches the notches of the Sunbelt to include Colorado and Utah as well as the Southwest.

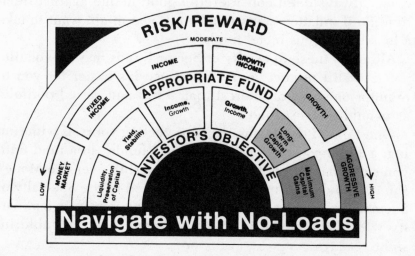

**Source:** No-Load Fund Investor, Inc., Hastings-on-Hudson, N.Y.

## Mutual Menu

Picking the mutual fund for you depends on many factors. Risk is of course the most important. What can your heart stand based on how much money you wish to earn? Age is a critical factor. If you are young and strong of constitution and looking for a fast ride with some possible bumps on the road to riches, you might want to chance a Performance Fund. If you are in your mid thirties, you are not over the investment hill yet, so you may be in for the long haul looking toward a retirement nest egg. For that goal you might want to consider Solid Growth Funds. The same goes if you are trying to save for college educations or a house. If you are looking for some cash flow while you are building that nest egg, your best bet might be Combined Growth and Income Funds. Finally, as you get older you may only want income, so Bond Funds are just what the doctor orders.

Once you have completed that assignment, you might think that you are ready for the big test: investing your money in a fund. Not yet, there is still some more homework. Call the toll-free number and ask for a prospectus and an application. It may take a week to 10 days to get the package. But keep track of how long because it will tell you about that fund's efficiency in general, something you may have gotten a feeling for while on the phone. These are important factors in picking a fund. If they are slow with new applications, they may also be slow in sending you your money when you ask for it. Or they may be slow with transfers and other transactions.

Check the address label for accuracy. If the phone salesperson or the computer operator didn't get the information correct, will the same thing happen with your transactions?

1. Call the toll-free number to request a prospectus and an application.
2. Keep track of how long they take to arrive.
3. Check the address label for accuracy.
4. Read the prospectus.

## Your Personal $$ Memo: Homework Time

To get a better feel for which fund is for you, go to your room and do your homework; if not to your room, to the library. This is really a lot more fun than school assignments because this time there is an immediate payoff. You are doing something for You!

Before you dive into any investment pool, you need to understand that there is a bottom and you can crack your head if you don't know what you are doing. So check out a few books in the Investment section of your library. See how a fund has performed over the past 5 years. This could be as easy as checking just a few publications:

*The Handbook for No-Load Investors*
published by the No-Load Investor, Inc.
PO Box 283
Hastings-on-Hudson, N.Y. 10706
It's an excellent tool; in addition they publish a monthly newsletter *The No-Load Invester*.

*Donoghue's Mutual Funds Almanac*
It includes five- and ten-year performances of more than 1,300 funds, plus toll-free numbers.

*Moody's Bank and Finance Manual*
A short but complete summary of hundreds of funds.

*Money Magazine*'s annual Mutual Fund issue.

*Forbes Magazine*'s annual Mutual Fund performance issue.

There are also a number of books on the subject, but due to time lags in the publication process they often don't have the latest information on a particular fund.

Reading a prospectus is a wild and crazy experience. There is a great deal of gobbledygook, and in a coming chapter we will sort through it with you. For now, though, look for the fund's investment record, its objectives, the structure of its management, and get an idea of the make-up of the portfolio. With almost any prospectus the good news is up front, but the bad news is often buried under the Bull (market) information.

There is often a section with a catchy title such as "Limiting Investment Risks" that will describe how much of the fund's assets will ever be tied into the securities of any single company or industry. The lower the percentage, the lower the risk. For instance, a $100 million bond fund invested equally in 100 bond issues protects itself against default. If two issues go belly up, you would lose only 2 percent of your assets.

But there is more to a prospectus than just numbers; it also explains the full scope of services such as check-writing privileges, telephone exchange or switching charges. It is a chance to get to know your fund before you are divorced from your money.

### Give Back to Get More

The obvious philosophy of investing, as we have said and will say time and time again, is: Buy Low, Sell High, and you will never lose. Of course you can't always do that. So, why not take some special kind of insurance called "Dollar-Cost-Averaging" where you invest a fixed dollar amount every month or quarter. By doing this you buy some shares at high prices and others at lower prices, and over the long haul the result can be a lower price per share. It is a safe, sane and reduced-risk way to invest.

Often a corporation passes along some of its profits to the shareholders. These are called *dividends* and they are normally paid quarterly. Well, when a Mutual Fund is a shareholder, it too receives dividends and passes them along to the members of the fund, in the form of a dividend check. If you are worried about what you are going to do with those pesky little dividend checks which will arrive every so often, why not tell the Mutual Fund you don't want them. Oh, you want the money, but you don't want the checks. Look into the fund's Dividend Reinvestment Plan. The Plan automatically reinvests your dividends to buy fractions of shares as well as whole shares in your name. These are often called DRPs or what we like to call Drips because they act like a leaky faucet. Each Drip is small, but eventually they form a larger pool of water, or in this case a larger pool of money in your account. Dividend Reinvestment Plans are a form of automatic dollar cost averaging.

### Remember Your Uncle

Everyone hopes you do well with your Mutual Fund investments, including your favorite Uncle Sam. Especially your favorite Uncle Sam. One thing you must realize is that once you are out of the realm of IRAs almost everything has tax consequences. About the only way around that is to stop earning income, or to invest solely in tax-free funds. Before you consider tax-free funds, remember they often have much lower yields than taxables, so unless you are in the top brackets the yield may be too low to offset the tax advantage.

With Mutual Funds you don't just pay taxes when you sell, but a number of times as different things happen. When a fund earns dividends from its investments (even if it's just interest) that money is distributed to shareholders so that the fund doesn't get stuck paying federal income taxes on the earnings (definitely a case of passing the buck). You must report that income whether you get a check or it is reinvested in the fund. These distributions take on different tax faces, and the fund will tell you what money needs to be declared as ordinary dividends or capital gain distributions.

Ordinary dividends must be reported on your 1040 federal tax return as ordinary income. That means it is taxed at whatever your adjusted tax bracket is.

Capital gains distributions are treated differently.

### Wait Watchers

Uncle Sam used to encourage long term investing, by giving a wonderful tax break on long term capital gains (profit made from investments). If you held on to an investment for more than six months, when you sold it you were taxed on only 40 percent of your profits. But no longer, now all capital gains (long or short) are considered regular taxable income taxed the same, no matter how long you hold them. If you are in the 15 percent bracket, your tax will be 15 percent of your profit. If you are in the 28 percent bracket, the tax rate is 28 percent. Of course as with anything else to do with the IRS, there are complications and confusing tax tables, so it is best to check with an accountant or tax preparer to determine your liabilities. Aren't tax laws fun? Be aware; they are continually changing.

All of that gets us around to the ease of declaring all capital gains distributions from Mutual Funds as long term, even if you have only been part of the fund for a few months. Normally a fund will make a once-a-year capital gains distribution to its shareholders, and the amount will be broken down on the IRS form 1099 which you will receive from the fund.

Even some income from tax-exempt Bond Funds is sometimes subject to federal taxes if the fund earns taxable income from interim investments or capital gains distributions from the sale of portfolio securities. Once again refer to that 1099.

## Full Gainer or Belly Flop?

When you sell your shares in a fund, even if you transfer from fund to fund within a family, you may have either a capital gain or a capital loss. You will need to keep careful records. Different IRS rules apply when you move out of a Mutual Fund than when a fund distributes capital gains from the sale of its holdings. We are talking about you selling your shares of a fund. A capital gain can be offset by a capital loss if you happen to be so unlucky as to have a loss. If you have any questions about taxes, always check with your tax preparer or the IRS since every case is different.

Once you have been invested in Mutual Funds for a while and have become more comfortable with the investment world, you may want to start buying stocks. Before you take that big step, you do need to have some understanding of how stocks are exchanged. We "share" that information in the next few chapters.

# 7

## Taking Stock in the
## Stock Markets

We don't know what you think of when someone says: "The Dow Jones Industrials closed up today after being down yesterday." For years we were impressed by just knowing which way the market went, but we never had the slightest idea as to what that figure meant. Well, the Dow Jones Industrials figure is an indicator of what 30 of the most-watched stocks do. We can't say for sure that there has been a conspiracy to keep the workings of Wall Street a secret from the American public, but it is not nearly as difficult to understand as the people who run the markets want us to believe.

The Dow Jones owes its name to 2 people: Charles Dow, who more than 100 years ago quit school at 16 to become a reporter, and Eddie Jones, a Brown University dropout. They got together to form the company, which now owns the business newspaper *The Wall Street Journal*. In 1884 they began publishing the average closing prices (final prices of the day) of 12 well known stocks. By 1928 the list had grown to 30 mostly blue chip stocks.

Every day Dow Jones takes the price of one share of each of these thirty industrial stocks, adds them up and divides the figure according to a special formula. The Dow, as it is called, shows whether the price of stocks in general on the New York Stock Exchange goes up or down. Of course, individual stocks go their own way to the point that when the Dow is up as many as one third of the stocks on the New York Stock Exchange may be down, but the Dow Jones averaging formula works out to be accurate when compared with the other measures such as Standard and Poors and Value Line.

## A Proud Owner

When you buy stock in a company, you are buying a share of the company. There may be millions and millions of shares, but if you own one, it makes you a part owner of the company and shareholder in the equity of the corporation. The companies sell the shares to raise money. Often they keep a majority of the shares for themselves so that they can maintain control of the corporation, but still each shareholder owns a piece of the action (a percentage of the business). This practice of shareholding is almost as old as time and it hasn't changed much in the past several thousand years, except that it has obviously become more sophisticated and much larger in scope.

Back before Columbus, merchants used to pool their money so they could build ships and sail to faraway ports to sell their goods. After they bought new products to carry back to their home port, they would share the profits, or if it didn't go well they would share the losses.

Soon after the American Revolution, on May 17, 1792, a financial baby was born that would grow into the New York Stock Exchange. A group of 24 merchants and auctioneers worked out a system to meet every day during regular hours to buy and sell the bonds (loans) of a very young United

States government, as well as shares in insurance companies and banks.

During the Industrial Revolution in the nineteenth century, there was such rapid growth and demand for money that the business of selling stock in companies took on a much greater significance. Almost everything was a gamble because none of these new companies had any track record and the world around them was rapidly changing with the advent of the steam engine, the telegraph and eventually the telephone. Those with money were caught up in a whirlwind of tossing the dice to the extent that huge fortunes were made but many were lost. At that time anyone who wanted to be involved in the stock market had to have a great deal of money. And it was not until just after World War I that the small investor began to join in on the fun. The stock markets soared and the people roared through the 1920s until the crash of 1929 when most investors suddenly became small investors or nonexistent investors. Since then stock markets have come under more control, including the careful eye of the Securities and Exchange Commission.

## How the Stock Exchange Works

The way the stock exchange works is fundamental supply and demand. If you wish to buy stock, you purchase it through a broker (licensed salesperson). The broker places an order with the stock exchange at a price determined by how much that stock is in demand. The more people who want to buy it, the higher the stock price will be. The reverse is true when you sell; some other investor has to be interested in buying. Again, the law of supply and demand applies. If you wish to sell a particular stock and not very many people want to buy it at that time, you may have to settle for a lower price than you had originally hoped for. You, the seller, never know who the buyer is and vice versa because this exchange is done through stock brokerage houses (licensed businesses for the buying and selling of numerous investments).

Say you want to buy 100 shares of Bubblz Company. You have heard it is a good deal and it is selling for $10 a share. (Most transactions are in round lots of one hundred shares; anything else is called an odd lot.)

With that in mind, you would phone your stock broker to initiate your order. The broker would then suggest that you buy at either $10 a share, if it can be purchased at that price, or at "market." (A market order is whatever the best available price might be at the time; it could be higher or it could be lower.) If you decide not to buy at market and you stick with your plan of $10 a share, it is called a limit order. There is no deal unless a stockholder wants to sell at that exact price. But, perhaps you make a decision to purchase Bubblz stock with a market order. Your broker then uses a computer to send the order to the brokerage house's clerk on the floor of whatever exchange carries Bubblz.

The broker on the floor gets the message to buy 100 shares of Bubblz at "market." Immediately the floor broker goes to the post on the floor where Bubblz is traded and asks "How's Bubblz?" The person who answers is called a specialist. A specialist is the broker's broker on the stock exchange floor, who controls the price of a particular stock through the use of a special account to buy-up or sell-off shares. This control of supply and demand helps smooth out wild price swings. In the case of Bubblz, the specialist says "ten to a half." It could end right here with the broker buying it at 10½, which is "market." But a broker's job is to get the best possible price for a customer, and based on the way Bubblz has traded recently, the broker believes it can be bought at 10¼. So the bid is made, "a fourth for a hundred." That's a quarter of a point lower than just offered. If you and your broker are in luck, then still another broker will enter the crowd with an order to sell 100 shares for 10¼ and, hearing your bid, will yell, "Sold!"

After the specialist on the floor completes the sale, the brokers report the transaction back to their telephone clerks so that you can be informed that you are the proud owner of 100 shares of Bubblz at 10¼. You then have until noon on the fifth business day to come up with the money; in this case, it would be $1,025 plus commission.

---

### How Special Is the Specialist?

A specialist on the trading floor of a stock exchange is much like a traffic cop during rush hour. The job is to keep everything flowing without a major crash. With stocks, should there be a rapid sell-off of a company such as Bubblz, the specialist, seeing how this could cause the stock to collapse, would buy up as much as possible to keep the price from hitting rock bottom. After absorbing the overabundance of supply, the specialist holds on until some of the demand returns, at which point that inventory is sold off. Also, the specialist has a job to do if a stock price rises too rapidly. A stock which rises too fast can create a major sell-off by profit takers, which in turn could cause the stock to plunge more rapidly than new orders could absorb, possibly creating financial calamity for the company, for no apparent reason. To make sure that doesn't happen, the specialist sells some more of the inventory with enough supply to meet some of the demand. It takes a delicate balance to slow the rate of increase without stifling the rally.

---

Even before you hear whether or not you have made a deal, a record of the transaction has been entered into the huge computers at the stock exchange; that entry activates what everyone calls the "Ticker," the teletype device that lets everyone read the transactions. They are transmitted to thousands of displays located in brokerage offices, businesses, banks and home-computer networks in hundreds of cities in the United States, Puerto Rico, Canada, and several European nations.

Not every stock is traded on the New York Stock Exchange (NYSE); there is also the American Stock Exchange.

AMEX, as it is known, is the second largest exchange, listing more than 900 companies. In fact, many of the AMEX listings are considered medium-size companies, but there are some large ones that prefer to stay right there where they feel very comfortable. A number of today's huge corporations were conceived and nurtured on the American Stock Exchange. The AMEX also lists government securities and Put and Call options.

Some people tend to look down on the AMEX; not simply considering it a junior exchange, they also feel it is too pedestrian. They may not know it, but their unjustified opinion is rooted in history. Before 1953 the American Stock Exchange was known as the New York Curb Exchange because for years trading was actually done outside on the curb. That was a long time ago though, and it moved indoors in 1921.

Times have changed; it is part of the big-time now, and every day millions of dollars' worth of prestigious stocks are traded on the floor of the American Stock Exchange in New York City.

That's not all, folks. There are several more exchanges. Number three in organized size is the Midwest Stock Exchange, which was built out of the Chicago Stock Exchange. And the list just keeps on growing with other regional exchanges such as the Pacific Stock Exchange, Philadelphia, Boston, Cincinnati, Spokane, Honolulu, and the Salt Lake City (The Intermountain Exchange) Exchanges. These all work on the same basic principle: Securities are bought and sold by auction.

But that is not the only way things are done. There are thousands of other companies whose stocks are not listed on any of the exchanges; these securities are sold over the counter via negotiation. Instead of the securities being tossed into a pool, from which anyone may dip, here the buyer and seller work together through brokers to agree mutually on a value and price.

## Over the Counter and Through the Woods

The over-the-counter market is watched over by an umbrella organization known as the National Association of Securities Dealers (NASD) which is the self-regulatory agency of the industry. NASD represents more than 4,000 broker-dealers in OTC stocks. As with the NYSE and AMEX, it operates under the authority of the Securities and Exchange Commission. NASD polices all OTC activities and has the power to expel members found guilty of unethical behavior. It is also charged with making investing easier for all parties concerned, which is one reason why NASDAQ was born. The AQ of NASDAQ stands for Automated Quotation System. It is a computer system designed to speed up the transactions. When NASDAQ (pronounced NAZ-DAK) was brought online in 1964, it created the world's longest trading floor, stretching 3,000 miles from coast to coast, connected by phone lines and microwave. This electronic exchange allows security dealers in thousands of offices to set up immediate contact between buyer and seller.

While not every OTC stock is listed on NASDAQ, 4,500 of the more than 7,000 over-the-counter traded companies are handled through the automated quotation system.

In some cases the deals are still handled on the phone, but the computer has given both the buyer and seller a better feel for what the market will bear so that they can more easily agree on a price.

## In the Pink

Prior to NASDAQ there was a way to determine at least representative prices for over-the-counter stocks, and it is still a helpful reference tool today. We are talking about the Pink Sheet published by the National Quotation Bureau, which is a privately owned, price-reporting service. Brokers or dealers who wish to have their prices listed report the latest trading prices in the afternoon. Then, while the rest of us are in bed, these prices are compiled and printed, and the Pink Sheets are distributed the following morning. Is it possible the name derives from the color of the compilers' eyes?

The Pink Sheet is a very comprehensive list, and each edition quotes more than 10,000 prices. Consider the effort and time involved in compiling it when compared with the speed of an automated quotation system. This means that it is not up-to-the-minute because of its once a day publication schedule. But the Pink Sheet is still valuable because it also carries those 2,500 other securities not handled by NASDAQ.

It is interesting to note that while NASD has determined that there are 600 NASDAQ securities which qualify to be listed on the NYSE, and another 1,000 which could be listed on the AMEX Board, these companies apparently prefer the technological efficiency of the NASDAQ system.

You might get the impression that these over-the-counter traded companies are small and possibly fly-by-nights. Not necessarily; for instance, many insurance companies, banks and even high-tech companies such as Apple Computer and Intel are traded OTC. You can also find many household names on the OTC listings such as Nike, Coors and Hoover. And the over-the-counter market is where you find most new issues—new companies just starting out with their first major public offering of stock.

## So What's the Difference?

There is a big difference between the stock exchange system of auction and the OTC method of negotiation. NASDAQ helps both the buyer and the seller as they each attempt to get the best prices. This is possible because it is a competitive, multiple market-maker system, connecting interested parties from all over the country. In contrast, the exchange system is a single specialist operation composed of those private brokerage firms which only do business on the exchange floor. Remember, the specialist's job is to maintain some stability in the stock price by buying-up or selling-off stock in his inventory. This is an attempt to solve the problem called whip-saw, or wild swings of price.

With OTC there is no specialist; instead dealer-brokers play that role by creating their own inventories of securities, hoping to find customers who wish to buy them at a higher price later on. These are called *market makers*, and there can be any number of market makers for any one issue. For example two or more brokerage houses can each create its own inventory of an OTC stock in order to facilitate trading, but these inventories also buffer those possible wild swings in price.

While there is always a specialist in the exchange system, there does not have to be a market maker with over-the-counter trades. Instead, your broker may have to deal directly with another broker who represents the stockholder on the other side of the deal. It's an excellent example of a free and more competitive market system. The OTC broker-dealer does not have to accept the quoted price but has a chance to get a possibly better price through NASDAQ for his or her client. It is a rather simple system of consulting the computer and receiving a representative bid price and a representative ask price on that stock. If the price is right for the customer, another keystroke shows the actual quotes of at least five firms "making a market" in that issue. For convenience, the best price appears first. Then the trader (your broker) makes contact with the market maker and concludes the transaction directly. The trade itself is then settled and cleared through a subsidiary of the NASD.

Another difference between over-the-counter and the exchange system is commissions. Many OTC transactions take place on what is known as a net-price basis. Instead of a commission the broker making a market in that stock (or warehousing the stock) earns a profit on the sale, much like other merchants, from selling the stock for more than it was purchased, or by buying it from you for less than it can be expected to sell. In this case it is called either a mark-up or a mark-down. That mark-up or mark-down is supposed to be kept at no more than five percent according to NASD guidelines.

If your broker is not making a market in that particular OTC stock, then you will pay a commission and you may also be subject to a mark-up or a mark-down. Be sure to ask how much a transaction is going to cost you, because if you are not careful you may lose all of your gains or potential gains to those nasty extra charges.

Now that you know where and how it all happens, it's time to learn to know when to do it. As in love, you can't simply start groping blindly; you need to understand the subtle signals that indicate it is all right to go on to the next step. If you rush things, you could find yourself slapped silly.

# 8

## Stocks and Bond-age and Some Kinkier Options

You should never get tied-down to an investment before you know what you are getting into. Although you may be intrigued by some sumptuous stock suggestion from a friend, don't touch it yet! Make sure you have some feeling for the stock market and how you might feel after it does a number on you. You also need to read the annual report and prospectus. While the prospectus may seem like a document written by lawyers for bankers, and seemingly designed to confuse buyers, it does have important information. Some of it is actually readable and understandable with pertinent details that affect you: what the company is worth, how much it is in debt, where it hopes to grow and who is running the store.

This is only the beginning of the homework. You also need to check the growth of the stock, its volatility, its price earnings ratio, its dividends and so on. After checking it out and determining that some investors have doubled, tripled and

---

### Your Personal $$ Memo: The Pondered Prospectus

You really can learn a great deal from these "wonder-filled" documents; a case in point is one prospectus we received recently about a new stock issue which we shall call Buy-O-Fraud. (If we used the real name the company might get cranky.) Within the first few paragraphs, the underwriters of the stock issue explained that the management of this company had no working experience in the highly technical field they were tackling, nor did they ever expect to get any experience personally because they planned to leave that in the hands of one person. The prospectus went on to explain that while this person had created this technique, he had never been successful at capitalizing on it and his last venture had gone bankrupt. Beyond that, the man was in his late sixties and in failing health.

You can't find a more honest approach. Because all of the possible pitfalls are pointed out, there is no way a Buy-O-Fraud investor could ever charge fraud.

Despite the open and honest warnings, millions of shares were offered and sold. As often happens with a new offering, enough demand was created that the stock price shot up and the original investors made a bundle by getting out early. As they sold off, the price tumbled to the point that those who bought later may have a difficult time recovering their investment.

---

quadrupled their money, you may be hot to trot. Wait just a minute!

Now that we have stimulated a desire to get into the market, we should caution you that there are no guarantees when it comes to stocks, bonds or options. About the only truisms we can provide are that over the long haul, stocks have outperformed bonds when it comes to beating inflation, and more people have been burned by options than have walked away with cold cash.

## Stocks and Bond-age

So you want to buy! Well, whether its stocks or bonds, it is a cash purchase. Cash means money in a spendable form such as a check or maybe a loan from your broker. In either case once the order is placed, your money is due in full within 5 business days. After the payment has been received, you have the choice of leaving the certificates with the broker registered in a street name or you can have them sent to you in your name.

If you choose the street name, that means dividends (if there are any) are paid to the broker, not to you, but are credited to your house account. While this works best for frequent traders, it can create a big problem should the broker go under. That would mean your certificates could be tied-up for months or years in red tape. Without your certificates, you can't trade or get out should the stock crash or should you need the money even for an emergency.

The way around that possibility is to have the certificates sent to you in your name. While they are often exciting to look at, they are not suitable for framing and should be kept in a safe-deposit box. Stock certificates can easily become legal tender in the hands of a forger. Safety is the best strategy if you are holding onto the stock for a length of time.

## What Type of Stock to Buy

You have some choices because there are common stocks and preferred stocks.

**Common Stocks** are for the common, everyday person such as you or us. With common stocks, you are buying a portion of the company, and even though you are not much of an owner and you are not making management decisions, you can join in at annual meetings or vote by proxy. Each share counts as one vote, and the more shares you hold, the more clout you carry. Just before an annual meeting the corporation will send you notification and a proxy card that gives you the power to exercise your feelings on certain matters. If you give your proxy to others, then you don't have any more say than that. But if you attend an annual meeting, you have a chance to speak your mind.

As a holder of common stock, you benefit from the good fortunes of the company as the stock prices and dividends increase, dividends being the portion of a corporation's earnings which is passed along to the shareholders.

On the other hand, your fortunes will decline if the company's fortunes decline. The reasons for such a decline can be varied, from the company's profit picture becoming very fuzzy to simply the perception on Wall Street that something isn't right. At other times a drop in stock price may have nothing to do with the corporation; the economy as a whole, or the periodic paranoia of the investment community may be responsible.

A corporation is under no obligation to pay dividends. Dividends must be declared by the board of directors and are based on performance and past history. Therefore, common stocks are usually priced lower than other stocks, such as preferred stock.

**Preferred Stock** might be your preference if you are looking more for income than for growth. Because, while both common and preferred stock represent shares in the same company, in some cases the dividends paid by preferred stocks can be three times those of common stock. In general, preferred stock is also less of an investment risk than common stock, but more so than bonds. Some say preferreds have the worst of both worlds because these have neither the enforceable claim of a bond, nor the opportunity to share in the possible profits of a rapidly rising common-stock price.

However, you are buying risk insurance. If the company ever bellies up, preferred stocks have first claim on the remaining assets after the outstanding bonds are taken care of.

Some preferred stocks are cumulative, which means dividends accumulate if a company skips a quarter or a year. When dividends do resume, preferred stockholders usually get their dividends just before common-stock holders receive theirs.

## What Should Turn You On?

When it comes to love everyone has a different answer, but when it comes to stocks the turn-ons are much the same for all of us, so long as we have matured enough financially to understand what it is that we are getting into.

There are a number of conditions which affect the market's behavior, and they are areas you can keep an eye on simply by reading the newspaper, watching the nightly news and being aware of the world around you by listening to the radio. Any given stock can be affected by a combination of the following factors: the economy, world conditions, monetary policy, interest rates, stock valuations, sentiment indicators and the general state of the market.

## Pump Harder, Peddle Faster

The business cycle is much like a bicycle: It goes up and down hills. Getting up hills can be tough, and coming down can be fast and dangerous. The term *business cycle* can refer to the economy in general and its periods of contraction and expansion, known to most of us as recession and recovery. The effects of business cycles can be different from industry to industry, depending on the economy as a whole. For that reason you need to read some of the signs, not just the Dow Jones Index but also get a feel for the Standard and Poor's 500. That way you will be able to tell if the stock-market averages have been on an upturn or downturn during the past 12 to 18 months. It is also important to understand what the experts predict for the future, so you should learn to read into the government statistics that come out each month. Later on in this book we will run down what these statistics are and what they mean to most of us. These indicators are supposed to be above politics and are broad-based enough to withstand some of the whipsaw of day-to-day living.

## Money Makes the Money-Go-Round

Without money to grow, a company will stagnate and the stock price will be affected. On the other hand, a company that is not growing by leaps and bounds might instead pump out large dividends. Many times companies decide to sit on the sidelines waiting for a different monetary policy on the part of the Federal Reserve Board that will cause interest rates to come down. This makes expansion much more affordable. Just about the time the Fed starts to loosen its grip on the money supply is often a time of stock-market growth, and many companies and their stocks are dragged out of their wallowing holes and into the rushing waters of profits. So, keep an eye on interest rates and the monetary policy. (Both items were discussed earlier when we were talking about where to stash your cash.) These are things to keep in mind for all investment opportunities.

## Eyeing the Goods

A good shopper wants to get the best for the least. You want good value. It can be difficult to tell sometimes with a stock; there are no real advertised bargain-basement type sales for stocks, but there are bargains. You just have to know where and how to look. When someone says a stock is undervalued, it means that the selling price is way below its true worth. How can that happen? It is because the stock market is controlled more by emotions than by real bottom-line thinking. For example, if enough investors somehow believe a stock is about to take off, it can become a self-fulfilling prophecy because they begin to buy aggressively. That in turn can push the price higher, attracting even more attention and more investors. The stock markets may be the purest form of supply and demand; when more people want to buy a particular stock than want to sell it, the price begins to take off. And the opposite is also true. As you will learn soon, the price/earnings (P/E) ratio is a good indicator.

There are times when you will read in the newspaper that a certain company is posting record profits, but at the same time the stock price is going south faster than a flock of geese in the fall. How can that happen? Well, the stock market is a funny place where history is very important, but everyone is betting on the future. The plummeting stock on skyrocketing earnings can suggest that the company's profits six months down the line will come in line with reality and be lower. On the other hand, there are more than four fingers and a thumb; there is also the situation of a company reporting lower earnings and the stock taking off anyway. This suggests that the outlook, at least in the eyes of the investor, has improved.

You may get the impression that the stock market is unorthodox and unpredictable; well, you are right. The soothsayers who push up a particular stock, or yell "Sell!" on another, may be way off base in the long run. Remember, no one has yet developed the always accurate crystal ball, which leads us directly to those who think they have.

### Sentimental Journeys

By now you may have gotten the impression that the stock market as a whole is nothing more than a huge series of wishing wells connected by wires and computers. People simply throw in their money, close their eyes and hope. Well, believe it or not, many people do just that. There are a great deal of superstitions controlling the market and a number of sentiment indicators. For example, you may read about the great Superbowl Stock Market Indicator, where the market will either win or lose depending on which league wins. It may work for a day or two. (The same goes for the World Series Stock Indicator or the Presidential Election Indicators.) These are not serious long-term indicators; instead, they are all devices which have been invented by brokers or analysts trying to break the tension and add some levity to their lives.

The main sentiment indicator you should concern yourself with is whether or not the big traders are Bullish or Bearish. Bullish of course means the market is charging to make a killing; Bearish means it is either hibernating or retreating.

## STOCK MARKET ACTION SINCE 1832
### Net Change From Year To Year
### Based On Average December Prices

| President Elected | 4-Year Cycle Beginning | Election Year | Post-Election Year | Mid-term | Pre-Election Year |
|---|---|---|---|---|---|
| Jackson (D) | 1832 | 15% | − 3% | 10% | 2% |
| Van Buren (D) | 1836 | − 8 | − 8 | 1 | −13 |
| W.H. Harrison (W)** | 1840* | 5 | −14 | −13 | 36 |
| Polk (D) | 1844* | 8 | 6 | −15 | 1 |
| Taylor (W)** | 1848* | − 4 | 0 | 19 | − 3 |
| Pierce (D) | 1852* | 20 | −13 | −30 | 1 |
| Buchanan (D) | 1856 | 4 | −30 | − 7 | − 7 |
| Lincoln (R) | 1860* | − 4 | − 4 | 43 | 30 |
| Lincoln (R)** | 1864 | 0 | −14 | − 3 | − 6 |
| Grant (R) | 1868 | 2 | − 7 | − 4 | 7 |
| Grant (R) | 1872 | 7 | −13 | 3 | − 4 |
| Hayes (R) | 1876 | −18 | −10 | 6 | 43 |
| Garfield (R)** | 1880 | 19 | 3 | − 3 | − 9 |
| Cleveland (D) | 1884* | −19 | 20 | 9 | − 7 |
| B. Harrison (R) | 1888* | − 2 | 3 | −14 | 18 |

## STOCK MARKET ACTION SINCE 1832 (continued)
### Net Change From Year To Year
### Based On Average December Prices

| President Elected | 4-Year Cycle Beginning | Election Year | Post-Election Year | Mid-term | Pre-Election Year |
|---|---|---|---|---|---|
| Cleveland (D) | 1892* | 1 | − 20 | − 3 | 1 |
| McKinley (R) | 1896* | − 2 | 13 | 19 | 7 |
| McKinley (R)** | 1900 | 14 | 16 | 1 | − 19 |
| 1832–1903 totals | | 38% | − 75% | 19% | 78% |
| T. Roosevelt (R) | 1904 | 25 | 16 | 3 | − 33 |
| Taft (R) | 1908 | 37 | 14 | − 12 | 1 |
| Wilson (D) | 1912* | 3 | − 14 | − 9 | 32 |
| Wilson (D) | 1916 | 3 | − 31 | 16 | 13 |
| Harding (R)** | 1920* | − 24 | 7 | 20 | − 3 |
| Coolidge (R) | 1924 | 19 | 23 | 5 | 26 |
| Hoover (R) | 1928 | 36 | − 15 | − 29 | − 47 |
| F. Roosevelt (D) | 1932* | − 18 | 48 | − 2 | 39 |
| F. Roosevelt (D) | 1936 | 28 | − 34 | 13 | 0 |
| F. Roosevelt (D) | 1940 | − 12 | − 15 | 6 | 21 |
| F. Roosevelt (D)** | 1944 | 14 | 33 | − 10 | − 2 |
| Truman (D) | 1948 | − 2 | 11 | 20 | 15 |
| Eisenhower (R) | 1952* | 7 | − 3 | 39 | 23 |
| Eisenhower (R) | 1956 | 4 | − 13 | 33 | 11 |
| Kennedy (D)** | 1960* | − 4 | 27 | − 13 | 18 |
| Johnson (D) | 1964 | 13 | 9 | − 11 | 17 |
| Nixon (R) | 1968* | 12 | − 14 | − 1 | 10 |
| Nixon (R)*** | 1972 | 12 | − 19 | − 32 | 32 |
| Carter (D) | 1976* | 18 | − 10 | 2 | 11 |
| Reagan (R) | 1980* | 26 | − 7 | 13 | 18 |
| 1904–1983 totals | | 197% | 13% | 51% | 202% |
| 1832–1983 totals | | 235% | − 62% | 70% | 280% |

*Party in power ousted     D—Democrat  W—Whig  R—Republican
**Death in office
***Resigned

Source: The 1985 Stock Trader's Almanac, The Hirsch Organization, 6 Deer Trail, Old Tappan, N.J. 07675

## Animal Instincts

What we are talking about here is that you must understand the state of the market as a whole before you invest in anything. While not all stocks are brought down by an overall Bear market, not all take off with a Bull either. The market is constantly populated with both Bulls and Bears, and you need to understand how that will affect your particular area of interest. You may be Bullish on a particular company, but the market may be Bearish on that industry. You can get an indication of the general feelings by tracking several stocks in the industry.

If the stock of the company you are interested in seems way out of line, check with your broker for an analyst's report to see if the company may have a market edge on the others. It is the analyst's job to watch a particular corporation, know its management philosophy and its relationship to the industry as a whole. From that, you may learn that the market edge is because of a new product or that the corporation is headed in a new direction. Some investors find the birth of new ideas in established companies quite exciting, and they tend to push the price higher.

## Know the Field

Rule Number One for The First-Time Investor desiring the excitement of the stock market: Go for an industry that is familiar to you. This is important because it will tremendously cut down on your homework. This industry can be in the same field as your profession, a reasonable consideration since you constantly keep up with your own company and competition anyway. Because of that closeness you may have a much better feel for trends than the general public and be able to get in on the ground floor before a stock goes through the roof. (We are not talking about inside information, which is when someone involved in the overall decisions of a company trades on specific nonpublic information which can come only from his or her position at the top. Insider information is sometimes given to a friend so that he too can benefit, all of which is illegal and unethical.) What we are talking about is the gut feelings you take home from work. Are things going well or not? Using your own expertise can be quite helpful.

Another way to pick a stock is by using your hobbies. If you are an ardent movie buff, try studio stock or other industries which supply the studios. You are already reading volumes of material on that particular interest and will be able to get a feel for which way an investment might go. If you are really into records, stereos or other electronic gear, those industries might be the best place for you to start.

Not only do you already have a solid base of information, you are also more inclined to stay on top of a field that interests you beyond your investment interest. The key to proper trading is understanding the business you are invested in and recognizing its trends before the bulk of the investment community.

## Matter of Conscience

Your own ethical standards are also a consideration: Never invest in a company which you can't or don't believe in, or one which is running against your ethical grain. If you feel there are shady deals or the company is doing business with individuals or countries you don't approve of, do not invest in the first place, or make sure you get out if you already have invested. There is enough to worry about with investing without having that hang over your head.

## The Price of Loving a Stock

To determine if a stock sales price is a good one for you, it's important for you to understand where it stands in relation to the overall market and to know the stock's own highs and lows of the past 52 weeks. Ask yourself the following questions, and you should have a better feeling for the possible rapid extreme fluctuations of its price, known as its volatility.

1. Has the stock gone up as the market has?
2. Has the stock gone up while the majority of the other stocks declined?
3. How close to the 52-week high is the stock?
4. If it is at its peak, is the market in general still moving forward?
5. Is the stock near its 52-week low?
6. If it is at its low, is the market in general continuing to decline or has it started to move upward?
7. If the company pays a dividend, has it increased or decreased?
8. Has the company's dividend payment record been consistent or erratic?
9. Have the dividends increased as the company grows?
10. Are earnings being plowed back into the company for expansion or for research and development of new products?

## Which Beta is a Betta Beta?

Beta is more than the second letter of the Greek alphabet. It is a measure of a particular stock's volatility, relative to the stock market as a whole. Normally this is measured against the S&P 500 index. The S&P equals 1.00, so a stock that has a beta of 1.70 is more volatile than a stock with a .80. Many of the most successful professional portfolio managers buy into high beta stocks when the market is expected to take off because high betas have a better chance of rapid growth. When a down cycle is anticipated, low beta stocks are purchased because historically low betas do not fall with the same speed. The idea is that the lower a beta the less it will be affected by a rapidly declining market. Before you buy a stock you might want to ask your broker about the beta which is "betta now than lata."

## Buying by the Book

A number of investors also keep their eyes on a company's book value. That is the amount of money that would be left over if the company's assets were sold and after the outstanding debts were paid off. The theory is that if the company were forced into that situation by bankruptcy, the money left over, or book value, would be distributed to the shareholders.

Then you take your math one step further and divide the book value by the number of outstanding shares and immediately you have the book value per share.

These are important figures to investors because if a stock is trading below book value it is sometimes considered a good buy. One reason it might be considered a good buy is that the parts are worth more than the whole. In other words, the company could sell off part of the corporation and thereby increase the total value of the corporation.

## Know the P/E

The P/E (Price/Earnings ratio) is listed in the newspaper and tells you how much "Price" you have to pay for $1 of earnings. It gives you an idea of the investment community's general feelings about the particular company. This is accomplished by dividing the current market price of one share of the stock by the company's per share earnings. Earnings per share is of course the portion of each company's profit allocated to each share of common stock. A corporation with a $20 million after-tax profit and 2 million outstanding shares of common stock, would have an earnings-per-share of $10.

If you are so inclined to figure the P/E yourself, you will find the data in the company's earnings report. For example, a company that earned $4 a share over the past year and sells for $40 has a P/E of 10. That simply means it is selling for 10 times earnings, and investors are willing to pay $10 for every $1 of last year's earnings because they figure the future holds even higher earnings.

There is no such thing as a typical P/E, just as there is no such thing as a typical stock price. P/E ratios can run from as low as 1.4 to higher than 86.7.

The lower the P/E the more conservative the investment is considered to be. A stock with a high P/E is considered more volatile and may move higher at a faster rate during a Bull market, but it also tends to move south rapidly when the market is down.

It is important to remember the P/E is based on the past and you are betting on the future. So keep the figure in perspective by looking at an average of the last several years of earnings and divide that figure into the current stock price. History can give you a feeling for the future, because if a stock is trading at its highest P/E, there is more of a risk that it is riding for a fall.

These figures are available through several sources including the corporation's annual report, *Value Line Ratings and Reports* and, of course, your broker.

### Read the Reports

Earnings figures are very important, as they can tell you a great deal about a company. Projected earnings will also give you an idea of how the corporation is thinking. All of this is easily found in the quarterly and annual reports. If your broker doesn't actually have the reports, the broker will have the address so you can write for them. Another place to look for the information or address is in the public library.

Be careful! Don't try to read an annual or quarterly report

as you would a novel, from beginning to end. Instead you should read an annual report as you might an "adult" magazine, skimming the articles and looking for the stimulating figures and facts. When you find something tickles your fancy, go into that in some depth. You might be titillated by a new product or line so read through the report for all the news on that. Or, if you have a working knowledge of one division of the company and something in the annual report doesn't ring true, that is where you will want to give the report some serious attention. The company writes the report, so you must be aware that only the good information will be easy to find. Since bad news will be played down, you need to learn to read between the lines.

---

### Your Personal $$ Memo: Word Games

It doesn't take a terribly twisted mind to see the humor in the way the report writers try to hide the bad news without being accused of burying it.

A few key words or phrases that might signal some hidden meanings include "despite," "except for," "if this" and "Improvements are expected in . . ." Or as one president's letter I recently read began, "1984 was a year of adjustment . . ." I realized I didn't have to jump to the financial figures to determine that it was a bad year.

We especially love the annual reports that are full of four-color pictures of lots of happy employees standing around looking at sparkling new equipment. It sure does give you a warm feeling about the company and a sense of closeness to the people, but that kind of a report doesn't tell you very much and it might be using the glitz to divert your attention away from some very important, but not terribly encouraging, news. Enjoy the pictures and warmth, but remember investments are not emotional attachments to the employees, the management or the company. Corporations want to build your emotional involvement so you will stick with them in bad times. An investment decision based on that can be fatal to your financial well-being.

**—Bob**

Be on the lookout for braggadocio or otherwise cocky statements that say the company is expanding because of the general economic boom. That expansion may be too late, and when the next down-cycle hits (and it will), it could create inventory surpluses that drag down earnings.

If the company is expanding and current earnings are way up because of recent acquisitions, you might see these indicators as a flashing yellow caution light because the company could be adding too much debt.

### Bean Counters

We shouldn't make fun of accountants. They do count more than beans. The accountant's report or letter at the end of the annual report shows an independent audit of the books. This simply says the report was prepared in accordance with generally accepted accounting principles. If the letter expresses even the slightest reservation about anything, be sure to read on. It could be a red flag of possible red ink for your portfolio. Check the footnotes; they might show that the company has stepped in something it shouldn't have or that the company has changed some of the accounting rules. Other possibilities include changes in stock value because of splits or pending claims or lawsuits.

### Don't Lose Your Balance Sheet

The balance sheet, simply stated, shows what the company owns and what it owes. In checking over several reports, look for major differences between the company's assets and liabilities. One asset that might be a liability to the stockholder would be accounts receivable (money owed to the company). If that figure jumps without a corresponding jump in sales while money is tight, it is a signal that the customers are slow to pay and the company may have to borrow money at high interest rates to keep up cash flow.

Inventories can also become a liability if they grow faster than sales. Any company that is producing more than it sells has to cut back eventually. The sales figures can be found in the income statement.

## The Old Bottom Line

The income statement shows the record of operating activities over the year. It matches the revenues received against all costs. This is where you find the bottom line. Look to see if there was a net profit or loss. The first item to check out is net sales and the rate of growth. Just doing better than last year is not good enough; you want the rate of increase to be even more rapid than before, unless you are checking the stock out at the end of a recession; in that case consider the rate of decline in sales. When that rate slows, it might be the time to buy.

Don't forget operating costs. If income from sales is soaring and costs are being kept under contol, it is a good sign that profit margins are likely to increase. On the other hand, if operating costs are rising faster than income from sales, watch out.

## Debt Fret

A company's debt structure is very important. Current liabilities in the balance sheet will tell how much of the debt is due in the coming year. That must be paid out of current assets. As for long-term debt, the footnotes to the financial statement usually include a section detailing the interest rate that must be paid. You want to see if the company had borrowed when rates were low, which can help provide greater potential earnings in the long run. A company that borrows when rates are high can often be saddled with too much of a burden to continue expansion.

## Corporate Crystal Balls

Some people leave the financial analysis up to the experts and quickly look for items such as market-share trends. In other words, how much of the market does the firm control and how much has it captured or lost in recent years? Check to see if it is a healthy trend over the past five years, given the outside forces of the general economy and market cycles.

Check out the product lines. Normally the product lines are covered in great detail, including color photos. Why not put the information to use? If the company seems out of touch with the times, it might be time to let go of your own stock or not to invest in the company in the first place.

## Talking to Your Broker

About the only way you can be successfully involved in investing is to know what you are talking about. Every industry has its jargon, and it can be like a foreign language if you are not familiar with it. So let's eavesdrop on a typical conversation between a broker and a client:

> *Customer:* Susan, I just read something in the paper and I'm not sure what to do. This jerk has made lots of recommendations in the past, but I haven't had much luck with them. Though this one seems to be rather exciting.
> *Broker:* Joe, all you pick is losers. Why don't you forget about stock tips in the paper and use our analysts? These people work day in and day out studying each company, its management, its financial situation and its long-term goals. These analysts are like high-priced private

eyes who are also forecasters. Their job is to project a company's future earnings.

*Customer:* But what makes them any better than this investment columnist?

*Broker:* Joe, any columnist is a generalist. These analysts are specialists who live and breathe the few companies or specific industries they are paid to worry about.

*Customer:* Still, is the analyst any better than the local weatherman who can't seem to predict what's going to happen from one hour to the next?

*Broker:* Certainly! Though you must remember that these specialists can be burned by intervening forces that are beyond forecasting.

*Customer:* But this is a new issue that looks as if it will be a spectacular growth stock.

*Broker:* Joe, the new-issue market is risky. By definition, most times it's a new venture with no track record. The price the underwriter assigns to it may not have any bearing on reality. There is no guarantee it's going to grow, and the company is underscoring the risk by offering units. With each share you buy, you get a warrant, which is a chance to buy another share of that stock at an assigned price at a later date. It's like a loss leader at the supermarket, something to grab your attention.

*Customer:* Wait, Susan, the last penny stock article I read said this underwriter's last two offerings were very successful and the underwriter has a proven track record.

*Broker:* Joe, just because penny stocks sell for under $3 a share doesn't mean they are a bargain. A number of them are good buys but many are also very speculative. On top of that, you will have a hard time following your investment because penny stocks often are not listed on the financial pages. In order to find out how your stock is doing, you would have to call me to check out the Pink Sheet here at the office.

*Customer:* That Pink Sheet comes out every day, so what's the problem other than my constantly tugging at your ear?

*Broker:* The Pink Sheet, as you know, has the over-the-counter listing of numerous stocks, but it doesn't give the latest price. In order to get that info for you, I would look in the Pink Sheet, find out which firm was underwriting or backing the issue, phone them, and they could tell me the spread between the ask and bid price.

*Customer:* Bid and ask price . . . spread?

*Broker:* I was afraid you might not really know what you are getting into. The ask price is the lowest price the seller is willing to take while the bid is the most you are willing to pay. Sandwiched in between you will find the "high-priced" spread.

*Customer:* Okay! But, what are those over-the-counter stocks I see in the paper?

*Broker:* Those are companies that have grown beyond the Pink Sheet and have been picked up by one of three exchanges of the National Association of Securities Dealers known as NASDAQ. To continue to be quoted, the companies must maintain total assets of $500,000 plus capital and surplus of $250,000.

*Customer:* Even those don't sound like very big companies to me.

*Broker:* Well, actually there are many "very" large companies listed on the NASDAQ; it's just their decision not to go to a bigger board such as the American or New York Stock Exchanges. The older exchanges have some very stringent rules which often mean a bit more stability.

*Customer:* Do you mean Blue Chip stocks?

*Broker:* Sure, you won't find those on NASDAQ because Blue Chip stocks are considered to be the highest quality investment-grade stocks, with a long and unbroken record of earnings and dividends in good times and bad times. In this case a long history is more than twenty-five years.

*Customer:* Let me tell you that there are still no guarantees with a Blue Chip! The last high-quality stock you recommended had been paying a high dividend and you wanted me to go long-term because it had all the indications of a forthcoming split, but somehow I took a blood bath and was saved only when the stop loss order was triggered last week. Where was the quality with that one?

*Broker:* Hold your horses. Playing the market has been compared with the race track because, even though all the winning signals are there, sometimes your pony doesn't come in. While there are no guarantees in the stock market, there is a difference because you can limit your losses with a stop order. Of course, you know what a stop order is. That's when you tell me or another broker how far the stock can fall before it's sold. You are protecting yourself from losing everything by exercising a stop order. But, even with a stop order, you can't be sure you will get that exact price because the stock can fall faster than the broker can act.

A stop order is also great for protecting your gains when a stock is on the rise. You simply use a floating stop, so when your stock moves up you simply tell me, your broker, to move that stop order higher. Playing with stop orders gives you a chance to ride along; as the stock moves up, you are still able to name the price you want should it start to fall.

*Customer:* So a stop protected me from losing everything. But what happened to the split?

*Broker:* We can't predict everything. As I told you, it looked as if you would realize two shares for each one you owned if the split had occurred. Apparently the company didn't need to expand its stock base to make it more attractive to investors.

*Customer:* Something I find confusing about a split is if the company had issued one milion shares originally and then called for a split it would have two million shares. But each share would then be worth half as much as before. So why all the excitment about stock splits?

*Broker:* That one is simple. Sure, each $50 share all of a sudden became two $25 shares, but often the stock price rises right after a split because the public gets turned on by the lower price of a stock. Of course that could be a false indicator of a stock's value. You see, the company's net assets didn't increase, only the number of outstanding shares. What we expected was a two for one split, but there can be three for ones, four for ones, three for twos and even reverse splits where two shares become one.

*Customer:* Isn't that the same as a tender offer?

*Broker:* No way! Don't get those confused. While a tender offer can be a corporation buying back its own shares, usually it's another company or individual who wants to buy up enough shares to take over a corporation. That can be lucrative if the stock has been undervalued on the open market. Or if there is a greenmailer in the wings.

*Customer:* Greenmailer? Is that the same as a blackmailer?

*Broker:* Some people might say that, because a greenmailer is a corporation or an individual who targets a company and wants to make it look as if a takeover is underway. A not-so-simple act, which can push the stock price higher. This may scare the target company which, in hopes of avoiding a takeover, might make an even better tender offer. That act alone could bid the stock even higher yet. It's usually at that point the greenmailer bails out with a hefty profit. It's something some of the very big boys have gotten into recently, but it's not considered totally aboveboard.

*Customer:* Susan, this is all beginning to make a lot more sense. About the tip I found in the paper, maybe I better do some more homework. Could you send me your analyst's opinion on Upsen-Down, Inc.?

*Broker:* Joe, consider it in the mail. No matter what you decide you are on the right track. You are trying to make an informed decision and not just acting on a tip. I will be more than happy to help you with that. Bye! Or should I say *Buy-Buy!*

## Time to Buy

So, now you feel like going all the way! You also want to make all the right moves so you don't embarrass yourself. You will never be thought of as clumsy if you use some finesse. Ask yourself these questions and if the yeses add up substantially, it may be time to buy.

—Do you see an end to the business downturn?
—Is inflation deflating?
—Are corporate profits starting Up?
—Are interest rates headed Down?
—Is the Fed allowing the money supply to grow?

—Are your friends pessimistic about the market? Friends
are fun, but they may not be the type of investors who
recognize that the stock market is more attractive when
prices are depressed than when prices are headed
through the roof.

—Has the rate of decline slowed, as you would find in the
final stages of a Bear market?

—Has the market dropped back to the low point once or
twice and then rebounded? If so, it may be ready for a
strong forward leap.

—Is the stock in an industry still in favor?

—Does it have a high beta? (Which is a sign the stock
could take off with the rest of the market.)

—Does the stock have a high P/E ratio? (A high P/E means
the stock is more volatile and could move faster than
other stocks.)

While each person will have his or her own reasons for
buying a stock, these are important questions to ask with each
tip or suggestion you wish to follow. But please, don't buy
any stock until you have done your research. Homework
didn't stop when we left school.

### Oh, to Sell with It!

Once you buy, there will come a time when you feel you
should sell. Your hope, of course, is that you will sell the
stock for more than you paid. If you remember correctly, that
is one of the main keys for creating a fortune: Buy Low, Sell
High, and you will never lose money.

So, knowing when to sell is probably much more important than knowing when to buy. For that reason we have also
put together a little checklist to help you determine when
you should consider selling a stock. Like all other check-
lists, this one is not foolproof, but it can help you make your
own decision with the feeling that you have given consid-

eration to a number of different criteria. If a number of your answers are yes, you might want to consider selling.

—Has there been an economic recovery for a year or more? The economy works in cycles and it may be ready for a slowdown.

—Has the market been rising rapidly for a year? Nothing goes up forever.

—Has more stock gone down than up over the past 60 days?

—Is your stock about to plunge below its past 52-week average?

—Is your stock increasing slower or falling faster than the Dow Jones averages?

—Are more stocks hitting lows than highs? A serious danger signal in a supposedly strong market. (Check low column in the newspaper listings.)

—Are interest rates heading up? Could be tough on businesses which need to expand. It could also entice people out of stocks and into bonds, causing stock prices to fall.

—Has your stock fallen by 15 to 20 percent, if listed on the major exchanges, or 20 to 25 percent for issues from the more volatile OTC?

—Has a favorable development failed to materialize, such as increased earnings, a takeover or a new product taking off?

—Is the P/E of your stock higher than its 5-year average?

—Has the P/E for your stock risen 50 percent in a short time? This is very important unless you feel the company's prospects still look great. The stock could become overvalued, and you might be better off with a stock that is undervalued, where your profit potential could increase.

—Is sales growth starting to deteriorate, profit growth heading south and the company's competitive position in the industry starting to slip?

—Is the company saddled with high-interest long- and short-term debts? They can be very serious if the company heads into a slump.

—Oh yes, ask yourself if the competition has better products? If so, get out now!

No investment decision is simple; there are always a number of factors which must be considered. But, remember, you should never have any serious emotional attachment to an investment. Loving a stock more than your own financial worth is not a healthy relationship. When it is time to sell, you shouldn't hold on out of loyalty. Remember, when the company did well, it wasn't just doing well for you. But when it does poorly, you may be the only one hurt. The people running the company may have already sold their portion. You may have no way of knowing. Let your wallet guide your loyalties.

### Bonding Without Binding

Some people feel terribly tied down by bonds, constrained and unable to wiggle free. Others love the sense of security that comes from knowing who is master and what can be expected.

When you buy a bond, you are loaning money to a corporation. A bond is really nothing more than a loan or, as they say in financial circles, a debt security. These are not short-term small loans though; instead they are normally for 20 or 25 years and sold in $1,000 increments. As with any other type of loan, you are paid interest for use of the money until the maturity date, when you are repaid the principal amount. One of the drawbacks of bonds is that you don't necessarily share in the good fortune of the company because your rate of return is set in stone. No matter how much better the corporation does the rate won't change. On the other hand, you have some protection should the company not do well. In bad times a corporation may not pay a dividend to common stockholders, but it must pay the interest due to the bond holder.

Not all bonds are created equal; there are several different kinds and the cost and yield can be affected by the types of bond.

**Discount Bonds** are older bonds available on the open market. They are sometimes difficult to sell because their set interest rate is different from prevailing rates. New bonds are issued at a fixed price and fixed interest rate. Many older bonds are then sold at discount because their initial interest rate was lower. Discount simply means the bond's trading price has been dropped to make up the difference by compensating for the higher interest rate. As with newly issued bonds, when discount bonds mature you get the full face value. In the meantime, you are buying and holding on to a bond which has a relatively low set interest rate in comparison with today's yield. But you are still seeing a higher yield because of the difference between the discounted price you pay for the bond and its fully mature face value.

---

### Your Personal $$ Memo: Discounting Can Be Disquieting

You own a 20-year $10,000 bond paying 10 percent. That means that $1,000 a year is paid in interest. Then all of a sudden interest rates jump to 15 percent and you need to sell. Not very many people would be foolish enough to be interested in a bond with such a low yield, so you must discount it, meaning that your bond is no longer worth $10,000 on the open market, so in order to make it attractive it would have to be discounted to $6,666 creating a yield equal to 15 percent.

On the bright side, should interest rates fall, your bond could increase in value. A dramatic drop could make a very significant difference; for example, a 5 percent interest rate could make a $10,000 bond worth nearly $20,000. Please understand that these rates are rough; the formula is very complicated, so complicated that brokers need to refer to *Yield to Maturity Charts* and a *Bond-Basis Book*, which handle all of the messy math involved.

**Zero Coupon Bonds** are wonderful for people who are fed-up with having to clip coupons from their bonds in order to receive the interest. Zero Coupon Bonds have no coupons and also pay no periodic interest, though they do promise big appreciation by maturity.

Zeroes give you a chance to buy larger bonds for less cash up front. For example: a $1,000 8-year Zero Coupon Bond would cost $302. The result is a yield-to-maturity that is effectively over 15 percent. As you can see from the arithmetic involved, the investment would be tripled in 8 years. All of this happens automatically. The one possible drawback is that many people feel they don't have to pay income taxes on that interest until the bond matures. Not True! You will still have to pay the IRS out of your pocket as if you were paid that interest each year. Some advisors feel Zero Coupon Bonds are great for IRAs or Keoghs because an investor is free of those tax hassles.

**Junk Bonds** deserve their name. Because all of a sudden they can become worthless junk. Junk Bonds are lower quality bonds, often considered below investment grade. But that can mean super-high yields because of the super-high risks. There are some Junk Bond issues which offer rates 5, 10 and 15 percent higher than triple A bonds, in order to attract money. These are not, you should understand, for The First-Time Investor. Junk Bonds take a great deal of homework and, even more than that, a great deal of intestinal fortitude.

**Convertibles** are not always cars which allow you to raise the roof, but are also a type of bond. Convertibles can be converted into common stock in the same company. Exactly when you can make the conversion, how many shares you can exchange per bond and the price you will pay are spelled out in the bond offering.

At first glance these may not seem very attractive because they do pay less interest than regular bonds, but unlike regular bonds, convertibles allow you the opportunity to enjoy some of the good fortunes of a company. You are betting that the company's stock will rise enough to make the conversion privilege more valuable.

Why would a corporation offer convertibles? It gives the company a chance to borrow money at a lower interest rate than the company would have to pay with an ordinary bond.

## Look Before You Leap

Before buying bonds, consider why you want them. We realize that First-Time Investors can be of any age, so consider these factors.

If you happen to be over 40, looking for long-term security income and don't need liquidity, bonds could possibly provide a comfortable investment for you.

If you are in your twenties and thirties, you may seriously want to consider something with higher potential growth, with an eye to the future.

Some important factors that should be mentioned include bond issuance: When you buy a bond it will usually be registered in your name and the interest collected directly by you. However, there is an older type of bond, known as a Bearer Bond, which is not registered in your name. These have coupons which you clip on certain dates and redeem for cash. This caused a great deal of headaches for the IRS, so all bonds issued now are registered. The only place you can find these older unregistered bearer bonds is in the secondary or discount market.

Four things to constantly consider with bonds are **Risk, Earnings, Averaging** and **Maturity**.

# Risk!

Risk? Yes, there is risk, but you can minimize it by going for Quality which in turn provides some safety. As with all investments, some bonds are safer than others, while some are very risky. Of course, there are some advantages to the risk because the higher the risk the higher the yield.

To help all investors determine the potential risk several services publish ratings after studying the fiscal health of each company. These ratings are published by Moody's, and Standard and Poors. The highest rating for Moody's Investor Service is Aaa. The top of the heap for S & Ps (Standard and Poors) are rated AAA. While these ratings do not guarantee a return, they are the best assurance at the moment that the issuer is credit worthy. Both services are highly regarded in the financial communities and either one can be used to evaluate the risk of any bond issue. To give you an idea of how the ratings read, we have listed a few categories below:

| MOODY'S | | S&Ps |
|---------|---|------|
| Aaa | Highest Quality | AAA |
| Aa | High Quality | AA |
| A | Good Quality | A |
| Baa | Medium Grade (somewhat speculative) | BBB |
| Ba | Speculative (some defensive qualities) | BB / B |
| B | Highly Speculative | CCC |
| Caa | Bonds which could be in default already, also those not paying current interest due | CC / C |
| C | Lowest Rating | D |

Remember, these ratings are not a promise of performance, only an evaluation.

Sometimes you may be interested in a bond which is offering a high yield but not listed as a Junk Bond. Read the prospectus and you might find that it has all the makings of junk. One example is a communications company that raised more than a billion dollars despite an ominous future. The offering papers plainly stated that the issuing company might not be able to pay the interest payments, let alone redeem the principal.

Of course the communications company might come through in the end even though the prospectus read: ". . . based on current levels of operation (assuming no growth in revenues) the company's cash flow would be insufficient to make interest payments on the debt securities." How would the company cover those obligations? Well, it would have to use other funds, to the extent available, to make such payments. Even though it was all there in black and white and the rating services called it highly speculative, the underwriters banked on people not reading everything. That faith paid off, with the underwriters going to the bank, while the bond holders may eventually be taken to the cleaners, if the prospectus forecasts the future accurately. Of course, there is always the chance the company could take off and have no problem, though that isn't in the current cards.

One way to reduce risk while investing in bonds, is to go for diversification. Don't invest in just one bond issue or company, but also use Bond Funds. Some fund portfolios contain short-term bond holdings, while others are longer term. But your risk-reducing factor is that each fund holds hundreds of diverse bonds.

### Earnings

Earnings in this case are described as the return, current yield or yield-to-maturity. The *return* is what you receive either quarterly or upon maturity, depending on the type of bond. The *current yield* is the income earned, based on the bond's relationship to the fluctuations of the bond market. *Yield-to-maturity* has to do with bonds bought on the secondary market and is the actual yield between purchase price and maturity, a complicated formula that forces even bond dealers to refer to a special set of tables. To make sure you have a fixed yield, you buy a new bond and hold on to it until maturity.

Not everyone does that, and as we have mentioned, bonds are sometimes bought and sold at a premium or discount. Remember, deep discount bonds were originally issued at face value, but now sell much lower than before because interest rates in the general market have gone through the roof, leaving the bond's original yield in the basement. In order to make up that difference, the bonds sell far enough below face value to bring the yield up to current market interest rates. On the other hand, if the bond is paying a higher interest rate than the current market interest rate, you pay a premium to buy that bond on the secondary market. That means the price you are paying for the bond is higher than the original issue price. You must take into consideration whether the income earned will offset the difference between the higher price you pay for the bond and its value at maturity.

## Averaging

Averaging the purchase costs is another version of dollar-cost-averaging: purchasing small amounts of a particular investment, some at higher prices and some at lower prices, thus averaging your overall purchase cost.

With bonds you dollar-cost-average by making sure your holdings mature at different times. When one bond matures, you reinvest that cash in another bond which matures after the final bond is set to be redeemed. It's an investment game much like one we all played as children, leapfrogging. This tends to average out the effect of market interest changes.

## Maturity

Maturity is the life of a bond, the time from original issue until you must be repaid. Long-term bonds have maturity dates of 20 or 30 years, while intermediate bonds become mature in 5 to 10 years. If you wait until the maturity date, you are guaranteed to get your principal back. To get that kind of guarantee your money will have to remain tied up for a long time. While bonds are not considered very liquid, you can always redeem them early by selling on the secondary market; though, as we have explained, you chance losing money if the interest rates have generally jumped beyond the yield of your bond.

There is always the chance that you won't have control of the exact time you can redeem a bond. Even if you are more than pleased with the yield and the stability of a company, your bond could be called and redeemed early, but that doesn't mean you will lose your initial investment, only that you will have to make an investment decision earlier than you might have wished. The call provision in the prospectus will help you to determine just how callable a bond might be. The prospectus will list the procedure for "calling the bond," where you are forced to redeem the bond at a stated price prior to its maturity. The prospectus will also explain the earliest that the bond can be called. Often a bond is called if interest rates have dropped dramatically. Registered bond holders are notified by mail, but those who have bearer bonds may not find out until it's time to clip a coupon and are told they cannot. When that happens a bearer bond holder will simply lose the interest from the time the bond has been called.

One final point on bonds: You may have wondered why your broker hasn't highly recommended that you put your money into bonds? Well, it could have something to do with self-interest. Commissions on bonds are smaller than those for stock transactions.

## Only Iron Stomachs Need Apply

What we have discussed so far in this chapter is concern with basic investing. You may have an overwhelming desire to go further than that. Before you do, take heed. Our suggestion is that you take your time and become comfortable with the simpler things in your investing life. The First-Time Investor really has no place playing in the dangerous world of Margins, Options or Short Sales. They may sound sexy and exciting, but you can be hurt terribly even if you are well experienced in the investment facts of life.

With that warning stated, we also believe that you should have some understanding of these areas in case someone attempts to entice you. You are less likely to tumble head over heels if you know where you are headed and can watch your step.

## Buying on Margin

After reading all of this you may find yourself "hot to trot." You want to buy some stocks or bonds, but you can't get the money you need in order to invest because it happens to be tied-up in other places such as a house or some other tangible asset. Well, Wall Street has an expensive answer, and it works if you are simply a creditworthy person; it's called buying on margin. In other words, it is a chance to buy stock on credit. The margin is the amount of cash you have to put up, usually 50 percent or more, and you borrow the rest from the broker. The Federal Reserve Board decides how much of a margin is considered safe for the economy as a whole and then the exchanges and brokerage houses set their own tighter rules. Because you are borrowing money you have to pay for it just like any other type of loan. The interest rate can run ¾ percent more than it costs the broker to borrow the money from a bank. Because the loan is covered by the stock itself (acting as the collateral) you don't have to pay back the margin loan until you sell the stock.

Of course there is, as they say on Wall Street, a serious downside to buying on margin and that is if the stock falls in price. If that happens you will have to put up more money to fulfill the margin maintenance requirements. The New York Stock Exchange has what is known as the 25 *percent rule* which means that if the stock drops by 25 percent, you must make up the difference. Each brokerage house has its own, possibly stricter, rules. So depending on the percentage, if you fall below it you either have to make up the difference or sometimes pay off the margin account. That is what is called margin call and it comes collect, so to speak.

## My Favorite Margin

Why might you do this? It is called having *leverage*. And, because you are using leverage to increase your holdings you can own twice as much for half as much out of pocket cash. Why don't you want to do this? It is a gamble, and while it is good for gamblers, it is not good for First-Time Investors. Nevertheless, the concept is something you should understand, so we shall continue. One example of leverage most people understand is a mortgage. For instance, if you bought a $50,000 house outright and sold it for $60,000, your $10,000 profit would equal a 20 percent return. But if you had borrowed $25,000 through a mortgage then the $10,000 profit would be a 40 percent return on the money you actually put out. You were gambling with less and making more.

With stocks it will be the same as with real estate; it's a way of using borrowed funds to add to your portfolio, in this case hoping the house will rise in value, but if it doesn't, or it falls in value, you could lose even more money when you sell. In our example if the price fell to $40,000 and you had paid $50,000 cash, your loss would be 20 percent, but if you had leveraged and borrowed $25,000, the $10,000 dollar loss is equal to a 40 percent loss. When you lose with leverage, you assume all of the loss. Either way you have lost $10,000, but the percentage of loss is different.

In the stock or bond market when you use leverage, you are also increasing your potential profit or loss. When the margin is set at 50 percent, you can buy $5,000 worth of stock for only $2,500; the rest is borrowed. Remember, you don't have to put up any more money unless the stock price plummets by 25 percent or less, depending on the current rules. If you then sell that stock for $6,000, the broker takes out the $2,500 borrowed and you get $3,500 dollars. That works out to be a $1,000 appreciation (less commissions and interest on the loan) which is a 40 percent return on your investment instead of only 20 percent, had you put down all of the money. Of course, as we mentioned in the mortgage example earlier, if the stock drops your loss is magnified. You can lose twice as fast too. Should the stock drop and you have to sell for $4,000, you still pay the broker $2,500 plus commissions and interest, leaving you with less than $1,500 and a loss of more than 40 percent.

## This Warrants Attention

An *outstanding warrant* in investment circles is not something that can arrest your development, but instead can possibly help your portfolio grow by leaps and bounds.

Warrants are nothing more than a fancy investment-type "come on" sold with new issues by the issuing corporation. Looking ahead, the corporation realizes it must pave the way for the future sale of securities and that it needs to entice people to buy now and purchase later. You see, when you buy warrants, you are buying options which give you a chance to purchase the common stock of a company at a specified price by simply making a cash payment and turning in the warrant. Most warrants have a time limit during which you can exercise them and buy that common stock. Obviously your hope is that the stock will have risen in price beyond the face value of the warrant. These are marvelous little devices because you not only can get a great buy on stock, you have yet another chance to make even more money. As a stock rises in price and the time approaches to exercise the warrant, the warrant becomes more valuable. That means there is a market for warrants and they can be sold independent of the actual stock through a broker.

---

### Your Personal $$ Memo: Act Fast, Offer Limited

Once warrants expire they are worthless, which is why many consider this another form of gambling. You are betting that the stock will rise in price beyond the amount you paid for the warrant plus enough over and above that to make a nice immediate paper profit. Doesn't that sound like a great money-making scheme? Watch out because you can also be on the wrong side of the bet and lose a bundle.

---

### The Kinkier Options

You may remember we touched on Option Funds in the Mutual Funds chapter; this is where we tell you more about options as an investment in and of themselves. Options are a risky game for the investor who is sophisticated enough to understand the ups and downs of the stock market. They might be right for someone who feels he or she has a special insight or who owns a crystal ball that might give an indication of future stock movements. Options provide the opportunity to make a bundle by making only a small wager. Any stock trade is a gamble, so the thought process with options is: "Why put all the money on the line?"

If a stock is currently trading at $50 and you believe that it will be trading at $60 in a few months, you could always buy the stock now and ride it out, but that would mean spending at least $5,000 for 100 shares (commissions not included). Why do that if you could be assured of picking up the stock later at the price you want to pay without putting up all of that money, especially if you only had to lay out one-tenth of the total, in this case $500?

The definition of an option is the right to buy or sell a certain number of shares (always in even lots of 100) of a listed stock at an agreed-upon price by a specified date. That agreed-upon price is called the strike or exercise price. The attraction is that the most you can lose is the price of the option, and most of the time people buying options do lose that.

Someone who already owns stock can sell options; these are called *covered calls*. This is considered by some as a conservative move because it is a chance for the stock owner to increase the yield on the holdings whether or not the option is exercised. That is because the option seller gets to pocket the premium no matter what happens. If the option is exercised, the stock is in effect called away and must be surrendered, but the most the stockholder can lose is the furture growth of the stock.

Statistics show that more than 70 percent of the options expire without being exercised, which means the persons wanting to buy stock through options didn't get the chance but lost only the cost of the premiums.

## Head Spinning Yet?

Don't be upset if you are confused by all of this, as we will call upon some easy-to-follow examples in order to put the Put and Call into perspective.

Buying a call option is when you pay a premium for the right to wager that once you actually take possesion of a stock it could be sold immediately for more than you will actually pay for it. For example, if you have a strong feeling that a stock currently selling for $50 a share will go through the roof several months down the line, you can buy a call with a strike price of $55. If the stock hits $58, then the right to buy it at only $55 dollars becomes more valuable. But you don't really want to exercise that right until the stock rises above the strike price by enough to cover the cost of the premium and the commission and still deliver to you a tidy little profit. Basically the stock needs to appreciate 10 percent to get to the strike price and another 10 percent to make the exercise worthwhile.

In a boom or Bull market those premiums can be rather large. The value of a call generally increases as the price of the stock increases. It's another case of supply and demand. As the stock rises, it attracts attention, and people want to get in on the good fortune.

Selling a call means you are paid a premium by the buyer to sell the stock at an agreed-upon price if the option is exercised by the call buyer. Your hope is that the stock will not rise enough for the option to be exercised during that time limit. It is a chance to earn money while you hope the market slips or at least doesn't take off. If it does, all you have lost is the future earnings of the stock, but you have your money to invest anywhere you wish.

If you are "bearish," expecting a falling market and think that a stock you own is heading south then you might look for some protection. That's when a sophisticated investor, one who is able to watch the market on a daily basis with a strong feeling of expertise, buys a put. The idea is that the stockholder pays someone to buy that stock by a specified date at a set price. This can be a cushion if the stock is currently trading at $55 and you purchase a put with a strike price of $50. Should the stock drop to $45, you could exercise the put option and sell the stock for $50, saving the $500 you would have lost had you been forced to sell at the current lower price. The person who sells the put to you, is of course betting that the stock won't drop that much and you won't exercise your option. If you sit tight, the put seller loses nothing and keeps the premium.

You might be under the impression that you must own the stock in order to sell a call. That would be called a covered option, but that is not always the case. You can actually make naked calls, which means writing a call against stock you don't actually own. When you don't own the securities, it is called an uncovered option.

Basically with a naked option you can be caught with your pants down as the stock rises. If the stock is called, you would have to buy the stock to cover the action and deliver it to the new owner at an excessive price. It is a big gamble which could result in a large cash loss.

### Coming Up Short!

Are you ready for some Wall Street sleight of hand? A chance to sell something you don't own and make a profit by buying it after you have sold it. This is called a *short sale* and it is legal, though it is one of the most dangerous financial strategies even an experienced investor can attempt. Get ready to follow the moves, at no time do the fingers really leave the hand. Convinced that a stock is about to fall in price, an investor borrows a certain number of shares from his broker, then turns around and sells those shares at the current price.

"NO DEAR, I AM SURE THAT IS NOT WHAT THEY MEAN BY SHORT SALE. . ."

Our gambler's hope is that the stock price will drop, so that when he is forced to buy it, he is paying less than he sold it for. That is his profit margin. This is a sell-high, buy-low philosophy which looks good on paper but in reality can leave our original investor at the short end of the stick. He can lose if the stock doesn't drop or if it rises, because no matter what happens he must buy it. The broker, who handles all of this, loves the transaction because he has commissions from a sell, 2 buys and a borrow order.

## How to Lose Even More—Faster

If you ever have the urge to play in the commodities or futures markets, pause for a moment and recall the words to a famous song: "Whatever will be, will be. The future's not ours to see . . ." The proof of that in the commodities market is that more than 90 percent of the investors lose more money than their original investment.

The markets have changed a bit in recent years, but not the odds. No longer are you limited to losing with just commodities such as pork bellies, soybeans, sugar and coffee; now you can even speculate on the future of interest rates through Treasury Bond Futures. Add to that the chance to bet on the action of the stock market as a whole through Index Options. There are others, but the odds are just as stacked as ever against the investor—First-Time or not.

## Read and Reap

Now that you have read this chapter, you may get the feeling that investing in stocks, bonds, options and futures is a rather simple and painless procedure. Well, it can be very difficult and hurt terribly if you don't do your homework and know what and who is seducing you. In love, and even in lust, we are often blind to the true motives of a seducer. With investing, the warm smile, the caring conversation, the tender touch and romantic talk of untold riches can be the kiss of financial death. The First-Time Investor can only become a sophisticated investor by being able to see the subtleties of the process.

As with a marriage, a relationship with a broker can either be mutually satisfying or an unholy nightmare. Be prepared, because a relationship with a broker is not like the sharing give-and-take of a love liaison. You, the investor with your own money on the line, really should be in control of the total situation. It's a cold, hard fact of life, and those facts of life face you in the following pages.

# 9

## How NOT to Become
## Broker with a Broker

If Hamlet were alive today he would be puzzled by the new question of the ages: To Go with a Broker or Not to Go with a Broker, that is the question. Whether it is nobler in the minds of men to suffer the commissions and omissions of outrageous, fortune-hunting brokers. Forgive us, oh great Bard. But the point is: Do you, The First-Time Investor, really need to have a stockbroker?

A relationship with a broker can be like a love affair; you have both wildly wonderful weeks and terribly traumatic times. The courtship begins with the broker holding your hand through the first few transactions. It makes you feel good inside. You begin to think he or she won't ever hurt you. You give more trust; the broker takes more chances. He or she makes you feel even better and seems to have found your "Gee Whiz" spot. Every time your broker tickles it, you give in more. Soon the broker has you in the palm of his or her hand. Will you continue to be manipulated? Probably, until you feel that you are being used. But, when will you notice that? Probably when it's too late, or when you have earned more money for the broker than the broker has earned for you.

It is a fact that the broker comes out ahead whether you win or lose, because the broker earns commissions when you buy or when you sell. You need to know whether the broker is more interested in you *or* in the commissions. You must remember that no matter how friendly a broker seems, this is a business affair to the broker, not a love affair. You must also be businesslike and establish early on that your financial goals should be the main priority.

## The Mating Dance

Finding a good broker is a lot like finding the right date. Very few of us are lucky to find the love of our life on the first date. Most of us have searched and dated many other people before deciding on the "perfect" match. With a broker you need to do some old-fashioned courting. An introduction through a mutual friend can help get things started on the right foot. So, put down the yellow pages! Instead, ask your friends or relatives whom they might recommend, and why. Learn something about the reputation of the brokerage house as well. Don't stop with only one recommendation—get several names and numbers. Call, speak to the broker and request a chance to sit down and talk face to face. Make sure there is no charge. The idea is for you to get a feel for the person. You are the client; the broker works for you because you pay the bills through commissions.

During the interview don't just talk about *your* desires and hopes. It is a given that you want to make money the most comfortable way possible. And that is the key. Find out what the broker's trading style is. Is the broker conservative or speculative? If you are cautious you don't want someone who will be getting you in and out of stocks at breakneck speed. If you want to take it slow and easy until it feels good, you need to explain that you may not go all the way with your investment plans until you have solidified the relationship. How often can you expect a call from the broker, and how often can you call? Some frank and honest discussions about style are important in the beginning. As with love, you must feel a bond of trust. This person will control something that is very important to you, *YOUR* money! And don't forget to find out how much commission the brokerage house charges!

---

### Checklist for Choosing Brokers

Keep this list in mind as you are interviewing the person who is in the running to run your investments. If you go into this kind of a relationship blind, you may never see your money again.

1. Ask the broker directly, "What is your trading style?"
2. Is the broker conservative or speculative? And does it match your style?
3. How often will the broker phone you with tips?
4. How often can you call for advice or handholding?
5. How much commission does the brokerage house charge?

---

Do you feel that what you have to offer may not attract someone? Don't sell yourself short. Sure, you may not have a big portfolio to catch the broker's eyes, but size isn't all that counts in the beginning. You are just starting to plant your seeds. If the chemistry is right and the two of you hit it off, you could both find financial happiness. But as with first dates, that is a bit much to expect the first time out.

Many brokerage houses will see the small investor as someone to be taken care of after the high rollers have been

## The Big 7

Seven might be considered a lucky number in gambling, so it's not strange that we should have seven major questions you should ask a broker before your make your pick.

1. Ask about the broker's history: educational background, securities background and tenure as a broker.
2. Does the investment information come from personal research or from the brokerage firm's in-house analysts?
3. What is the broker's specialty? Have the success stories been in blue chips or speculative issues? Bonds? Options? Futures? Tax Shelters? What does the broker consider his or her weak areas?
4. Ask to check out his or her past recommendations in good and bad markets? This can be done by checking with references, but keep in mind this information may have been sanitized.
5. Does the broker recommend a sell price at the time you purchase? Will it be long or short term (for capital gains taxes)?
6. Does the broker's portfolio contain the same stocks as are being recommended?
7. Finally, ask what reasonable investment goals you can expect? There can't be any promises, but try to get an honest feel. This may be about the only way you can keep track of a broker's performance.

made happy. That means your broker may not have the time to offer to satisfy your needs at first. For that reason brokerage houses often assign their new sales representatives (brokers) to smaller accounts. While you might get the freshman's undivided attention, this is not a time for you to be with another First-Timer. Experience does make the *broker*. If you don't feel comfortable with the person a brokerage house assigns to you, ask for another. Be bold; it is your money and you can take it somewhere else.

## What to Look For

The ideal broker doesn't have to wear a certain style of clothes or have a clean desk, but should be someone who will patiently answer your questions and give you the tools to help you make decisions.

Something we can not stress enough is that if the broker isn't asking you questions about your temperament, you should ask yourself why not. The broker needs to know if you are a risk taker or if you like quiet, methodical moves. Your investment temperament should match his or hers. Sometimes the questions may seem a bit too personal, and if they are, you should speak up. Some brokers use this technique to find out about your style. The initial interview should be a real give-and-take. Also, try to attend free seminars or meetings frequently offered by brokerage houses. These will help you develop a sense of the kind of houses they are.

## Love Can Be Blind, Investments Can't Be

You are not finished with your homework yet, not by a long shot. One of the key things a broker should do to help you get started is to provide research on the investments in which you are currently interested. Most brokers are provided with this information by analysts within the brokerage house. An analyst's job is to research specific companies to determine their profit potential and understand everything there is to know about the corporation's philosophies from top management down to middle management. One of the most important functions of the analyst is to determine how much the company will earn in the future. When reviewing the material, you should always ask about the analyst's track record. Normally a brokerage house protects itself by ridding itself of analysts with poor track records, but ask anyway.

You should also compare the information the broker gives you with your own research. Certainly you are hiring an ex-

pert, but you need to make the final decision on any stock buy, and you should be confident that you have covered every possible base. You really don't need to be reminded, but it is your money and your broker won't cry with you if you lose it because you went into something blindly. Researching a stock is not difficult. We suggest you read the annual report, check recent financial statements (your broker can get these), and then visit the local library to get some more investor information from *Standard and Poors* as well as *Value Line*. Also check the newspaper financial pages and financial magazines for any tidbits that might help you make a decision. That's right; you make the decision not the broker. Have we said that enough times to get the point across?

## Join the Club

If you still don't feel comfortable with a broker or if you have had some difficulty finding one, may we suggest that your key may be a club. Not a country club or golf club, but an investment club.

If someone says investment club to you, what comes to mind? For many it might be an old building with lots of stuffed chairs and couches where rich old men sit and discuss their Blue Chip stocks all day and half the night. But, that isn't what an investment club is at all. Investment clubs are small groups of people, sometimes just from the neighborhood, who pool their money and their knowledge to gain firsthand practice in the art of investing. Many are newcomers to the game and they don't have a lot of money to put on the line. So for $20, $30, $50 or more a month each member of the club adds to the mini-mutual fund. The members research stocks and when they make a decision, they buy the shares in the name of the club. If the stock makes money, everyone benefits; if it loses, everyone shares that loss as well. But, remember, the main reason for the club is to learn how to use the market without risking too much of your own money. The National Association of Investment Clubs in Royal Oak, Michigan, will register and help clubs with a monthly magazine called *Better Investing* and a step-by-step layperson's guide to analyzing stocks. Write:

> National Association of Investment Clubs
> P.O. Box 220
> Royal Oak, MI 48068

They have had more than 5,000 clubs registered through the NAIC and would be more than willing to help you set up your own for a small fee of $25 per club plus $6 per member.

### Going It Alone

If you want to go solo, you can best make your first move by reading this book. But it's just an appetizer. After reading it, serve yourself a main course—an investment course. You can find one nearly anywhere through community colleges, extension courses and other adult education programs. Some of the courses are more specialized than others. But even with a basic course, you can still learn a lot about investments and what kind of investor you are. Best of all, they are not that expensive.

Then you can continue your education at your local library where you will find a variety of investment tools ranging from *The Value Line Investment Survey*, to Standard & Poors *The Outlook* and *United Business & Investment Report* as well as other first rate magazines such as *Money, Forbes, Inc., Fortune, Changing Times* and *Barron's*. These are invaluable vehicles to help you down the road to riches. Of course there are the daily newspapers such as *The Wall Street Journal* and *Investors Daily*.

There may be as many as 1,000 stock-market guides and advisory services out there. To get a handle on what you might be interested in, you might want to contact:

> Select Information Exchange
> 2095 Broadway
> New York, NY 10023

The exchange publishes a catalog of advisory services as well as their subscription prices. They can range from $50 to more than $500 per year, though most are between $65 and $175. The nice part is that they are tax deductible.

Anyone can publish a paid advisory letter. Several we know of are in fact high-school dropouts; at least one is an electrician, one is a janitor, and another a hairdresser. There are no tests or qualifications required. The only thing they must do is register with the Securities and Exchange Commission. The SEC requires only that the publisher report annually about the service's financial condition, investment strategy, sources and methods of analysis. Your motto from this day forward should always be *caveat emptor*, meaning, let the Buyer Beware.

## Discount Brokers

A little experience can take you a long way. And once you have a little under your belt, you may want to start making some of your own moves. The best and least expensive move to consider is going to a discount broker. Discount brokers will never give you a sales pitch but will take care of your order while saving you up to 70 percent in commissions over a full-commission broker. Of course even a discount house has a minimum commission charge which can run between $25 and $45, depending on the house. Check with the one you choose. It might make the difference between making a trade or not wanting to spend the money on commissions.

To get an idea of how much you can save, a full-commission broker might charge $86 to sell 100 shares at $40, while a discount broker's cut would only be about $41 for the same transaction. With a discount broker you are not paying for the handholding you often don't get from a full-commission broker even when you pay for it.

It is important to keep in mind when dealing with a discount broker that you are calling all the shots; there is no help from analysts or the broker himself. So you sink or swim by yourself. Charles Schwab & Co. is one of the largest discount brokerages and has tried to redefine the differences between the two types of brokerage houses. Once called Full Service Brokers, Schwab calls them full-commission brokers because most discount houses now offer as many features as the full-commission brokers, including:

1. Security Safekeeping
2. Money Market Funds
3. Margin Accounts
4. Larger discounts for heavy traders
5. Cash Management Accounts.

The list of discount services sometimes exceeds that of full-commission brokers by offering longer hours, sometimes 24-

hours-a-day 7-days-a-week toll-free transaction numbers as well as faster transaction confirmation.

Many investors actually use the services of both types of brokerage houses. If the full-commission broker provides you with information and recommendations, you should have that broker execute the transaction, while making use of the discounter for other trades.

---

**Your Personal $$ Memo: One for All, All for One**

You may not believe it, but there could be a discount broker just about a block away from where you work or live. It's even possible that you may have paid him a visit this week and not known it was a discount brokerage house. Your local friendly banker could be in the business now. More and more banks, savings and loans as well as some credit unions are going into the discount brokerage business. One major example is Charles Schwab and Co., which was taken over by Bank of America. It seems like a perfect marriage, a bank and a discount broker. Of course this makes shopping more interesting because services and commissions vary.

---

### Even More of a Discount

There is a way to get around paying commissions to anyone. All it takes is owning a stock which has a Dividend Reinvestment Plan. This is without a doubt one of the greatest bonuses available to all investors—beginners or high rollers.

A Dividend Reinvestment Plan lets you make stock purchases, with small amounts of money, on a monthly or quarterly basis depending on how the plan is set up. All of this is done with little or no service charge. With no commission your money is working harder for you. There are hundreds of companies that offer this excellent service. One way to find out which companies do make the offer is to check the annual list published by Standard and Poors, cost $2. Write to:

Standard & Poors
Public Relations Dept.
25 Broadway
New York, NY 10004

Here is how it works: Any dividends earned by stock in your name can be automatically reinvested in the company in the form of partial shares. Beyond that, you may be able to purchase additional shares simply by sending money directly to the corporation's holding company. Doesn't that sound like fun? You don't have to deal with any kind of broker. Some companies even let you split the dividends so a portion is sent to you and the rest is reinvested in stock. And if that's not good enough, some companies make it even nicer by giving you a 3 to 5 percent discount on stock bought through dividends you reinvest.

There must be a catch, right? No, believe it or not, it's as easy as making love and just as sweet. All you have to do is:

1. Find out if the company you are interested in offers a Dividend Reinvestment Plan (DRP).
2. If it does have a plan, make sure at least one share is in your name. Shares in the brokerage house street name do not qualify.
3. As soon as the company has you on file, you will be eligible to join the program by filling out the form permitting the company to reinvest your dividends to purchase additional shares.

### Drips Make a Splash

You may already own stock in a company that offers a DRP. If none of those shares are in your name, you may not even know if the company makes such as offer. Many brokers don't voluntarily share that kind of information because they can lose potential commissions should you decide to buy more of the same stock through a DRP.

Before you consider buying only one share of stock to open a DRP, consider the cost of that one share. The rules say you need to have only one share registered in your name, but the company expects you to buy more than one share. Even if you use a discount broker, the cost of such a small transaction can be relatively high. The minimum transaction charge with most discount houses is between $25 and $45, so a single-share purchase is not cost effective, considering the commission could be more than the cost of that share.

---

## Freebies

DRPs are not the only way companies try to attract and keep stockholders. A number of companies now offer so-called freebies. American Recreation, Inc. lets stockholders with at least 300 shares bowl for free at its 26 bowling centers. The only restriction is that there must be unoccupied lanes.

Marriott Corporation offers as much as 50 percent off hotel prices to shareholders. Ramada Inns, Inc. offers up to 25 percent off on some rooms. Scott Paper Company sends stockholders a Christmas package that among other things includes tissue paper. General Mills offers discounts at its Red Lobster restaurants. Information about which companies offer freebies can be found in a $9.50 booklet from:

> Stock Holder Freebies
> Buttonwood Press
> 41 Park Ave.
> New York, NY 10016

---

One suggestion for a beginner might be to look into a service such as one at Merrill Lynch called a Sharebuilder Account. Bob has looked into this as a possibility to help his pre-teenage daughter begin her own personal portfolio. As she begins to earn money from after-school jobs, she can invest it in relatively small amounts in a sharebuilder-type account. This type of account lets you invest by the amount of money you send, not by the individual share. For instance, if Harmony sends in $25 (plus commission) to purchase a stock that sells for $50 a share, she will receive a ½ share through the sharebuilder account. It is one of the few ways anyone can accumulate fractional shares of actual stock. Another plus is the sharebuilder commission schedule is a great deal less than regular rates. One of the best benefits of all is that once you have accumulated a full share in a company that offers a DRP you can have Merrill Lynch mail the certificate (registered in your name) to you for a one-time charge of $5. The sharebuilder account is a great way for a beginner to get a feel for both the market and get started in dividend reinvestment plans.

The final benefit with a sharebuilder plan for stocks, DRPs and even no-load mutual funds is the advantage of dollar-cost-averaging.

## Winning by Being Average

We have been taught that we should always strive to be above average. But sometimes average is perfect and that sometimes is when it comes to investing. Dollar-cost-averaging is an excellent investment strategy for The First-Time Investor. As we just mentioned, it can easily be applied to those wonderful DRPs, sharebuilder accounts and no-load Mutual Funds. To make dollar-cost-averaging work, you simply invest the same amount of money at regular intervals. It requires that you consistently sink the same amount of cash into additional shares of a stock which you already own, no matter how much the price fluctuates. You decide how much money you can comfortably invest each month or quarter. But no matter how the market goes, you still contribute that same amount. You ignore the daily fluctuations of the market because you are not trying to guess when it will hit the bottom or when it will be the best time to buy. The idea is that you are putting in the same amount regularly, so that when the stock price is down, you end up buying more shares than when the price is higher. You are averaging your costs and the fundamental uptrend of the market over the long haul. It is possible to lose with this system if the stock you pick doesn't realize its growth potential or if you are forced to take the money out for something else.

So you want to be a bit more daring? Why not be more speculative and add some excitement to your dollar-cost-averaging? Simply vary the technique a little by increasing your periodic investment when the market is on the downside and then return to your regularly scheduled investment when the market starts to head up. The reasoning behind this strategy is that you increase the number of shares you buy when the price and market are down in anticipation that the price will rise. This way you end up owning more shares that you purchased at a lower price in order to realize a higher gain when you sell. Almost any way you look at it, dollar-cost-averaging is a great strategy when you have no way to guess which way the market is going.

| Purchases | Amount Invested | Price Per Share | # of Shares Purchased* |
|---|---|---|---|
| Jan. | $100 | $20 | 5.0 |
| Feb. | 100 | 15 | 6.7 |
| Mar | 100 | 12 | 8.3 |
| Apr. | 100 | 16 | 6.25 |
| May | 100 | 17 | 5.9 |
| Jun. | 100 | 20 | 5.0 |
| | Total $600 | | Total 37.15 shares |

*This example does not include commission charges. (The Sharebuilder Plan® offers commissions reduced up to 45% from regular Merrill Lynch rates on equities and up to 30% on Merrill Lynch mutual funds.)

**Source:** Courtesy Merrill Lynch.

## All Sure Bets Are Off

If you feel very confident about a stock, have done all the proper research and even have the cash to pay for it, you could go for broke. Go ahead and sink all of your money into that sure bet, but remember it could be an all-or-nothing proposition. Be forewarned; The First-Time Investor shouldn't play that game. We strongly feel that dollar-cost-averaging is the way to get started with stocks. It may not make you an overnight millionaire, but in most cases you will be able to sleep better, especially when the market is on one of its usual roller-coaster rides.


## Hot Tips Burn

Would you ever buy a used car from a stranger over the phone, without seeing it, without test-driving it or without getting a money-back guarantee? Of course not! Then why do so many people buy stock because they overheard a hot tip from a stranger or even a friend or relative? That's bad news because rarely if ever does that hot tip turn out to be worth anything more than hot air. By the time you hear something on the street, you can be sure lots of other people have heard it too, especially the big institutional buyer who can snap up a sizable chunk or block of stock, driving the prices way beyond a profitable reach for you.

From the never-say-never file, on the positive side, if you know a tipster and have watched and verified whether or not he or she called at least three consecutive winners, you may want to take a gamble. But buy yourself some loss insurance, so to speak, by setting a sell price in case the stock falls to that particular level. Still, as a rule, the only tips you should get involved with are the tips you leave for a waiter or waitress.

## One-Stop Investing

Time is money and some financial institutions are offering an opportunity to save both. If you are the type of person who doesn't have enough time to make your own bed, we have something that's made for you: a Total Asset Management Account.

Banks and brokerage houses everywhere are offering their own versions of these Asset Management Accounts. They all have one thing in common: They don't want to talk with you unless you already have between $1,000 and $20,000 in cash or securities. But if you leave that much with them, they will provide you with a supermarket of services such as Money Market Funds, checking accounts, credit cards, full service or discount brokerage services and Specialized Funds.

The first one on the block was the Merrill Lynch Cash Management Account, but nearly every brokerage house now has its own version and its own pet name. They are basically all the same, offering a chance to consolidate services and bookkeeping. There are fees involved, and they differ from account to account. But they are worth looking into if you happen to have that much cash lying around because they give you numerous investment choices.

## A Job Offer You Can't Refuse

If you believe in yourself and your ability to perform wonders for your boss, then you might be interested in a very good investment opportunity as close as your own job. An employee stock-option or savings plan could possibly be the best benefit that will ever come your way. Normally it's a chance for an employee to have between 3 percent and 6 percent taken out of his or her check through payroll deductions. The company often matches all or part of that amount.

The money is then either invested in the company's own stock or put into a special, professionally managed fund. A smart investor will take full advantage of this plan by investing the full amount in order to get the maximum matching funds. Some of the other benefits of a company stock option plan are that you don't have commissions to worry about and you can allow your fractional shares to accumulate. Once again, dollar-cost-averaging could play an important part in the growth of your portfolio. One final benefit is that the company keeps a record of all your transactions for you. Sounds like a great deal? It is!

## Financial Planners

The future is not ours to see! That's not just a line from an old song; it is also the truth. However, that doesn't stop people from selling their alleged talents to predict what can and will happen to your fortunes. You can get that kind of advice from gypsies, tarot card readers, palm readers, tea leaf readers, someone with a crystal ball, a spiritual advisor or even a financial planner. It might be unfair to lump all financial planners in with fortune tellers, but many do have the same track record. Don't get financial planners confused with stockbrokers. While some brokerage houses offer financial planning, the planners to whom we are referring are those who are not directly connected to the stock markets. These financial planners deal with a more diverse field of investments.

Finding an excellent, highly successful financial advisor takes a great deal of luck. Even though there are some highly qualified financial planners out there, there are many who are unqualified and don't know what they are talking about. The problem is that almost anyone can hang out a shingle that says he or she is a financial advisor. It is nearly impossible to find a "true" professional who will claim to be a jack of all financial trades. Many can give excellent advice in one area such as law, tax, insurance or estate planning, but each specialty is so complex it's difficult to have the proper background to cover every area adequately. Just as you don't go to a dentist to have your eyes checked, don't go to a real estate expert to find the best stock advice.

You don't always get what you pay for in the financial world. The cost of financial planning can be expensive and sometimes hidden. The majority of planners say they won't charge you anything for their advice and they don't. Instead they make their money off fat commissions earned when you sink your hard-earned cash into their suggested investments. It's a conflict of interest of the worst kind. Human nature being greedy, this can easily mean that you will be shown the investment that will more than likely be most profitable to the salesperson (oops, we mean financial planner).

An important fact to consider if you ever feel you need a financial counselor is to make sure you deal with a firm or individual that sells only advice and not investments. You want a counselor who is concerned about your future, not his or her future commissions.

If you still want to find a financial planner, go about it in the same way we suggested looking for a stockbroker. Ask your successful friends for recommendations. A quick look in the phonebook is not enough. A planner who advertises as being certified might only have paid for and passed a mail-order correspondence course. And he or she could possibly give you a course of poor information and high commission. However, it should be mentioned that the C.F.P. course and degree offered by Certified Financial Planners of Denver is recommended by some industry observers. For a list you can write to:

C.F.P.
9725 E. Hampden Ave.
Denver, CO 80231

for names of planners in your area who have passed the course and have practical experience. The list will also include background information and fees.

---

## Checklist for Financial Planners

To conduct your private investigation of this financial planner ask about the following:

1. Education. Any degrees in finance from an accredited institution?
2. Experience in the financial planning field?
3. What is the planner's track record to date?
4. How much will the advice cost? Make sure there are no products for sale or commissions to be earned.
5. Ask for references, clients in your portfolio range. Of course this may well be a sanitized list, so when you check with references ask the customers if they know of any other customers you could also contact.
6. Discuss you financial goals and ask how this advice will help you reach those goals.
7. Ask about diversification of your portfolio. You don't want all of your eggs in one basket.
8. Finally, ask to see his or her personal portfolio. While your goals will not be the same, you can get an idea whether or not this financial planner practices what he or she preaches.

---

No one gives this kind of advice for nothing. We keep saying stay away from those who claim "you pay nothing" because they are commission hungry. How, then, do the others earn their keep? They earn fees which are often based on an hourly rate or a percentage of income or assets. The costs can run an average of $50 to $200 for the initial work-up. After that, the annual fees can run between $500 and $4,000. But price is not an indication of quality. Be sure to understand the fee structure before you get involved. Remember, you will pay whether or not the advice pays off for you. Your only recourse is to go somewhere else for advice, or do it yourself.

There is an answer for someone who still wants a financial plan but is afraid to get involved with a financial advisor. If you fear being taken or don't want a major expense, there is always a computer service. We suggest the services of:

The Consumer Financial Institute
288 Walnut St.
Newton, MA 02160

All you have to do is fill out both the 48-question questionnaire and a check for less than $175 (based on their scale) and the C.F.I. computer will do the rest. You will receive a 30-page leatherette-bound, computerized financial plan tailored to your present financial situation and your stated goals. In addition, you will receive some research material to help you learn how to meet those goals. Of course, the information that comes from the computer is only as good as the information you give it. Remember the computer age axiom: "GIGO—Garbage in, Garbage out."

Another answer might be to contact your bank or broker. More and more are offering moderate-fee financial-planning programs. But, beware, both banks and brokers do have ulterior motives as they sell investment vehicles.

### Read All About It

The best source of financial advice may be yourself. Never underestimate your own financial savvy. All the information you need is only a few books away. Everything you could ever want to know about taxes, wills, investments and financial planning is at your local library or bookstore under Financial Planning or Personal Finance. Also, again, don't forget Investment and Financial Planning courses offered by local educational institutions.

## A Micro-Chip Off the Old Block

If you have the hardware, the marketplace has the software to help you with your financial homework. Almost every day more sophisticated personal-computer programs are hitting the stores for use in the home.

One of the most popular programs at the time we wrote this book was *Andrew Tobia$ Managing Your Money*. While we are not recommending this one in particular, it is an excellent example of an integrated home financial package. It happened to be 7 programs in one that prepared a budget, balanced the checkbook, calculated your net worth, managed your stock portfolio, calculated your taxes, estimated life insurance needs, analyzed loans and even helped with retirement planning—all for about $160, plus the cost of the computer of course. That is just one example; there are also some very sophisticated portfolio management programs from services such as Dow Jones or Hale System that will help you with record keeping as well as calculating a stock's value automatically, updating information from phone-linked services and keeping track of capital gains and goals. And these programs are easy to use. The multitude of computer-related magazines continue to review these products, and they are more up-to-date on the ever-changing world of computer programs than this or any other book.

## You'll Sometimes Walk Alone

Keep in mind as you start out that there is nothing wrong in allowing a broker to hold your hand; but don't allow him or her to sweet-talk you into going further than you feel comfortable. A broker can be a teacher, advisor and investment confidante, but you are indeed the master of your own financial fate. You should be prepared to make decisions based on more than just the information supplied to you by a person who makes money ONLY if you use his or her services.

The only way that you will ever know if a broker's advice is in your best interest is by keeping up with your investments on a regular basis. And because no company is an island, you must also be able to follow the general trends of the stock market, financial community and the economy. That may sound like a complicated task, but it is not that overwhelming, as you will learn in the following chapter.

# 10

## The Financial Page for Funds and Profit

For years, the first thing most of us have turned to in the newspaper is the comics, horoscope or sports. The First-Time Investor is not required to give up these habits, and we hope you never do. However, you shouldn't stop with these fun items. You should also read at least the front page and then turn to the Financial or Business section. On these pages you may find the clues to answer the riddles of riches.

In this chapter we will explain how to read the market quotes from the stock exchanges, Mutual Funds and bonds. We have put together easy-to-follow, step-by-step explanations of investment tables, graphics and government statistics.

After you have completed this chapter, you will also have a better idea of how the money supply, GNP, prime rate, and cost of living figures affect you and your investments. These will no longer be meaningless statistics, but will be stimulating and involving.

## Quotes that Count

Part of the joy of owning stock is being able to watch your money work for you. While there may not be daily news stories about your favorite holdings, chances are that you can still keep an eye on the action of the company through the stock market listings which you can find in most major newspapers. It may take some sampling at first because some papers carry more complete listings than others. Some will carry the complete NYSE (New York Stock Exchange) and AMEX (American Stock Exchange) composite listings; these are often called detailed listings. The listings for the OTC (over-the-counter) and regional exchanges are most often condensed because of lack of space.

Checking the listings on a regular basis is a valuable investment tool because you will be able to see whether or not your investment is working for you. We would suggest that if you want the best feeling for a trend, you should probably pay more attention to the weekly listings in the Sunday newspaper than those in the daily papers.

You will find the printed information rather straightforward because the printed listings give you the prior trading close, the trading period high and low, the net change and some data to give you an idea which way the stock has gone over the past year. Also packed into this one little line in the newspaper is information on the most recent dividend estimates as well as the price/earnings ratio.

When you first see the stock tables you might wonder, "How can anyone get all of that information from a single line of seemingly meaningless numbers?" The answer is easy, once you know the code, which happily is the same for both the New York and American Stock Exchanges.

Read through our example and then take your new-found skill and apply it to the listings of your favorite companies printed in the newspaper.

The abbreviation of a company's name is not always what

you will find on the tickertape or computer because each national news-wire service uses its own easy-to-understand code. So while you may need to take a wild stab, you will find that the abbreviation of the company's name does make sense.

Our example for the purpose of this exercise is Gulf + Western, abbreviated **GlfWst,** which is understandable. The line in the newspaper will look a great deal like this: (The numbers, obviously, will be different, but the essential interpretation will be the same.)

| 52-week hi lo | | Div | Yld % | PE ratio | Sales 100s | Hi | Lo | Last | Chg |
|---|---|---|---|---|---|---|---|---|---|
| **35** | **25⅛** GlfWst | .90 | 2.6 | 11 | 12300 | 34⅞ | 32½ | 34¼ | +1½ |

The first two figures are the 12-month High and Low. In the case of GlfWst the stock reached a high of **35** ($35 per share) at some point in the past year. GlfWst also reached a low of **25⅛** ($25.125) during the same time period. What this doesn't tell you is when either occurred.

| 52-week hi lo | | Div | Yld % | PE ratio | Sales 100s | Hi | Lo | Last | Chg |
|---|---|---|---|---|---|---|---|---|---|
| 35 | 25⅛ **GlfWst** | .90 | 2.6 | 11 | 12300 | 34⅞ | 32½ | 34¼ | +1½ |

The next symbol is of course the name of the company **GlfWst.** It is listed alphabetically and is probably placed at this point in the line behind the 12-month High and Low in order to separate history from current events, because nearly everything that follows the company name is the latest trading information. There are a few symbols which will pop up behind the names of certain companies. For instance, if there is a **pf** after the name that means it is preferred stock or a **Wt** stands for a warrant.

| 52-week | | | Div | Yld | PE | Sales | Hi | Lo | Last | Chg |
|---|---|---|---|---|---|---|---|---|---|---|
| hi | lo | | | % | ratio | 100s | | | | |
| 35 | 25⅛ | GlfWst | .90 | 2.6 | 11 | 12300 | 34⅞ | 32½ | 34¼ | +1½ |

The figure immediately following the name is the dividend, which is estimated, based on the latest quarterly or semiannual declaration.

| 52-week | | | Div | Yld | PE | Sales | Hi | Lo | Last | Chg |
|---|---|---|---|---|---|---|---|---|---|---|
| hi | lo | | | % | ratio | 100s | | | | |
| 35 | 25⅛ | GlfWst | .90 | **2.6** | 11 | 12300 | 34⅞ | 32½ | 34¼ | +1½ |

The 90-cents-a-share dividend in this case translates into the yield of **2.6** Basically this is the percentage return on the investment, determined by dividing the dividend by the current closing stock price and then represented as a percentage.

| 52-week | | | Div | Yld | PE | Sales | Hi | Lo | Last | Chg |
|---|---|---|---|---|---|---|---|---|---|---|
| hi | lo | | | % | ratio | 100s | | | | |
| 35 | 25⅛ | GlfWst | .90 | 2.6 | **11** | 12300 | 34⅞ | 32½ | 34¼ | +1½ |

The **11** in the GlfWst listing is the price/earnings ratio. That is the number of times by which the company's latest 12-month earnings per share must be multiplied to get the current stock price. In this case, GlfWst's stock price is 11 times larger than its earnings per share figure. As you learned in an earlier chapter, the P/E ratio is one of the most widely used tools for analyzing a stock because it tells you how much price you have to pay for $1 earnings. When a company's earnings per share are on the rise or expected to rise rapidly, you might see a higher P/E than with a company growing more slowly.

| 52-week hi lo | | Div | Yld % | PE ratio | Sales 100s | Hi | Lo | Last | Chg |
|---|---|---|---|---|---|---|---|---|---|
| 35 | 25⅛ GlfWst | .90 | 2.6 | 11 | **12300** | 34⅞ | 32½ | 34¼ | +1½ |

This is where you see what kind of action your stock is getting, as this tells how many shares were traded. They are listed in hundreds. This particular week GlfWst appears to have been hot, trading more than one million shares. If it's a very slow period for a particular issue, you may see the letter "z" preceding the number, which indicates the actual number of shares traded.

| 52-week hi lo | | Div | Yld % | PE ratio | Sales 100s | Hi | Lo | Last | Chg |
|---|---|---|---|---|---|---|---|---|---|
| 35 | 25⅛ GlfWst | .90 | 2.6 | 11 | 12300 | **34⅞** | 32½ | 34¼ | +1½ |

In the Sunday listings **34⅞** was the highest price paid for the stock that week. (In the daily listings you would find the highest price paid for the previous day.)

| 52-week hi lo | | Div | Yld % | PE ratio | Sales 100s | Hi | Lo | Last | Chg |
|---|---|---|---|---|---|---|---|---|---|
| 35 | 25⅛ GlfWst | .90 | 2.6 | 11 | 12300 | 34⅞ | **32½** | 34¼ | +1½ |

In the Sunday listings 32½ was the lowest price paid for the week. (The daily listing would show the lowest price paid the previous day.)

| 52-week hi lo | | Div | Yld % | PE ratio | Sales 100s | Hi | Lo | Last | Chg |
|---|---|---|---|---|---|---|---|---|---|
| 35 | 25⅛ GlfWst | .90 | 2.6 | 11 | 12300 | 34⅞ | 32½ | **34¼** | +1½ |

**34¼** was the last price paid at the closing bell. Watching these three figures—the highest price paid, the lowest paid, and the last paid—can give you a good indication of the volatility of the stock. In Wall Street jargon some call it the trading pattern.

| 52-week | | Div | Yld | PE | Sales | Hi | Lo | Last | Chg |
|---|---|---|---|---|---|---|---|---|---|
| hi | lo | | % | ratio | 100s | | | | |
| 35 | 25⅛ GlfWst | .90 | 2.6 | 11 | 12300 | 34⅞ | 32½ | 34¼ | +1½ |

Last but not least when reading the stock tables, you will find this figure and a plus or minus sign preceding it. Its purpose is to save you the time and trouble of doing the math. It indicates the net change from the previous week's closing price. In this case, GlfWst closed up 1½ points or up $1.50 per share over the previous week's closing. If this were the daily newspaper listing that figure would indicate the net change from the previous day's closing price.

Wasn't that easy? If you are still not comfortable, don't feel bad; studying the figures and explanations a few times should make it quite clear. Reading investment tables is much like learning a new language; about the only way it will sink in is to put it to use. So, why not start tracking some stocks you find interesting. Soon you will be very comfortable with those previously confusing columns.


### Over the Hump of Over-the-Counter Quotes

Not all market quotations are created equal. An excellent example is how the over-the-counter stocks are quoted. As you will remember from our previous chapter on exchanges, there is one and only one price for every stock. It is the price the market will bear. But things are different with over-the-counter for several reasons. There are three different formats for listing the daily or weekly quotes. The larger OTC-traded companies are listed on the *NASDAQ National Market* and the listings look somewhat like those of the New York or American Stock exchanges.

| 52-week | | | | Sales | Hi | Lo | Last | Chg |
|---------|---|---|-----|-------|----|----|------|-----|
| hi | lo | | Div | ratio 100s | | | | |
| 11⅝ | 6⅝ | Nike B. | .40 | 915 | 8⅞ | 8⅜ | 8⅝ | +⅛ |

The "hi" and "lo" are the actual high and low sales prices of the day, but in an earlier chapter we told you that OTC stocks were traded on a bid and ask basis. Well, that is still true. It is just that with these OTC stocks the market is very active, allowing for actual hard prices instead of bid and ask, so they are listed as the firm figure.

The second OTC listings could be called the *NASDAQ National List* or *NASDAQ Bid and Asked Quotations* depending on which newspaper you read. The name is not as important as the way the stocks are listed. This is where the bid and ask prices are shown as the highest bid and the lowest asked price. These are not fixed prices because the quotes are only representative buy and sell prices.

The Sunday newspaper will most likely carry the week's bid range in this type of form:

| | High | Low | Bid | Chg |
|----------|------|-----|-----|-----|
| Falstaff | 6 | 5⅞ | 6 | +⅛ |

That is fairly straightforward. The week's high was **6,** the lowest bid was **5⅞** with the final bid recorded being **6.** The resulting change over the week was that Falstaff rose by **⅛.**

The weekday listings are slightly different and include the number of shares sold.

| | Sales 100s | Bid | Asked | Net Chg |
|----------|------------|-----|-------|---------|
| Falstaff | 51 | 6 | 6¼ | . . . |

In this case more than 5,000 shares changed hands, and the bid (the most anyone is willing to pay) was **6,** while the asked price (the lowest anyone is willing to take in order to sell) was **6¼.** Because the bid did not increase from the previous trading day, there was no net change.

The final OTC-type listing is known under several headings including the *Additional OTC Quotes* or *NASDAQ Supplemental O-T-C*. This listing is very simple.


|  | Bid | Asked |
|---|---|---|
| Swenson's Inc. | 2¼ | 2½ |


That is quite straightforward and by now self-explanatory.

While most First-Time Investors don't start out in the stock market, we presented the stock tables first because those are the listings most people have seen before. It is also very helpful to understand how to read them so you can start planning future investments now by watching the action on corporations you find intriguing.


## Mutual Satisfaction

Shopping for a Mutual Fund might be easier if you read those tables in the Sunday newspaper. It is easier to make instant, though short-term, comparisons. Knowing how to read the Mutual Fund Tables is also important for keeping track of your own fund. For this example a dart thrown at the paper has taken us to State Street Investment Corporation's Growth Fund. The listings for Mutual Funds are often more straightforward than for stocks because the name is listed more clearly, and when there is a family of funds they all fall under one heading. With State Street Investment Corp., there

are at least three funds, but we will look only at the Growth
Fund which is listed as:

**StStreet Inv:**   NAV    Offer Price    NAV chng
**Grwth**          55.70   N.L.          −.44

While this line may not look as if it contains much information, it does tell you a great deal. **Grwth** is obviously the
fund's name within State Street Investment Corp.

StStreet Inv:   **NAV**    Offer Price    NAV chng
Grwth           **55.70**   N.L.          −.44

The **NAV** stands for the net asset value of each share. The
value of each Mutual Fund share is determined by taking the
total value of the fund's holdings, subtracting the small management fee and then dividing the figure by the number of
shares outstanding. Once again the wizards of Wall Street
have saved you all that math and provided the NAV for you,
which in this case shows that each share would cost **$55.70.**

StStreet Inv:   NAV    **Offer Price**    NAV chng
Grwth           55.70   **N.L.**          −.44

In this case, the **N.L.** indicates the fund is no-load (no commission or sales charge), meaning that the offer price is the
same as the NAV. If there is a figure in that column, it means
that the fund has a load and the commission is factored in,
and the figure shows the price you would have to pay in order to purchase a share from the fund.

StStreet Inv:   NAV    Offer Price    **NAV chng**
Grwth           55.70   N.L.          **−.44**

The final figure shows the change in the net asset value per share at the close of the stock market the previous day (in the case of Sunday listings it would be the net asset value change per share over the previous week). Some of the full-week listings will also show the high, low, close and change.

Mutual Fund tables may be the simplest you will ever deal with, but they don't need to be more complicated because, as you will remember, you are paying for professional management to worry about details.

## Bound by Bonds

Bond tables, unlike those for Mutual Funds, are crammed with information. We return now to Gulf and Western and a bond which is due to reach maturity in the year 2003. The bond market listing is as follows:

**60½   49**   GlfWn   7s03A   12.2   83   58   57   57½   +⅛

The first figures are the 12-month High and Low. In this case a high of **$605.00** and a low of **$490.00**.

60½   49   **GlfWn   7s03A**   12.2   83   58   57   57½   +⅛

By now you understand GlfWn stands for Gulf and Western, but those other numbers and symbols may be a bit confusing. The **7s03A** quite simply represents the original coupon or interest rate and the final two digits are the year of maturity. In this case the original interest rate was **7** percent, the s means that there was no fraction, the **03** means it matures in the year 2003, and the **A** at the end of the quote means this is the A series of bonds. GlfWn issued two sets of **7s03** bonds; one is the A series, the other, the B series.

60½   49   GlfWn   7s03A   **12.2**   **83**   58   57½   +⅛

The **12.2** represents the current yield, which is the annual percentage return for someone who buys the bond at the current price. The **83** represents the sales volume in $1,000 bonds.

60½   49   GlfWn   7s03A   12.2   83   **58**   **57**   57½   +⅛

Now it's time to tie some of these numbers together. If the original bond was issued with a 7-percent yield, why is it now 12.2 percent? That is because the price of the bond has fallen from $1,000 on the day that it was issued to a current trading high of **58** ($580) and to a low of **57** ($570). With bonds you always add a zero to these figures in order to get the actual price. Remember, with a bond the yield is increased by lowering the purchase price (discounting a bond).

60½   49   GlfWn   7s03A   12.2   83   58   57   **57½**   **+⅛**

This brings us to the closing price of the final trading day **57½** ($575). With bonds a ½ equals $5, while 1 equals $10. So, the net change of **+⅛** equals an increase of $1.25.

Doesn't it feel good being able to read and understand those market charts? As you have learned, they do begin to make sense, and with this basic training you should be able to follow the movements of the markets with ease.

### Newspaper Training

You may feel that there is a tremendous amount of seemingly obscure information in the daily and weekly newspapers, information which affects investment decisions; however, you will soon find this obscurity replaced with enlightenment. Reading between the headlines, you will eventually find the forces that guide the financial community.

Certainly you have seen the headlined statistics passed off on the news with great authority and no depth, a simple pronouncement that the GNP rose at an annual rate of 5.5 percent. The newscaster gives the snap analysis that this is good news and you feel better. But you are no better informed; instead you may be wondering just what is a GNP? Can you cuddle with one on a cold night?

## Meet Your New Friends

There is no need to be frightened by statistics. When you become familiar with them, they will be your friends. One important weekly set of statistics you will want to watch, because it will certainly have an immediate effect on the stock market, is the money supply. This is a measure of how much money is in the system and indicates how the Federal Reserve feels the economy is going. The Fed controls the money supply in order to control growth and contain inflation. A tight money supply can mean high interest rates and slowed growth, often reflected in a down stock market but an up bond market.

A less restrictive money supply means more money for loans and potentially lower interest rates, an important seed for growth in the stock market because it means cheaper money for expansion; meanwhile, the news is devastating for the bond market. Tying up money in long-term bonds that pay a low interest rate is not considered a desirable investment for most people.

These money-supply figures are released every Thursday afternoon after the markets close and are listed as the M-0, M-1, M-2 and M-3 which we detailed in Chapter 4. Newspaper articles often explain how these actually translate to either tight money or lower interest rates.

### Money Matters—It Sure Does!

Most people feel they already understand inflation figures because they can feel the effects of inflation right in their pocketbooks. But without familiarity with actual names and numbers, the figures can be somewhat confusing. There are two sets of inflation numbers each month: the Consumer Price Index and the Producer Price Index.

If someone says PPI to you, what is your initial response? A glassy-eyed, cold stare is appropriate! PPI is the government acronymn for Producer Price Index. It normally comes out one week before the other inflation index, the CPI (consumer price index). The PPI is an important indicator because it tells us how much more we can expect to have taken from our pockets in just a few weeks' time. The Producer Price Index, which used to be known as the Wholesale Price Index, measures the price changes of goods that are finished, completely processed and ready for sale to the ultimate user or consumer. Of course it's a bit more complicated than pure consumer inflation figures because the PPI includes things such as trucks, farm equipment and machinery which would be consumed or used by businesses. It also includes consumer goods such as food, clothing, appliances and cars that would be purchased by retailers for eventual sale to you and me. As you go deeper into the PPI you will also find it measures the flour that goes into bread and so on.

Information is collected on some 2,800 commodities by surveying 7,000 businesses through the mail. The data is weighted for seasonal and geographic differences; then the numbers are all crunched by computers, and we have the final figure. The Producer Price Index is considered a long-view measure of inflation.

### My! My! It's the CPI!

It's mysterious, it's more powerful than a locomotive, it's able to jump or fall, it affects all of us and it's seemingly impossible to understand. What is it? Well if it were inflation it would have bitten you in your wallet, but it's only one measure of inflation. It is the Consumer Price Index (CPI). Every month the government publishes this figure that can make us gasp! Or make us breathe a sigh of relief. But where does the CPI come from? That is what makes it so mysterious. Every month the government measures changes in prices, based on a fixed market-basket of goods and services that contains food, housing, fuel, transportation, medical care, entertainment, clothes and personal care. These are just some of the 385 major items in this market-basket. Prices are collected from 24,000 sources such as grocery stores, department stores, hospitals and gas stations. From those figures the government computes the cost of living. Now you know that the figures don't come from a crystal ball, unless that is one of the items in the market-basket.

The cost of living index, like so many others, does not give a totally accurate accounting of how much people spend. Any one customer or family may purchase different items and different quantities for their own market-basket. It does create an overall view from which we might see where inflation is headed in the short term.

Inflation can affect investments. When individuals have less money to spend on consumer goods, there are fewer dollars to invest, which could dramatically slow down the stock market. Also, inflation eats away at your portfolio, especially if you are locked into an investment which doesn't have an inflation-beating yield. While low inflation may result in lower interest earnings for those invested in Money Market Funds and bonds, keep in mind that you are not having to give up as much of that yield to inflation.

## Stats that Work for You

Unemployment figures are another government statistic which hit home because most of us have been unemployed at one time or another, or at least on the job hunt. The unemployment rate is not only an indicator of how much competition we face, but also an important economic indicator for an investor. The jobless rate cuts across the entire economy and can give you an early sign if things are headed downhill or back up. Remember, when people don't work, they don't earn money and they don't spend what they don't have, and that in turn can mean retail stores can't sell their goods and inventories start to build so the stores don't reorder, leaving the factories no alternative but to slow down producing so many goods. When factories have less work for their workers, overtime is cut first, then layoffs begin, adding to the unemployment spiral. For the stockholder this could mean decreased corporate profits, smaller dividends and possibly a falling stock price. This is a very simple treatment of the situation because all of those cutbacks can be good news for a corporation having to reexamine its methods, and can lead to a leaner, meaner operation which will eventually show higher profits. If you have done your homework before buying the stock, you may already know how a corporation handles high national unemployment or recession.

Just for background, the government doesn't go out and count every unemployed person in America each month. Instead the labor department conducts what is known as a "Household Survey" which canvasses 60,000 households. The interviewer tries to determine how many people live in the home, how many are older than 16 and what is their job status. These interviews are conducted nearly two weeks before the figures are released on the first Friday of the month. So, the unemployment rate is really a situation report on the previous month.

Who is considered unemployed? Someone who has not worked during the survey week but who has made an effort to find a job during the prior four weeks. Someone temporarily laid off or someone waiting to report to a job within 30 days is also considered unemployed. In the government's eyes, however, people on strike are considered fully employed, as are those who are paid for working 35 hours or more a week. They are called full-time workers, while those employed for only one hour to 34 hours a week are labeled as part-time workers. You don't have to be paid to be considered employed. If you put 15 or more hours a week into a family business, you are also counted among the employed.

Not everyone is counted even statistically in either the employed or unemployed columns. Those who have stopped working and stopped looking for work are not considered jobless; instead they are called discouraged workers.

## GNP Does Not Mean Good News People

Every 3 months the federal government reports the GNP, the Gross National Product, which is the broadest measure of the nation's economy. The name Gross National Product makes sense when you realize that it measures the output of all the goods and services in America, every item produced, sold, and consumed in America, whether it is a product or a service.

The GNP is divided into four categories:

1. Personal consumption expenditures (government talk for what you spend your money on).
2. Gross private domestic investment, (which includes home buying as well as investments by businesses including equipment, offices, factories and buildings).
3. Net exports of goods and services, which is the balance of trade between what this country imports and exports (how much we spent for TVs from Japan, against how much wheat we sold to the Russians).
4. Government purchases. Uncle Sam is the single largest consumer, so that what the government buys and how much it pays is very important to the economy as a whole.

The GNP is much like a sales report, as it only measures the sales of final products. That means that the steel in your washing machine, the cloth in your shirts or the flour in your cake mixes is in effect counted in the sale of the final product. This is a sneaky but effective way of factoring in all the goods and services. Once the government has these figures, it can determine if the economy is continuing to grow or if it is slowing. It is the indicator of whether or not the economy is in a recession or if inflation is out of line. This information gives the investor a chance to determine if the current movements of any investment are in line with the total economy. The Gross National Product is a broad but effective measure.

As we said, these figures come out every 3 months, though you are bound to hear GNP mentioned much more frequently. The government has seven chances to revise the figures. This isn't a game of playing with statistics or trying to fiddle with the economy; instead, when the first report of the GNP comes out about two weeks after the end of the quarter, it is based on incomplete data. Just consider the magnitude of the reporting system! So when the rest of the information comes in, the GNP is revised. This can happen a number of times after the first release. So, when you hear or read two different GNP figures, you must pay attention to which quarter they represent.


## Americans Produce

All investors should be interested in how much manufacturers are producing. So you should consider paying attention to one figure you might not hear on the radio or see on the nightly news which is the Index of Industrial Production. Newspapers often give this a detailed presentation because it reflects what is happening in the world of durable goods such as washer-dryers, refrigerators, other large appliances and cars. But that is not all; the Index of Industrial Production also measures nondurables such as the parts used in production of the durables, business equipment, construction supplies, food and clothing. The index also breaks down the data by industry product such as chemicals, lumber and transportation equipment. That breakdown can make life a bit easier for the investor trying to follow a particular field. Because the index covers manufacturing, which is quite sensitive to economic downturns, it is seen as a reliable indicator as to whether or not the economy has indeed slipped into a recession. On the other hand, because the industries covered are so sensitive to a recession, it can give an overstated view of the depth of a recession.

## A Housing Start Is Not a Home

The monthly Housing Start figures can give you an idea of how the construction industry sees the future economy. It is often the first sector of the economy to slow as the economy loses steam. Housing contractors look way ahead before breaking ground, which is when the Commerce Department considers construction on a housing unit to have started. Building a house may take months or years to complete and a builder depends very much on so many other sectors of the economy. Contractors as a whole have to look ahead at interest rates and the potential of the economy. They need to know that the economy will be able to deliver all the materials and durable goods needed for that house, but they also must know that the job market is strong enough to provide paychecks for the future inhabitants of the housing. So, if builders are not Bullish on the economy, they don't build; that feeling in turn can have a domino effect on not only the supply side of the housing industry but also the supply of housing. Fewer housing units being built can mean higher prices for homes and rent if the demand remains strong when the economy remains weak.

### Economic Forecasts

Economists as a practice do not forecast; they only suggest what might happen given certain data and changes to that data. Even with that they don't pull that data out of thin air. In place of tea leaves to provide a picture of the future, the Commerce Department has come up with its own economic crystal ball called the Index of Leading Economic Indicators. There are 12 components, which include the length of the average manufacturing work week, layoff rate for manufacturing employees, inflation-adjusted new orders for consumer goods and materials, the delivery speed of those goods, the rate of new business formation, contracts for manufacturing plants and equipment, the changing size of inventories, changes in crude material prices, stock prices, liquid assets and the changes in the M-2 money supply. This combination has historically moved up or down because the economy as a whole starts its own swing. Classic interpretation says if the LEI (Leading Economic Indicators) is down overall for 3 straight months, we are headed for a recession. As to be expected, if the index is on the rise for 3 additional months, we are headed into a recovery. The problem with the theory is that it is not foolproof. Since World War II, the LEI has forecast 9 recessions, when only 6 actually occurred, and like weather forecasts, it has missed predicting a few. The most notable was in 1973 when the index showed only a slight dip; meanwhile the economy was crashing into the worst recession since World War II.

## Now You Know It! Now You Don't

None of these indices will be the be-all and end-all when it comes to investing, but understanding what they indicate and how they affect the investment world will help you sleep a bit more comfortably, knowing that your decisions were not all made in the dark.

The business pages often provide quite detailed explanations of the figures and analyses by some of the best economists in the nation. Of course it won't take long before you realize that not all economists agree. Each bases his or her comments on different sets of figures in different economic reports. You as an investor will need to become familiar enough with each report to be able to pinpoint the information that will particularly affect the industries in which you are investing. It takes some time, but when it is your money that is involved, all of a sudden the homework becomes a great deal more interesting.

# 11

## Real Estate Creates a Real Estate

Are you prepared for the Hunt? A successful house hunter needs the instincts of a bloodhound and a deadly accurate aim to snag the dream house and the perfect mortgage.

In the beginning your largest holding is often your home. That could very well be a good idea because real estate does create a solid foundation for your estate. But homeownership is not for everyone.

If you are in the mood for househunting, one weapon *everyone* needs is a large down payment. The more you put down, the more you reduce the risk of being wounded by high monthly mortgage payments. You should never borrow the money for a down payment because the combined payments could totally destroy any quality of living you might hope to have. Also, most mortgage lenders won't give you the time of day if you need to borrow the down payment.

To every rule there is an exception. Never borrow money for the down payment *unless* you are lucky enough to borrow the money from a family member without a time limit to repay, or better yet, with no repayment at all. Any agreement such as that is strictly between you and the family member, though there is a chance Uncle Sam might be interested in whether or not the loan is really a gift.

## Location! Location! Location! Location!

It cannot be said enough that location is the most important factor in any home purchase. Not necessarily a fancy address, but a desirable or growing part of town, where prices are most likely to climb over a relatively short period of time. One example might be a rapidly growing area where continued expansion is controlled by certain immoveable barriers such as rivers or mountains, or possibly something equally immovable—zoning restrictions on further construction. Look for an upwardly mobile neighborhood. It would be wonderful if you could find such a thing before it begins to pick up too much speed on its upward climb. It takes some searching and homework, but it pays off in the long run. One source who might tip you off to such an area is a local banker. Even before the realtors, the bankers will have a strong feeling if an area is about to take off. That is because while realtors always hope prices will rise, mortgage writers bank on it. You want to follow the leaders, but not too far behind.

You don't have to be a great friend of a banker to get that information. Simply phone for an appointment to speak to a mortgage officer. During the appointment ask about the current rates and restrictions for different parts of the area. If a part of town is in rebirth, there might be concessions made in order to attract new money. If you have already picked a part of town you like, simply ask if the bank feels the real estate appraisals are in line with growth and if there has been a great deal of turnover. You might run into some resistance, but chances are if you appear to be a creditworthy person you can get some answers. Despite the attitudes of some bankers, they are all in the business of lending money, and mortgage customers are a very important source of income.

## 3BDR 2BR DR DN EIK GAR

Translation: Three bedrooms, two bathrooms, dining room, den, eat-in kitchen and a garage. After a while you begin to learn the househunting code. You learn it out of self-defense in order to save yourself the time and energy of looking at the wrong places. Size is your next consideration; once you have several areas to investigate you need to decide how much space you want, how much you really need and how much you can afford in that section of town. Consider, also, what future buyers might need from that property. Always respect the investment value of the house because you may want to trade up some day into a bigger and more expensive house. When that happens you want a desirable piece of property to sell for top dollar.

### Condos and Co-ops

The First-Time Investor should probably consider buying an existing *livable* home for the first time out. Building or renovating a house can involve expenses that cannot be recovered in just a few years of ownership.

A house is not a home, but also a home is not always a house. While the "American Dream" has traditionally meant a single-family home, that is not always the best answer. You might consider a condominium or some other type of cluster housing such as co-operative apartments (co-ops). These allow you to save on both building and land costs. An added benefit is that, with fewer walls exposed to Mother Nature, attached homes can hold down heating and cooling costs.

There are also some possible undesirable ramifications of common ownership. With a single family home, your family decides what improvements will be made, taking current budgets into account. With a condo or co-op your neighbors have as much say as you do and possibly more. They can tell you whether or not you can make changes such as putting up TV antennas or dictate the kind of flowerbox you can have in your window. So, you may have to give up a great deal of freedom. On the other side of the equation, you might also gain some delightful public facilities, such as a party room, game room, swimming pool, or sauna.

When you buy a condominium, you buy not only your dwelling, which may or may not be attached to the others, you also buy your share of the land and other things held in common with the other condo owners. These may include recreational facilities. None of these things are free, of course, because each month a condo owner is assessed a monthly maintenance fee that pays a management company to keep everything, including your roof and lawn, in tip-top shape.

One advantage to owning a condo is that in most cases you are not restricted in selling it, renting it out, or letting friends stay there for as long as you wish. Unless the bylaws specify otherwise, it is your castle, with someone else taking care of the moat.

A cooperative or co-op is much different because instead of buying an apartment you are really buying a share or a number of shares in a closed corporation which owns the building. This means you cannot do with the apartment as you wish, unless it is also the wish of the board of directors of the corporation. While the members of the board are also your neighbors, their interests may not be the same as yours. With a co-op, you do get many of the same tax benefits as owning a home, but, as with a condo, you also have to pay a monthly maintenance fee, also determined by the board.

Another important point to remember with common ownership is that there are common bills that are paid as monthly maintenance fees. There are controlled by a board of directors that decides if and when the common roads, roofs, or public areas should be repaired. Those fees could actually increase dramatically against your wishes. Boards have the powers of tiny governments, and they can also restrict pets or even children. There have been cases where owners have had to sell because they began a family after they bought and moved into a condo or co-op complex.

The co-op boards even have the power to decide if they want you living in their building and have the power of veto if you decide to sell. Of course they are restricted from barring anyone on the basis of sex, race, religion, or age. The board can even control the amount you are allowed to mortgage.

If you are attracted to a condo or co-op, "Buyer Beware" because sales pitches can be exaggerated. Make sure that all values, investment potentials, tax advantages, and vacancy factors are put into writing. Putting pen to paper seems to have the effect of pricking the balloon of overly inflated sales presentations. One more caution: Always check the credentials of the developer and builder.

### Park and Live

This may be a mobile society, but mobile homes are not really mobile. While you might be able to "move it" (realtor talk for selling it), you are often very limited in physically moving a mobile home. It is really made to stay put on a permanent site. These two- and three-bedroom mobile homes are for buyers with a very limited budget, but in recent years they have turned into decent investments by appreciating in value. It wasn't too many years ago that mobile homes depreciated much like cars or trucks.

Again, location is very important here because many areas have zoned against mobile homes. Although as they become more popular and mobile-home parks no longer look like trailer parks, new state laws are overriding local restrictions.


## Do You Really Want to Buy?

Your immediate response might be, "Of course!" Don't be too hasty! Renting may very well be more financially advantageous to you. Houses are not appreciating as rapidly as they did in the soaring '70s. Ten years ago you could realize a substantial appreciation and recover your buying, closing, moving and redecorating costs in just two years; now it can take more than five.

**Something everyone should keep in mind is that if you can rent for half of what your house payment would be, then it might not make much sense to buy.**

An excellent example could be Ron and Rhoda Renter, who have started househunting because they didn't want to keep handing over $410 a month in rent to a landlord. Their dream house costs $70,000, with a $10,000 down payment on a 30-year adjustable-rate mortgage. They figure they can afford the $720-a-month mortgage payments. They also expect they will sell the house in 10 years when their children finish high school. Does it pay for the Renters to buy? They might do better by investing that $10,000 in something else, according to a buy/rent analysis computer program used by Cornell University. The computer crunches the pluses and minuses of ownership and renting for each individual case, taking into account the costs of home ownership (mortgage payments, insurance, property taxes, moving costs, closing fees, down payment and of course upkeep and repairs). This provides a figure called the "equivalent rent" of the purchased house which can be compared with the current monthly rent paid on the apartment or house.

In this example Ron and Rhoda Renter would have a starting "equivalent rent" of $480 a month which would rise with inflation. The appreciation of the house for the ten years they hope to keep it is factored in. That means the "equivalent rent" is a great deal lower than the $720 a month mortgage payments. In order to reduce the "equivalent rent" to their current rent level, they would have to hold on to the house for 20 years. Mr. and Mrs. Renter might want to consider staying renters and putting the difference into other forms of income investment. Reading *The First-Time Investor* should give more than a few suggestions.

Remember, if you can rent for half of what your house payment would be, then it might not make much sense to buy.

Should you be interested in such an evaluation, write for more information from:

Buy/Rent Analysis
Consumer Economics and Housing Department
Cornell University
Ithaca, N.Y. 14853

The fee is small; at the time we wrote this book it was only $25.

### Realtor Sinks In

You have decided to buy, picked your location and have a feel for your affordable price range. Time to find a real estate broker. While you might be able to find homes advertised in the newspaper, or see *for sale* signs on lawns, your best bet is to see a professional. A realtor will have a better sense of the market than you can determine on your own, especially the availabilities and the price ranges.

The buyer does not normally pay the real estate agent anything. The agent is working on a commission paid from the proceeds of the sale. That in effect means the real estate agent is working for the seller, not the buyer. While this may smack of some kind of conflict of interest, realtors realize that the seller is moving out of the community and the buyer is moving in. With that in mind, they want to make sure that the buyer is happy and has the best possible deal because their reputation in the area is at stake. The fact that most realtors belong to multiple listing services means that you don't have to worry about missing too many homes within the range of your price and requirements. But there are still a few exclusive listings, so you may have to go across the street to another realtor in order to explore those exclusives on the other agent's books.

### Buying Means Paying!

Just as you must shop for a good real-estate deal, you need to shop for a good mortgage deal. This can include a few items other than just a reasonable mortgage rate. Consider these items, which we shall also discuss: application fees, the points and the possibility of prepayment penalties.

This is where having a sizable down payment can pay off. The more you borrow, the higher your monthly payments and the more the house will cost in the long run. If you have a low down payment, the lender might charge you something over and above the monthly mortgage payment. This added charge is called Private Mortgage Guarantee Insurance or PMI. It protects the lender against the costs of default and foreclosure.

When mortgage shopping, look for the subtle differences that separate the lenders. All mortgage lenders will charge you something called points. Points pay for the processing of the mortgage. One point equals 1 percent of the total loan. It must be paid in cash at the closing and can cost thousands of dollars. Look for the fewest points because, unlike other mortgage interest costs, points are not tax deductible. While some say they are nothing more than an extra few interest payments, Uncle Sam says they are simply the cost of doing business with a banker. Check to see if you are allowed to sell the house and prepay the mortgage early without penalty. It is something that can save you thousands of dollars. Some mortgage lenders won't let you off without paying a penalty should you sell before 2, 3, 5, 10 or even 30 years have elapsed.

### Name that Mortgage, in 15, 25, or 30 Years

The traditional home mortgage has been either 25 or 30 years with both the interest rate and the payments fixed. Each monthly payment covers the interest payment and begins whittling away at the principal. In the beginning about the only thing you pay is interest. An excellent example is a 30-year, fixed-rate, 11 percent $100,000 dollar mortgage:

| | |
|---|---|
| Monthly payments | $952.32 |
| Payment #1 breakdown | $916.67 interest |
| | $ 35.65 principal |

At the end of the first year you will have paid $10,977.77 in interest, but only $450.07 toward actually owning the house. You won't start paying more on the principal each month than you pay for interest until your 286th monthly mortgage payment. That is nearly 24 years after you buy the house. However, since mortgage interest on your home is tax deductible, a substantial deduction can be taken in the earlier years, thus reducing your personal income-tax bill.

## HOW MUCH A MORTGAGE CAN COST

There are many different mortgage options today, but to give
you an idea of financing costs, the following table shows the
monthly principal and interest payments required on a 30-
year, fixed rate mortgage for varying loan amounts (what you
still owe after making the down payment) and interest rate
levels. Lenders generally figure that buyers can spend up to
28% of monthly income on housing costs (mortgage payments, taxes and insurance).

| 30-YEAR FIXED-RATE MORTGAGE | MONTHLY PAYMENT OF PRINCIPAL AND INTEREST | | |
|---|---|---|---|
| | at 12% | at 13% | at 14% |
| $ 80,000 | $ 822.90 | $ 884.96 | $ 947.90 |
| $ 90,000 | $ 925.75 | $ 995.58 | $1,066.38 |
| $100,000 | $1,028.62 | $1,106.20 | $1,184.88 |

**Source:** Merrill Lynch

One way to save on paying that much out in interest is to
opt for a shorter-term mortgage. A number of people are
considering the 15 year, fixed-rate notes which are often 1 to
2 percent lower. While the monthly payments may be 10 to
15 percent higher, the total number of payments is cut in half.

| $60,000 MORTGAGE | INTEREST RATE | PAYMENTS MONTHLY | TOTAL INTEREST PAID |
|---|---|---|---|
| 30-year Conventional | 12% | $617.17 | $162,181.20 |
| 15-year Conventional | 11.50% | $700.92 | $66,165.60 |
| SAVINGS OVER THE LIFE OF THE LOAN | | | $96,015.60 |

# ARM Wrestling

One way to keep your monthly payment lower is to consider an Adjustable-Rate Mortgage (ARM) or an Adjustable-Rate Loan (ARL). Both mean the same thing. The interest rate floats and is periodically adjusted as interest rates change. The restrictions on how much or how often the mortgage rate and payment can be adjusted varies from state to state and even lender to lender. Some rules say no more than a 1-percent increase every 6 months; others allow up to 4 percent a year. Make sure you understand how much the payments and interest rate can fluctuate and what the lender uses as a measure to adjust the interest rate. Some use the rates for 6-month Treasury bills, which can be rather volatile. Others use 3-year Treasury notes which do not fluctuate as radically. Avoid any system that allows lenders to tie mortgage rates to measures of their own devising, such as the price they must pay in order to borrow money. As one congressional staffer testified, "Those systems are nothing more than a license to rip you off."

Ask questions and get the answers in writing. For instance:

1. What interest-rate index is used to determine the new rate?
2. How often can the interest rate be changed?
3. What are the limits on the changes in interest rate and payments?

In every way possible avoid the type of adjustable rate mortgage that offers you the same monthly payment no matter what happens to the interest rate. If the interest rate is adjusted upward, and you don't start paying that extra interest, it is just added to the loan as part of the principal. In the end you could owe more than you borrowed in the first place. It could come as a nasty surprise, when you try to sell the house or refinance, to realize that even though the house has appreciated you still owe the bank more money with nothing to show for it.

There is also a mix-and-match type hybrid, the fixed/adjustable-rate mortgage. Payments are set up as they are for the traditional 30-year mortgage, but at the end of 3 to 5 years you and the lender renegotiate the interest rate. This is done with a guarantee of renewal and is called the Renegotiable-Rate Mortgage (RRM).

## Don't Roll Over for the Rollover

If you go for a rollover mortgage, you could find yourself financially belly-up. The payments for a ROM are also set up as they are for a traditional 30 year, fixed-rate mortgage, except at the end of 3 to 5 years the loan has to be refinanced or the balance must be paid off. If the bank demands that you repay the loan, it is really nothing more than a balloon payment: a financially dangerous idea which could mean you lose your home by being forced either to sell or into foreclosure, which means the lender simply takes title and you get nothing in return.

## Upwardly Mobile Mortgage Checks

For those who expect their income to rise and who want to buy before the big bucks start rolling in, there is one type of pay-later plan that might work. It is called a Graduated Payment Mortgage or GPM. Payments increase according to a preset schedule. Again, be careful that you are not increasing the principal with this type of loan. Ask questions now, and demand that the answers be given in writing.

Some institutions are happy to play rich uncle for you and loan you the money to buy a house at a lower interest rate in return for a piece of the action. The lender simply gets a

share of the profits when you sell or refinance. Be forewarned: Some of these Shared Appreciation Mortgages
(SAM) contain language that allows the institution to demand its share before you may want to sell or refinance. Even
though this time limit is detailed in the contract and might
not be exercised, it can be a severe financial shock if there is
a knock on the door demanding the money—now.

### Assume If You Will

Everyone has heard that you should never assume anything;
forget that for a moment. Though currently it is more difficult than a few years ago, you might consider assuming a
mortgage. Older mortgages often carry relatively low interest rates. Two potential problems: the lender may not allow
it, and assuming an existing mortage means you must come
up with a much larger down payment or a second mortgage
to complete the deal. When you assume a mortgage, you must
give the seller the difference between the balance and the
selling price. Many VA and FHA mortgages remain assum-
able, while many conventional loans have a due-on-sale
clause. That three-word clause means the balance must be
repaid to the lender immediately upon sale, so there is no
way the mortgage can be assumed.

### Creative Financing

There are a number of fad mortgages, variations on the mortgages we have mentioned, and as financing has become more
creative, new types of mortgages that continually pop up. So,
one of your first househunting moves should be to stop off at
local banks and other lenders to pick up their brochures.
Then ask your realtor to explain them in more detail and also
to tell you of any possible pitfalls. If a deal sounds too good

to be true, check it out with your accountant or a real-estate attorney. Over the past 5 years more than a million families have lost their homes because they did not understand the loopholes of their creative financing.

## Time to Beg

The actual searching for a loan does not happen until after you have found the house, made an offer and had it accepted. Some have likened this mortgage search to begging for money. If you are prepared, the process can be much less distasteful.

Don't worry, you really don't have to beg. Well, at least you don't need to get down on your knees and beg. Asking for a loan is not something that comes naturally to most people. We have been taught not to borrow unless it's necessary. But buying a house makes it necessary, so here are some suggestions that should make it a bit easier.

Rule 1. Start your loan shopping where you are most comfortable and probably known, at your own bank or savings and loan. If you already have a relationship such as a savings or checking account, you have a bargaining chip. Whether you get a loan depends on whether the lender thinks you will repay it, so they check your income and credit history. If you have had any credit problems tell them up front. Honesty pays because it gives you a chance to explain the extenuating circumstances.

Rule 2. Remember that when you are asking for a loan you are conducting a business transaction, so dress and act accordingly. (Read that to mean conservatively.)

Rule 3. If you are turned down for a mortgage, don't hesitate to ask why. You are legally entitled to an answer. Remember, each bank is different; one may see you as a risk, while another is willing to take that risk.

Getting a loan is easier if you speak the language. The language in this case is bankerese. It is relatively easy once you understand a few terms, and within a few days you can amuse and astound your family and friends. But the most important advantage is that with a little study you can understand what a banker is saying when you are trying to get a mortgage. For instance principal is no longer the parent figure in school, but the figure at the bottom of a loan; the actual amount of money you borrow is the principal. Balance is not what you attempt to do before you fall into default; balance is the amount you owe at any point on the loan.

Default is not placing blame: Default means *you* have failed to make the payment on a loan during the time or in the way specified in the loan contract. Forfeit is what you do when you default. You give up something to the creditor. In the case of a mortgage, it is the house. If you default, don't pay back on time, the lender can repossess or take away your collateral. That's a tough way to learn the language of loans.

## Home Is Where the Mortgage Is!

The application forms for a mortgage seem endless, and the lender will ask you for more financial information than you may have compiled in your life. For the purpose of complete record keeping later, you should keep a copy of the completed form. If all goes well, you should know within eight weeks if you have been accepted. If not, you may have to go through it all again with another bank.

You have the mortgage application, have paid the down payment and have sent in change-of-address cards, but are you home free? *Free* is definitely the wrong word to use. Before you can own that mortgage you must repay a bundle more, and it could run into thousands of dollars. First, you will pay a loan set-up fee called points. One point equals 1 percent of the mortgage, so each point for a $60,000 loan would be $600. Seldom could you get off that inexpensively, as most mortgages require three or more points be paid. Also, the property must be appraised; that's two or three hundred dollars. The property must be inspected to make sure the house isn't about to fall down or being eaten by termites. Then there are the prepaids.

You must pay the balance of that first month's interest. Also, in order to protect their investment the lenders collect property taxes in monthly installments. Sometimes the first year's taxes must be paid to the bank in advance. Prepaid homeowner's insurance makes sure that the house, property and mortgage are all covered in case of disaster. Another insurance bill is title insurance to make sure the people selling it have the right to sell and that there are no liens on the property. Utility balances must also be paid, such as the remaining oil in the oil tanks. Transfer and recording taxes must be paid before the sale is final, and if you haven't run out of checks or a balance in your account, the house may be yours.

## Home Sweet Mortgage

Congratulations! After all of that, you probably consider yourself a homeowner, but you are not. You are a mortgage owner; the lender owns the house until the mortgage is paid off or you sell.

Earlier we mentioned how little of your monthly payment is actually applied to retiring the mortgage and how much is interest. On that $100,000, fixed-rate, 11 percent, 30-year mortgage, you would pay the lender $242,832 in interest over the life of the loan. A truly depressing figure. Don't get down; why not whittle down your mortgage and save tremendous amounts of money in the long run? *Unless your mortgage has a prepayment penalty clause, you can probably cut that thing right in half.* All you need to do is add money to each month's check to be used to prepay the principal. As you now realize, the interest is based on the outstanding balance. So as you cut into that balance the interest payments will be cut dramatically. This also has the effect of closing out the mortgage earlier.

Some lenders won't let you close out the loan earlier, but you can still cut down on the principal. Following our example of the $100,000 loan, simply adding $25 a week to the payment would save you more than $39,000, even if you had to hold on to the mortgage for its full 30-year life. On top of that, each payment after the tenth year would get smaller each month.

### Other Real Deals in Real Estate

There are other ways you can build your estate with real-estate holdings, but they can be tricky.

We would not suggest that The First-Time Investor consider dealing with rental real estate or commercial property such as office buildings, shopping centers or parking lots without doing a considerable amount of research into these areas. This book is designed to help the beginner get a solid footing; the people investing in these types of real estate deals are already off and running. This is not to say you may not qualify to join them soon, just that you should seek qualified advice from specialists in the field before you put even $1 into income property.

One type of real estate investment which may be all right for the more experienced of you is a Real Estate Investment Trust. These REITs are a chance to buy shares in real estate deals much as you would buy shares in a corporation. Many REITs (or "reets" as they are pronounced) are listed on the New York Stock Exchange, the American Stock Exchange or traded on the over-the-counter market.

Basically REITs offer you a chance to invest in property

without putting up a great deal of cash. The Real Estate Investment Trusts own property and make mortgage and other types of loans to developers. REITs are often broken down into two types, Equity REITs or Mortgage REITs. Equity REITs actually own apartment houses, condominiums, hotels, nursing homes, office buildings, industrial plants, retail stores and shopping centers. Mortgage REITs are the lenders offering mortgages and short-term construction loans. However, in an effort to protect themselves against rising interest rates, Mortgage REITs often demand a piece of the action. Further, there are a few hybrid REITs which mix their assets between equity and loans.

If you are interested in this type of investment action, homework is very important. People do lose money in real estate as millions of people learned the hard way in 1974 when the bottom fell out of the REIT market. To find out more you might consider writing for a copy of a highly respected newsletter, *Realty Stock Review:*

> Audit Investments, Inc.
> Dept. G
> 230 Park Ave.
> New York, NY 10169

The newsletter gives detailed analyses of REITs and other real-estate stock. When you receive your free copy, you will realize that the annual subscription for the twice-monthly publication is $198. The continuing homework may not be cheap, but it is a lot less expensive than blind decisions which can backfire. Since REITs are an investment, the cost of a subscription is tax deductible.

Real Estate Investment Trusts are not tax shelters, though they do offer some tax benefits. Check with your broker and your accountant before becoming involved in any REIT.

Homeowners already enjoy the most popular tax shelter in America, personal real estate. But your tax preparer may suggest that you should consider even more shelters.

# 12

## To Get Out of the Tax Storms You Need Shelters

The First-Time Investor should never forget the three big lies:

1. The check is in the mail.
2. I will never lie to you.
3. You will never have to pay taxes with this shelter.

Many shelters leak, and it is a fact of life that the federal government is tearing down a number of shelters because they were used to dodge taxes, not to provide shelter against them. Many other shelters such as exploratory oil-drilling projects, research and development shelters and limited partnerships are available only to those who have extra cash to lay on the line.

The IRS commissioner has said that the four fastest audit triggers are, "Tax shelters, tax shelters, tax shelters and tax shelters." For that reason our advice to anyone is not to get involved in any tax shelter without first consulting at least

"I COULD HAVE SWORN THIS CAME WITH A GUARANTEE
NOT TO LEAK!"

one certified public accountant and/or a tax attorney. If the shelter is then given a clean bill of health, go somewhere else for a second opinion. The cost of the exercise is relatively small compared with the cost of a failed shelter or IRS penalties and fines. Also, there is a chance that the consultation with the CPA may be a tax deduction, but check with the CPA on that as well.

Now that we have put the caution bug in your ear, we do want to say there are some tax shelters for The First-Time Investor. Your first is the shelter over your head, your own home. Others include your IRA, which we discussed at great length in a previous chapter, tax-exempt bonds, annuities, universal life policies, and possibly rental properties. We also must mention that because no tax shelter is set in concrete, Congress can change the rules at any time. Some of the old familiar shelters can easily be dismantled by the time you read this, so we advise you to check carefully with your accountant or attorney before taking shelter from tax storms.

With every tax shelter there are several types of risk to worry about: The business/investment risk, tax risk, inflation risk and psychological risk.

The idea of a tax shelter is not to take money away from the U.S. Treasury. On the contrary, Congress has decided that one way to entice people into investing in the future of America is to give the people a few extra dollars with which to dabble. A tax shelter is designed only to reduce your income-tax liability from passive investments, not regular income, so that you can invest in something which both you and Uncle Sam hope will pay off. For you the payoff will be more money in your portfolio, for Uncle Sam the payoff is that a portion of that increased portfolio will eventually be his.

Some argue, "Why make more money, when all I will have to do is pay more taxes?" Sounds reasonable, but it is silly! Wouldn't you rather turn $1 into $5, give the government $2 and have $2 more than you started with?

### Lean-tos Can Fall

One of the wonderful old standby income-shifting shelters had been the Clifford Trust. It was a chance for you to transfer investments to your child's name for ten years before reverting the investments back to you. You got the investment back, the child got the benefit of the income from the investment and it was taxed at the child's rate rather than your presumably higher rate. It was one way to build an education fund for your children and to keep Uncle Sam's greedy little fingers off much of the income. Did you notice the word "was?" A very important word because Congress determined that this was being too generous, so the Tax Reform Act of 1986 took away the important income-shifting benefits of Clifford Trusts.

You can still set up Clifford Trusts; you will pay taxes on the earnings of the trust just as if you had kept the investments in your own portfolio. If the trust is set up by a grandparent or other relative, he or she gets to pick up the tax tab.

The Uniform Gifts to Minors Act (UGMA) is still alive and well, allowing you to put as much as $10,000 a year ($20,000 if you and your spouse give together) into a UGMA account without being subject to the gift tax. But keep in mind that only the first $1,000 dollars of income generated each year by that account will be taxed at the child's rate, after that its at your higher rate. If you invest for growth instead of income and don't sell the assets before the child turns 14 creating a capital gain to be taxed at your rate, the child and you will be way ahead of the tax man. One way to postpone taxes while building a child's account is to buy Series EE U.S. Savings Bonds, as long as they won't mature before the child does (tax maturity in this case is 14). Another possibility could be zero-coupon municipal bonds. They pay no taxable interest. Instead you buy them at deep discount, for instance paying $400, and when the bond matures you get the full $1,000. As you can see, a Uniform Gifts to Minors Act account can be a wonderful investment vehicle for a child, but it isn't the tax shelter or even lean-to it used to be.

## Helping Your Government Help You

The next tax shelter is from the "You scratch my back, and I will scratch yours" category. State and local governments offer you a chance to protect some income if you invest in their debts. Municipal bonds can carry a federal tax exemption on the interest earned, as well as exemption from state taxes in the state of issue. Thirteen states and the District of Columbia don't tax municipal-bond interest at all. Municipal bonds often offer a lower yield than corporate bonds, but that tax exemption more than makes up for the difference for someone in a 28-percent tax bracket or higher.

Is there some risk involved? Most certainly. Consider the case of the bonds issued by the Washington Public Power Supply System. The bonds were tax exempt, but the utility ran into serious problems in building its nuclear power plants and defaulted on more than $2 billion in bonds. One more risk is that rising interest rates can depress bond values prior to maturity. Therefore, it is wise to consider shorter maturity bonds of ten years or less.

Another problem for the small investor is that most municipal bonds are offered in large denominations, no smaller than $5,000, and the brokerage fees can be staggering. For that reason most advisors recommend reducing the overall effect of the high brokerage fees by purchasing municipals in lots of no less than $25,000.

Before you feel completely left out, remember we mentioned that there are tax-exempt Municipal Bond Mutual Funds. Not only are you allowed to invest much smaller amounts, you are also more protected because of the diversification of the fund.

One further option might be checking with your brokerage firm to see if they offer Municipal Bond Unit Trusts. These Unit Trusts often hold a portfolio of twenty or more issues and each unit costs only $1,000. The trust pays a fixed rate of interest, possibly more than a point higher than mutual funds, but you pay for that with a lack of liquidity. There is a maturity date with the municipal bond unit trusts, and if you need to get out before that you may not be able to sell back at full face value because outside bond market forces can make the portfolio value fluctuate.

## Buy Now, Pay Later

When you invest in any of these so-called tax shelters you are using after-tax dollars, but they do shelter income from the investments from taxes either completely as in many municipal bond situations, or until you cash in the investment, as in the case of annuities. Insurance companies like to protect that money from taxation until you retire, when your tax bracket will presumably be lower. This is one of the drawbacks of annuities; they are not liquid unless you pay a severe penalty which, depending on when you pull out, may cost more than the interest earned.

Annuity payments may require a one-time investment of $5,000 or more, or they can call for smaller periodic payments. In either case you should consider the investment side of the situation. Check to see if the annuity pays a variable rate, or if you are locked into a fixed rate for the life of the contract.

Insurance companies also offer something called Universal Life Insurance, a variation on the theme of Whole Life. Part of the premium goes toward covering the insurance costs; the rest is put into a tax-sheltered savings account. The difference is that while Whole Life policies offer only 3 to 5 percent interest, Universal Life offers a variable rate that is more in line with rates for long-term bonds. The two main drawbacks are steep commissions to open the account and lack of liquidity.

## Using Someone Else's Shelter for Your Income

Probably the most popular tax shelter is being a landlord. The laws allow a 27½-year depreciation on the cost of the buildings. Landlords who like to make their rental properties more comfortable to live in by renovating older buildings have the added advantage of some write-offs for some of the improvements. Still, rental property ownership is very complicated, and that is why we suggested in the previous chapter that before you consider such a step you learn as much as you can about raising the money, leveraging the purchase, maintaining the property and dealing with tenants. And ask yourself how you will handle the calls in the middle of the night about the heating or plumbing problems.

If you are considering going solo into rental property, your two closest friends and advisors will probably turn out to be your accountant and your plumber. You will need to feel comfortable calling them at any time to request assistance.

If you really do like the idea of being a landlord, but you don't want to go it alone, you might consider a limited partnership with some friends. You can pool your money, diluting each partner's risk, and start small with an eye to selling and buying bigger properties. We know of several public school teachers in San Diego, who did this in the mid 1960s and were able to parlay their small individual investments into some sizable real-estate holdings. At that point they were able to liquidate their partnership and each go off on his own to build an even larger personal fortune. In this case a small partnership sheltered enough money long enough to grow into a windfall for everyone, not just the teachers but also the taxman.

### Big Time, Big Trouble

It has been estimated that Uncle Sam loses about $24 billion each year to questionable tax shelters, which is why the IRS is questioning each one. To avoid becoming entangled in that mess, avoid any tax deal which promises to shelter any of your active (regular or portfolio) income. Regular income is, of course, wages or salary. Portfolio income would be dividends, interest, and capital gains. So, what kind of income can shelters be used to protect? Simply put, only passive income or earnings from other so-called tax shelters such as rental

**Your Personal $$ Memo: Check with a CPA**

Remember the advice at the beginning of this chapter. Have a CPA check out any tax shelter because should the IRS disallow, say, a $5,000 Tax Shelter, that is only the beginning of the bad news. The second shocker is that the IRS charges 16 percent interest on additional taxes owed, compounded daily. So if you owe an additional five grand, that interest charge is an automatic minimum $870. If the IRS believes your story that you were hoodwinked, you may be off the hook after that. But, if the auditor feels that you should have known better, you will be hit with a negligence charge of 5 percent for underpayment plus another 50 percent of the interest. That works out to be $250 for the underpayment plus $435 in interest. As if that were not enough, if it is determined that you claimed too much depreciation or too big an investment tax credit because the shelter inflated its assets, you could be hit up for another 30 percent of the total amount due, in this case $1,500. If everything is taken care of right away at the audit, your total bill may be kept down to $8,055. All of that hassle, when all you were trying to do was shelter $5,000.

properties or passive income limited partnerships. If you try anything else, you are doing nothing more than sending an engraved invitation to the IRS for an audit.

If you want to be involved in sophisticated tax shelters, work through a reputable brokerage firm and deal only in public programs that have to be registered with the Securities and Exchange Commission. Sponsors of private tax-shelter programs do not have to file financial disclosure statements. Also, the larger public programs diversify the shelter's investments, thereby lowering your risk.

Another advantage of dealing through a broker is that it takes less up front to get in on the ground floor, a minimum investment of between $5,000 and $10,000 when compared to the $25,000 often needed to get in on a private shelter offered by a tax attorney or financial planner.

## Land Barons Beware

We have discussed many of the advantages and disadvantages to real estate as a tax shelter, but one more word of caution: If you are approached to join a real-estate partnership program (public or private), be aware that past partnerships have flooded the market with new construction that may not always have been needed. Beware of those shelters with an eye toward more large office buildings in large cities. The risk may be very high because of over-construction and high costs. Before you enter any real estate tax shelter, understand the goals of the program and study the market trends. They may have changed between the time the prospectus went to the printer and the ink dried.

## Don't Take a Drilling

You may remember when oil was called black gold; now some people call it crude crud because many oil and natural gas drilling operations crashed as the price of oil dropped.

The bad times are not expected to last forever because energy consumption continues to grow and Mother Nature hasn't found a way to mass-produce new reserves of oil and gas. This means that, in the future, oil and gas shelters may once again become profitable ventures.

These shelters encourage new drilling by allowing the immediate deduction of most of the drilling costs, and if the well is a gusher, there are continued write-offs on a percentage of the gross income because of, among other things, the oil and gas depletion allowance.

Before you so much as take out your check book, check with a CPA and, of course, read the prospectus closely. General partners have different requirements, and you may get locked into something more expensive than you had planned. Make sure that your liability is limited only to the amount you have invested. Be sure to pay attention to how much of your investment will be used for the actual drilling or exploration and how much for administration. Find a program that has as much of your own money as possible working on the project before the general partners get to take out their share. Some general partners are more greedy than others, and the terms should all be spelled out in the prospectus.

There are two major types of oil and gas shelter programs, exploratory and developmental. Exploration is extremely risky because wildcatting, as it is called, means looking for petroleum where you think it might be but aren't sure. Developmental programs are less risky because they search for oil and gas in already established areas. As with many tax-shelter offerings, there is some middle ground with what are called balanced programs which offer both exploratory and developmental wells.

## A Get-Away Shelter

If the first and best tax shelter is your home, then after all we have said, the second-best tax shelter may be your second home. It has been said that one reason Congress did not eliminate a second home as a tax shelter is that members of Congress have at least two homes. Even with that in mind, they didn't mind complicating the rules a bit.

The second home, or vacation home, can fall into one of two tax categories: a residence or a nonresidence. If you stay there for more than fourteen days per year, or more than 10 percent of the time you rent it out each year then it is considered a residence. But it still provides some tax relief. You may deduct in full your mortgage interest and real estate taxes. Add to that the possibility of being able to deduct some expenses and depreciation, but never more than the total rent you receive. There are a few more goodies, but again this is where an accountant comes in.

If you almost never use the second home—that is, if you stay there fewer than fourteen days or 10 percent of the total days you rent it, it qualifies as a nonresidence. That means, of course, there is no limit on the losses you can deduct. Did we say "no limit"? There is a limit really because you can only deduct losses from other passive income—income from other rentals and limited partnerships—but you can no longer use paper losses to shelter salary income. It is not quite that simple either, because of passive loss rules for active investors with a gross adjusted income under $150,000, so check with an accountant. Another drawback to the nonresidence rules: the wonderful mortgage interest deduction isn't so wonderful. It is being phased out because in this case it is considered consumer loan interest like credit card interest.

So, what do you do? Many second home owners are changing their ways, using it more for themselves and getting to use the mortgage interest deduction for a second residence.

## Covering Your Shelter

The first rule in protecting yourself when dealing with tax shelters is to remember that you are not trying to dodge taxes, only to defer them for higher profits. Stay away from private partnerships unless you are totally familiar with the investment area, the general partner and the other investors. And don't forget: There is less of a chance of IRS problems with a public partnership.

When examining a tax shelter, have the sponsor give you a copy of the IRS ruling or a tax opinion issued by a reputable legal or accounting firm. You want to make sure the shelter qualifies for the projected write-offs. IRS rulings take time and money, so quite often all that will be offered is a tax opinion of a legal or accounting firm. An IRS audit of a similar offering by the sponsor, which gives a clean bill of health, may be some degree of comfort, but it is not a guarantee that the deductions will be allowed in this new offering.

Demand that the sponsor provide a detailed track record showing successes or non-successes in similar ventures. You stand a better chance if the sponsor has been in business for more than just a few years. Finally, don't just check references but also check to see if the sponsor has the proper regulatory authority to sell the shelter. In other words, is the sponsor registered with the Securities and Exchange Commission?

Some shelters are being advertised as active investments, but they may be playing fast and loose with the rules. One such offering which tax attorneys tell us is questionable demands that when a husband and wife invest, the wife for instance is listed as an employee of the shelter. Then for two weeks a year she actually goes to the site and performs labor in order to legally appear on the books. It is a scheme that appears to meet the IRS tests, but tax attorneys warn that you would probably fail in an audit. And, with the tighter tax rules, anyone dabbling in shelters has about a 100 percent chance of an audit.

# 13

# Gold and Silver Are More than Jewelry

Not all that is gold glitters. But there certainly is something sensual about gold. But The First-Time Investor should be aware that it is very easy to be hurt when swept off your feet in a moment of passion.

Imagine having had the foresight to have bought gold in 1974 when it was selling for a $150 an ounce and then being able to make a killing in 1980 by selling it at $875 an ounce.

Now imagine all those people in 1980 who rushed out to get a piece of the action and then had to sell their $875 gold for the 1985 price of $347, just wishing that they had sold 2 years earlier when it was worth $87 an ounce more. Losing more than $500 an ounce cannot be considered fun. Any investment can go south on you, but few as rapidly as gold.

Silver has made some headlines over the past few years, but in the long haul it hasn't turned into a goldmine either. Still, since it is cheaper by the ounce, it seems more affordable for the beginner. Don't be fooled. The U.S. Government is selling off its reserves on the open market. It is a long-term program, which will keep the price low. That is not all; there are silver mines being discovered constantly, which will keep the supply high. This will satisfy demand and keep the price down.

If this hasn't discouraged you from considering precious metals as an investment, then we shall pass along some suggestions on how to proceed cautiously but wisely.

### The Inflation Insurance

About the only certain hedge against inflation is gold. It is one of the few investments that is considered currency in its current form. It is spendable in every corner of the world, and it is something available to even the smallest investor.

Gold is seen as a security blanket by many people. If the world economy were to collapse and paper money became worthless, goods and services could always be obtained through the trading of precious metals, gems and jewelry.

Some advocates of gold say that short of such catastrophes, even 20-percent inflation could wipe out conventional investments, while the value of gold could soar manyfold. There is, of course, no guarantee, because in recent times of extended inflation gold has consistently lagged. Also, when inflation has fallen, gold has often taken a beating. Still, there are those who feel that if 10 percent of your portfolio is made up of a combination of gold mining stocks and gold bullion, you have bought solid inflation insurance.

Those who want gold because they feel it is disaster insurance probably should not get too excited about gold Mutual Funds. Most invest more in gold mining stocks than bullion, and while they might make good investments, there is little you can do with Mutual Fund shares in a catastrophe where paper money is already considered worthless. The doomsayers believe in the end the only investment that counts is the precious metal itself.

## Bullion Bars Not Cubes

One way to buy gold is by the bar. You can purchase the economy-sized 1 ounce bar or, if you like, the giant-impress-everyone-even-your-enemies-size 400-ounce bar. You might want to keep the smaller one on a chain around your neck, but the larger one is certainly not for the coffee table. About the only recommended storage places for gold are safe deposit boxes or special depository banks. If you take possession in that form you must pay for shipment and insurance, and you must have the bar assayed (weighed and approved) before reselling it.

If you want to hold such large amounts of gold, you might do better by not taking physical possession of the precious metal. The alternative is to buy gold certificates, which are really receipts showing how much gold you own and where it is stored. You pay for that storage, and for insurance, but you don't need to worry about shipping or assaying. Of course you may never actually see the gold, so you must be sure that you are dealing with a reputable broker who has a long and substantiated history. Recently, there have been news reports of some gold certificate dealers being indicted because they not only never had the gold behind the certificates, but they didn't even bother to rent any storage space, even for show, in a despository bank. It was a very low overhead, high-return venture. The poor people holding the certificates found out just how worthless paper can become when there is no gold backing it.

## Gold to Go

Some people might like the security of hearing their gold jingle in their pockets. Keeping loose gold coins is inviting trouble; keeping gold coins in a safe place is much wiser. They are certainly more spendable in a national or world disaster than a gold bar, and they don't need to be assayed when you sell them. That is because gold coins are pre-weighed and certified for their purity during the minting process.

For years the most widely traded and most controversial gold coin has been South Africa's Krugerrand. While people don't fault it for its purity, the apartheid content is more than many can handle, so Krugerrand sales are dropping world-wide.

The new kid on the block is the "Angel" from the Isle of Man. That small, self-governing British dependency in the Irish Sea, equidistant from England, Scotland and Ireland, has decided to compete with the Krugerrand head to head. The Angel, like the Krugerrand, will be 22 karat or .9167 fine gold, which means it has been alloyed and hardened with copper so it will not wear down as rapidly as purer gold. The Isle of Man also certifies that the Angel will contain no South African gold; instead, the metal will reportedly come from Welsh mines, recycled Victorian gold and some gold purchased on the open market in Europe.

Currently the second most popular gold coin in the world is the Canadian Maple Leaf. The purists love it because it is .9999 fine gold. While that means each coin contains exactly an ounce of gold without any added alloy, it is soft and not as suited for jewelry or constant handling as the Krugerrand or Angel.

These gold coins, plus some others not considered top of the line by a number of investors, may be purchased through dealers and are retail-priced for the value of each coin's gold content plus a premium which often runs 3 to 4 percent depending on the quantity ordered.

## Hi-Ho Silver

You may remember all of the hubble-bubble when the Hunt brothers' silver bubble burst in the early 1980s after the price soared to nearly $50 per ounce and then took a dramatic fall to a fraction of that. Silver does not normally make such dramatic moves; during the 1970s it maintained a relatively smooth increase in value at an annual compounded rate of more than 20 percent. Its history since then has not been as rewarding. Those who have dealt in silver ingots believe in a long term, buy-and-hold strategy. Others feel that the last person who put silver to good use was the Lone Ranger.

## A Gem of an Idea

Imaginé buying a white 1.5-carat round-cut diamond for $9,360 and turning around 5 years later and selling it for more than $30,000. That kind of 27-percent annual gain has been quite possible in the gem markets. Then why aren't more people putting their investment dollars into precious stones and making a killing?

There are two reasons; the first is that most people are too sentimentally attached to their fine jewelry, such as engagement rings, to part with them and, second, gems bought to be worn are seldom of investment quality, meaning you can't get even retail prices for them when you sell.

Gems as investments are not a game for The First-Time Investor; leave it for the professionals. If you feel you must invest in precious stones, make sure you deal only with a reputable dealer who has a longstanding reputation of handling only investment gems and not jewels for jewelry.

## A Hollow Ring

If you love to buy jewelry, do so for the enjoyment of wearing it and sharing it. Don't buy jewelry with the expectation that it will be a shrewd investment. About the only jewelry with any investment value are the antique relics kept in the royal vaults or the safe deposit boxes of a few very wealthy people. The point we just made about diamond investing is worth repeating. Amateur investors have neither the expertise necessary nor the money required to make the right purchases.

About the only thing we can do is be good consumers when we shop for jewelry for our own fulfillment. Remember a few rules, such as the karat mark representing the percentage of gold in an item. 24K means it is made of 100-percent pure gold, with each karat representing $1/24$ parts gold. But pure gold is too soft to be used in jewelry without alloys added to make it stronger. So, if jewelry has a mark that says 14K, it has 14 parts pure gold and 10 parts of alloy. The amount of alloy is determined by subtracting the number of karats from 24 (the mark of pure gold). Anything less than 10K can not be called gold under U.S. law. Always look for that karat stamp because only karat gold jewelry IS gold.

Yes, there is another carat measure. No, we didn't spell anything wrong. The carat with a "c" spells out the stone weight of diamonds.

### Dust Is a Collectible

Collecting stamps, coins, limited edition plates, numbered-specially pressed records or Goofie Glasses is a wonderful hobby and very rewarding for the serious collector. Collecting can be personally rewarding, but often not financially because there is no established and regulated market for collectibles. Coin and stamp collectors have the closest thing to a real market through recognized dealers and trading organizations. As for the rest, collectibles are often nothing more than a restful mind game.

You can better spend your time learning about more valuable forms of collection, such as collecting higher yields on other investments such as T-Bills.

# 14

## "T" Time for T-Bills and Other Government Desserts

If you find the risk involved in some investments hard to swallow, Uncle Sam may have some tasty little numbers for you to nibble on. Some of the sweetest are U.S. Treasury Bills (or T-Bills for short). They are considered the most marketable fixed-income securities in the world. The reason is simple: Would Uncle Sam default on U.S. Treasury issues? Unthinkable! If Uncle Sam goes belly-up, you can forget about every other investment you have anywhere with the possible exception of gold bullion and silver.

It may be hard to imagine an investment where you are sure that every cent will come back to you, but that is Uncle Sam's money-back guarantee when you buy securities through the Treasury Department. The guarantee simply states that all Treasury securities are backed by the full faith, credit and taxing power of the U.S. Government.

You might even consider that you will be doing your neighbors a favor because if people didn't buy T-bills, bonds or notes, the government might have to raise taxes constantly to cover its expenses. Instead T-bill buyers are lending money to their powerful Uncle for anywhere from 3 months to 10 years.

"HEY BUDDY, CAN YOU SPARE A GRAND?"

In order to make the process more interesting and easier for the investor, the Treasury offers a wide variety of securities that ranges from T-bills, bonds and notes to securities issued by federal agencies. There are also U.S. Savings Bonds, but we discussed those in Chapter 2. This time we are talking about the big-time government securities.

An easy way to gain experience with this type of investment is by trying the T-bills. They have the shortest term. They mature in 3, 6 or 12 months and are redeemed at the face value of $10,000. Of course, you don't pay that much money for them, you buy them at discount. The difference between the purchase price and the maturity price is the interest you earn. Yes, you do have to pay federal income taxes on that interest. Uncle Sam knows who you are, but you are protected from state and local taxes.

It is possible to sell T-bills before they mature, though on the secondary market you face losing some money if the interest rates have risen sharply since you bought it. That loss is because the price of the bill has been forced into a deeper discount in order to make up for the higher interest rate.

Take note of the Treasury Notes, which are considered medium-maturity notes because they have a maturity date of between 1 and 10 years. However, you don't have to wait that long before you receive some of the interest, because the interest is payable every 6 months. It also doesn't take a great deal of money to get in; if you are willing to tie up the principal for 4 years or more, the minimum purchase price is only $1,000. If you want the principal back in less than 4 years, the minimum purchase price is $5,000, which can be increased in multiples of $1,000.

If you like being bonded to an investment, Treasury Bonds have the longest maturity of all, but the lowest *overall* minimum purchase. Your money is tied up for 10 years or more, but you can get in for only $1,000, which can be increased by multiples of $1,000. The interest is also payable every 6 months. One psychological benefit of Treasury notes and bonds over T-bills is the way they are sold. T-bills are sold in book entry form meaning you receive receipts from the Treasury instead of certificates. Treasury notes and bonds can be either book entry or in registered form, which means you receive an engraved certificate with your name or ownership information printed on it, suitable for framing.

## Color Yourself Patriotic

So you want to put some green into these red, white and blue investments? There are two ways to do it: either through the federal system or commercially. If you follow the federal route, you can purchase government securities through the U.S. Treasury in Washington D.C., or at any of the dozen Federal Reserve Banks or their more than two-dozen branches around the nation. If you do it that way, there is no service charge, automatically increasing your yield a bit. You do pay a commission of between $25 and $50 if you buy them through commercial banks or brokers.

You don't actually need to go farther than a mailbox in order to buy directly from Uncle Sam; you simply submit a government form called a tender. When you do this make sure you have checked off that you want to bid noncompetitively. Competitive bidding is for banks and professional buyers. By being noncompetitive, you will pay the average of the competitive bids accepted by the Treasury. There is no way of knowing what the exact price will be when you submit your tender form, so you must enclose a certified check for the full face amount of the T-bills, notes or bonds which you plan to buy. Once the auction is held, the Treasury will send you a check for the difference between the face value and the discount price. This check is not your interest payment; therefore, it is not taxable; it is just a refund for overpaying. But, the amount is the same as the interest the T-bill, note or bond will pay. When the T-bill, note or bond matures, you get the full face value which of course includes that interest, which is at that point taxable. T-bill auctions are held every week for the 13-week and 26-week varieties, every 4 weeks for the 1-year type. The actual days of the auctions vary depending on which type of security you wish, so check with the Fed or your broker for more details on these money-back offers.

There is one more way in which you can invest in U.S.

Treasury bonds without putting up large amounts of money. Through brokerage houses you can buy what are known as "strips." Each brokerage house has its own pet name, such as CATS, a trademark of Salomon Brothers, Inc., or TIGRS (pronounced tigers), a trademark of Merrill Lynch. No matter what the name, they essentially are the same, created by "stripping" a U.S. Government note or bond into its two primary parts, the interest and the principal of the bond or note itself. Both types are sold at discount and make only one payment at maturity.

If you invested $100 in a strip that offered 12-percent yield to maturity you would earn $1,000 in 20 years. With the same yield $10,000 invested now would grow to $100,000 in 20 years.

Just because these are Zero Coupon Securities, you don't pay zero taxes until they mature. Quite the opposite, because the IRS recognizes the discount on strips as interest income. So each year you have to pay tax on the 12 percent earned as if it were ordinary income even though you won't see the money that was earned until the strip matures. That is one reason why many of these instruments are sold to be part of an IRA or Keogh, or for an account in a child's name for educational planning. (The little one is presumably in a lower tax bracket.)

### More Choices and Chances

If you want to back the American Dream, you can also invest in Federal Home Loan Bank Securities. The Federal Home Loan Banks loan home mortgage credit to the nation's thrift institutions. The FHLB securities do not come with the federal guarantee, but they are backed by mortgages, cash and Treasury securities. The FHLB securities carry maturities from under 1 year to 20 years. The minimum purchase is $10,000.

## Fast Money

Are you the impatient type who doesn't like to wait very long to get your money back? Well, your friendly Uncle has a suggestion. Consider the securities issued by some other federal agencies, which allow you to start immediately seeing a return, not only on the investment, but on the actual principal as well. Some of these are also backed by the full faith and credit of the federal government, the rest by the issuing agency itself. The risk is minimal because until now no agency has ever defaulted, but you do reap a slight reward for the slight risk, as most offer higher yields than Treasury obligations. The most popular are those from agencies which back home and farm ownership.

Some of the names are fun such as Ginnie Mae, Fannie Mae and Freddie Mac. The Maes and Macs used to be very expensive, with minimums ranging from $25,000 to $1 million, but now you can get in on the ground floor for as little as $1,000, depending on the kind you want. These are a different type of investment than you might be used to, because you don't get any money back when they mature. But, you haven't lost your money; instead, you have gotten it all back plus interest before the maturity date. Unlike bonds, the Maes and Macs are called pass-alongs because they are pass-through certificates. That means they pass along part of the principal with each monthly interest check. This can be handy if you need a constant cash flow, but it can be a pain if you have to figure out each month where you are going to put all that money. Another potential hassle is that sometimes these mortgage securities are paid off early and you could be sent a surprise payoff check of a sizable proportion one month. So, these are not for everyone.

## Mae We Talk?

*Ginnie Mae* is the name given to the Government National Mortgage Association, which holds only those mortgages insured by the Federal Housing Administration (FHA) or the Veterans Administration (VA). This means Uncle Sam backs Ginnie Mae all the way.

Your investment can run from an initial minimum of $25,000 for a new certificate from a government securities dealer or a broker, to as little as $1,000 for shares in a Unit Trust or Mutual Fund whose portfolio consists entirely of Ginnie Maes. There could be a sales charge for the unit trust, which is something to keep in mind when considering yield.

*Fannie Mae* or the Federal National Mortgage Association for long, and *Freddie Mac*, the Federal Home Loan Mortgage Corporation are both federally charted. While they are not explicitly backed by the federal government as are Treasury securities, they are guaranteed by agencies tied to the government, making them nearly as safe.

There are fun names and government agency offerings such as *Sallie Mae*, the Student Loan Marketing Association, which is to student loans what Ginnie Mae is to mortgages; *Sonny Mae*, the State of New York Mortgage Agency and *Nellie Mae*, the New England Education Loan Marketing Corporation. Also, there are securities available from the Small Business Administration, the Tennessee Valley Authority and the Farmers Home Administration; even the U.S. Postal Service delivers its own securities.

# 15

## Go for It!

You remain a First-Time Investor until you have put out the money and started to reap the rewards. Don't be afraid to get started. Making money should be, and can be, fun. Look for investments you truly find interesting because it is easier to follow the financial fates of something you enjoy.

As you begin to move into the investment world, you need to maintain a positive outlook and keep plugging. Most of us don't like discussing our failures, but there is hardly an investor who hasn't made a mistake and lost some money. You need to learn to cut your losses and learn from your mistakes. The only way to know when things are going south is by keeping up, doing your homework, keeping good records and being organized.

The only way to get there is to start investing right now. You begin that by setting up your 3-month security net, opening an IRA or Keogh and setting realistic goals.

Only you can set those goals, and only you can meet them. So they must not only be realistic, but specific. First, decide whether you are after growth or income or a combination of the two. That decision depends on your professional, financial and marital status; the number of children you have or plan to have and, finally, your age. A young person should be looking for growth during the time when more risks can be assumed, while someone closing in on retirement may be looking for income in order to finance a more comfortable lifestyle.

During those in-between years your strategy will shift. A single person with no family responsibilities might be willing to take a more aggressive stand with investing, but young couples tend to become somewhat more conservative if children enter the picture.

One of your goals could be educating your children. Planning for a college education must be done early. For example, just $2,000 invested at the baby's birth, left untouched in CDs, could grow to more than an average year's tuition, room and board by the time the freshman year comes around.

If a goal is to become financially independent, you need to specify at what point you want that freedom. You are not doing yourself much of a favor if you do not pinpoint a date; if you are vague, your whole portfolio will reflect that lack of direction. Once you have that date firmly in mind, you will adjust your investment strategy to meet the goal.

If the time-line is retirement, decide when you plan to retire, how much money you will need in order to support your lifestyle and keep that picture in your mind as you make all of your investment decisions.

Before we leave the subject of goals, don't just list them and file the information away for future consideration. Put them into action immediately. Remember, if you don't act, no one will do it for you—procrastination can be expensive.

### Risky Business

As soon as you begin to invest, you will recognize your risk factors if you don't know them already. Whenever you are faced with an investment decision, ask yourself, "Can I tolerate the risk involved and still sleep at night?"

There is a very good chance that you will be able to expand your risk tolerance by continuing to keep informed. Our biggest fear is of the unknown, so learn all you can. Read the business pages daily, starting as soon as you put this book down. Keep up with the various financial magazines; after a while you will find the ones that you enjoy reading and find financially worthwhile.

## Actually Doing It

The first major step you take in investing should be a money fund, to hold not just your 3-month security net, but also to build an investment reserve.

The second step should be some sort of Mutual Fund, to get a feel for the world of investing and enjoy the sense of relief that comes through Mutual Fund diversification. This is where you can first start putting dollar-cost-averaging to work. By investing the same amount in the fund each month, no matter which way it is heading, you protect yourself against an avalanche. By averaging the cost of your investment, you will not be hurt as badly as those who only bought when the fund was up.

The third step is actual stock ownership. Probably the most important rule for an early sense of comfort is to buy investments which you truly find interesting. They can be as close as your career or hobby. If you love computers or word processors and constantly read Hi-Tech type magazines, then that might be an industry worth considering.

## Nervous Yet?

If you are too unsure of yourself to go it alone, consider joining an investment club, which offers a chance to learn and possibly profit with others. Even if you don't profit, the mistakes won't cost as much because every member of the club shares in those as well.

## Walk Don't Run

When you are on your own, don't go hog wild in the beginning. Stick with only one or two stocks and learn from them. After a while, build into a more diversified portfolio with about a dozen stocks. At that size it remains manageable. But don't rush it, because it is easier to learn from a few mistakes than to have everything you have built come crashing down around you only because you lacked the proper experience to handle the task.

As you build the portfolio, look into dividend reinvestment plans that offer the chance to pick up extra shares by paying little or no commission. These plans are another way to cut your risk factor through dollar-cost-averaging.

## The Taxman Will Always Be There

Be aware of your tax liabilities, but don't make investment decisions based solely on tax avoidance; they should always make good investment sense.

Ask an accountant if tax shelters or tax-free investments are even necessary. If you are interested in a tax shelter, consider whether or not you would put your money there even if there were no tax benefits. You need to be assured that the risk is not increased because of the tax benefits. An extremely important point to consider is whether the sponsors have a successful track record with similar investments and with the IRS. Finally, make sure most of all that there isn't even the slightest chance that the IRS will throw the whole mess right back in your face, leaving you with a staggering tax bill.

## Orga . . . Organ . . . Organize

Everything must be taken in steps, especially organization. As you make the first moves toward investing, you should also make your first efforts toward organization. We have organized a list to help you in that direction:

1. Set up a safe deposit box at a bank for holding stocks, bonds and other investment documents that could be negotiable if they fell into the wrong hands.
2. Keep good financial records from day one. The least expensive and easiest way to start is with a looseleaf notebook to record the purchase price, date (for capital gains information), dividends, capital gains distribution and regular entries of the current quotes for every investment. This forces you to pay attention to the movements of the investment without having to rely on your memory. The second record-keeping item for your home is a fireproof strongbox of some type to hold insurance papers, a copy of your will and other important records or documents you can't afford to have destroyed in a fire.
3. Next, you should invest in a file drawer and set up individual files for ease of organization. These should include:
   a. Checking and other Bank Accounts—include the names of the banks, addresses, account numbers and phone numbers.
   b. Time Deposits—Name of institution, date of maturity, account number, principal, interest rate. Listed in that order you will have a visual trigger for rollover times.
   c. Money Fund Accounts—List the name of each fund, address, toll-free number and keep all statements for each account.
   d. IRA, Keogh, 401(k)—List where each is invested and the account number.
   e. All Securities—This is where you keep all stocks or Mutual Fund information by name, number of shares, serial numbers, purchase price, date, and the date when each will become long term.
   Also, keep all stockbroker correspondence informa-

tion including name, address, phone number and account number.
**f.** Insurance Information—List the policy type, number, amount and agent information.
**g.** Credit Cards—List all card numbers and toll-free
emergency numbers. It is also a good place to keep the
receipts and monthly bills.
**h.** Tax File—This is very important for holding on to
receipts for deductibles, capital gain or loss records, and
previous returns.

This is just a start toward organization. If you are fortunate
enough to have a computer, there are numerous programs
available to make the task even more orderly and even entertaining.

## Life and Death Decisions

For the most part investment decisions are not matters of life
and death, but the next two are just that. We need to discuss
Life Insurance and Wills. First of all everyone should have
a will. Imagine being remembered at your funeral for only
one thing, the tangled legal mess you left behind by not
leaving a will. Wills can be very simple and inexpensive, or
they can go on for more pages than this book and cost a fortune. As long as you have one, the only people who will care
about the length are the attorneys.

Life insurance is another matter. Not everyone needs it,
though you should consider some coverage in the beginning. Most of us make the wrong decision when it comes to
life insurance becasue we listen to agents who are only in it
to make a buck.

Rule one with insurance is that you should never consider
life insurance as an investment. It should only be looked at
as temporary protection against your early death. Anything
more than protection means you are paying a great deal more

than you should. Rule two is that you might consider dropping it after the kids are grown, the house is paid off, your pension is set, and you have accumulated a nice portfolio.

The two basic types of life insurance most people get involved with are Term and Whole Life. Term insurance is basic protection, and it is inexpensive when compared with whole life. A $200,000 nonsmoker term policy might cost only $218 a year. A $350 annual premium for whole life might only buy you $20,000 worth of protection. Term is without a doubt the way to go—no pun intended.

The reason for the difference is that only a small portion of a whole life premium goes for actual life insurance; the rest is invested, often for a retirement plan. The problem is that insurance companies traditionally have paid only around 5 percent annually on that investment. As you have learned, you can do a whole lot better putting that difference in a Money Fund or, eventually, CDs.

---

### Your Personal $$ Memo: Life Insurance Shopping

Life insurance shopping is very difficult because rates vary tremendously. Shopping can be made a great deal easier through a service that for $50 will save you hundreds of dollars over a period of years by finding one of the best life insurance rates in the country for your particular needs.

If you already own a policy and Insurance Information, Inc. cannot find you a better deal you get your money back.

> Insurance Information, Inc.
> 134 Middle Street
> Lowell, MA 01852
> 1-800-472-5800

---

### This Is It

This is our final "Heart to Wallet" talk. You already have a better understanding of the world of investments than most

than you should. Rule two is that you might consider dropping it after the kids are grown, the house is paid off, your pension is set, and you have accumulated a nice portfolio.

The two basic types of life insurance most people get involved with are Term and Whole Life. Term insurance is basic protection, and it is inexpensive when compared with whole life. A $200,000 nonsmoker term policy might cost only $218 a year. A $350 annual premium for whole life might only buy you $20,000 worth of protection. Term is without a doubt the way to go—no pun intended.

The reason for the difference is that only a small portion of a whole life premium goes for actual life insurance; the rest is invested, often for a retirement plan. The problem is that insurance companies traditionally have paid only around 5 percent annually on that investment. As you have learned, you can do a whole lot better putting that difference in a Money Fund or, eventually, CDs.

---

### Your Personal $$ Memo: Life Insurance Shopping

Life insurance shopping is very difficult because rates vary tremendously. Shopping can be made a great deal easier through a service that for $50 will save you hundreds of dollars over a period of years by finding one of the best life insurance rates in the country for your particular needs.

If you already own a policy and Insurance Information, Inc. cannot find you a better deal you get your money back.

> Insurance Information, Inc.
> 134 Middle Street
> Lowell, MA 01852
> 1-800-472-5800

---

### This Is It

This is our final "Heart to Wallet" talk. You already have a better understanding of the world of investments than most people. Make use of that edge you have on them and get started. It is your future, and you really do have control over it. This book is not the be-all and end-all book of investments; it is designed as a primer, so that you have a full comprehension of the basics and are able to go on to the more advanced texts with the knowledge gained from *The First-Time Investor*. Nothing would make us happier than if you felt confident enough to tackle some of those books now that you have read this.

The sexual innuendoes and related double-entendres in this book have not been gratuitous because there are so many parallels between sex and finance—the entanglements, involvements, commitments, the chances to reap returns, to learn from our losses, to be enriched, to be fulfilled.

Sexual maturity goes hand in hand with financial maturity in the high rolling, who's-on-top world of the late twentieth century—a world in which both sex and finance call for awareness, flexibility and finesse.

Remember from Chapter One that rule Number One is: **Take Care of Number ONE!** This translates to: Don't ever be the inactive partner in your love affair with—**MONEY!!!**

So . . . . . . *GO FOR IT!*

# Glossary

**Adjustable Rate Mortgage**—A mortgage with an interest rate which can be adjusted at specified intervals. The bank or savings and loan association determines that interest rate based on a particular index of its own choosing outside its control, such as U.S. Treasury bill rates.

**Annualized Yield**—The return on invested capital over a period of one year, taking into account the effects of compounding.

**Annuity**—Though sold by life insurance companies, these contracts are nearly the opposite of traditional life policies. Instead of contributing now to a lump sum to be paid to your survivors, with an annuity you pay regular premiums which will be repaid to you with interest until you die. The repayment, or distribution, usually begins at retirement.

**Application Fee**—When applying for a mortgage, this is the first bill you pay the lender, even before you have borrowed anything. The application fee is designed to cover the cost of the initial paperwork and is often less than $100. This is not to be confused with points, which are the loan origination fee and can run into thousands of dollars.

**Ask Price**—The price offered for a security in an over-the-counter transaction. Normally this is the lowest price a seller will offer.

**Asset(s)**—Property, securities or anything that has a cash or exchange value.

**Asset Management Account**—A convenience or combination account offered by brokerage houses or banking institutions that combines checking, savings, credit-type cards and investment services.

**Balance**—With checking accounts this is the bottom line. The amount in your account after all the checks and fees have been subtracted. With a mortgage a balance is how much you still owe on the total mortgage including the future interest due.

239

**Back Load**—A charge which is attached to some no-load Mutual Funds. While with a no-load you don't have to pay a commission or service charge when you set up the fund, when there is a back load you could be charged up to 5 percent should you cash in the fund in less than five years.

**Balanced Fund**—This is a Mutual Fund designed to provide low risk and high return through a balanced combination of preferred stock, common stock and bonds. These funds can provide a safety net when the stock market as a whole is falling, unlike funds which are invested only in stocks.

**Bankers Acceptance Notes**—A promissory note, a fancy name for a private loan guarantee between bankers and the import/export business.

**Bear Market**—Much like a hibernating bear, the market retreats into deeper slumber and is characterized by a prolonged period of falling stock prices. This is often brought on by a fear of a declining economy.

**Bearer Bond**—A bond which is not registered in anyone's name, and the interest is paid as coupons are clipped by the bearer. While these are no longer issued, those issued before the regulations changed that have not yet matured can still be purchased in the secondary-bond market.

**Beta**—The measure of a particular stock's volatility relative to the stock market as a whole. The higher the beta the more wildly the stock could swing as the market conditions change. A stock with a lower beta will normally rise and fall more slowly than the market. High betas are for those with strong stomachs; low betas, for those with a low threshold for risk.

**Bid Price**—This is the highest price a prospective buyer is willing to pay for a security such as an over-the-counter stock.

**Blue Chip Stocks**—The common stock of a company with a reputation of quality management as well as a long record of profit growth and uninterrupted dividend payments. While most Blue Chips have high prices, they often provide a low yield.

**Bond**—In effect, it is a loan to a corporation or the government or, as is said in financial circles, it is a debt security. These can be long term (20 to 25 years) or short term (8 to 15 years) and pay interest on a regular basis. At the end of the term, it matures and your principal (initial investment) is returned.

**Bond Fund**—A Mutual Fund that invests solely in corporate bonds. Not all Bond Funds are created equally. Some deal in more speculative issues in order to increase the yield. It is important for your own sense of risk comfort to understand the bond fund's investment strategy.

**Bond Market**—While bonds are purchased through a brokerage house or trust department, they are traded through a central Bond Market which is a separate part of the trading floor of the stock exchanges.

**Book Value**—The amount of money that would be left over if the company's assets were sold and all outstanding debts were paid off. An important figure because if a stock is trading below book value, it is sometimes considered a good buy.

**Bull**—Someone who is very optimistic, ready to charge into the market with the belief it is about to or going to continue to climb. Of course, someone can also be bullish on other things such as the economy or industry.

**Bull Market**—A charging stock market, or one continuing to rise with a great deal of stock and bond trading. The anticipation of an expanding economy or lower interest rates can set the bulls running. Bull Markets typically run out of energy after a few months, though that doesn't necessarily mean they become Bear Markets.

**Business Cycle**—A repeated sequence of events in the life of a corporation, affecting the cash flow and profitability of a company. It can refer to the expansion and contraction of both business and the economy. In relation to the economy the business cycle charts recessions and recoveries with the effects on growth, employment and inflation.

**Buying on Margin**—A chance to leverage your investment by putting up a partial payment on stocks and borrowing the rest from the broker. If the stock rises (increases in price) this could increase your actual yield because you had less of your own money tied up in the investment working for you. If the price falls below a certain level, you are forced either to put up more cash or to sell the securities. This is a highly regulated practice.

**Call Options**—By paying a premium you have the right to buy lots of 100 shares of a stock at a specified price before a specified deadline. This is for the investor who basically bets that a stock will rise rapidly and wants to pay a lower price than the specified higher or strike price. Those who sell call options get to keep the premium whether or not the option is exercised. If it is exercised the owner must surrender the certificates and does not profit from the much higher selling price. That profit goes to the person buying the call.

**Callable Bond**—A bond which can be paid off early by the bond issuer, though often if this call provision is exercised, the bond issuer must pay the holder a premium. The exact callable features of each bond are spelled out in the prospectus. The basic reason for bonds being called is when interest rates fall significantly and it is financially advantageous to pay off the higher interest bearing bonds and float a new issue at the new lower interest rates.

**Capital**—Any form of wealth (money, personal property, real estate, stocks or bonds) that is available to be used to create even more wealth.

**Capital Gain(s)**—The profit you earn from any investment. The difference between the price you pay to buy an asset and the increased price at which it is sold.

**Capital Loss**—The negative difference between the price paid for an asset and the lower price for which it is sold. (This can be used to offset capital gains in the same year for federal income tax purposes.)

**Cats**—see **Strips**.

**CD (Certificate of Deposit)**—A timed loan from you to a bank, which pays a predetermined interest rate. CDs can be written for varying lengths of time from a few weeks to a number of years. The money in a CD is not considered liquid (available to you) without your facing severe penalties for early withdrawal.

**Clifford Trust**—This is one of the goodies that Uncle Sam changed dramatically with the Tax Reform Act of 1986. It used to be a wonderful way for parents to set up a trust for their children with the added pleasure of income-shifting. In effect it meant taxes on the trust's income were based on the child's rate, not the parent's. Congress decided that was too generous, and now until a child turns 14 the taxes will be based on the parent's rate not the child's. If you wish to set up a Clifford Trust, see an accountant.

**Closed-end Mutual Fund**—Operates with a specific and limited amount of shares. These are often listed on a stock exchange and are traded as any other listed security. Most Mutual Funds, however, are open-ended and create new shares to meet the demands of investors.

**Closing Price**—The final price of the final transaction at the end of the stock exchange's trading day.

**Collateral**—The asset the borrower provides in order to protect the lender against default. In the case of a mortgage, the house is pledged as the collateral, and if you don't make the payments, the lender has the right to seize the house and sell it to cover the balance of the loan. The lender also has the right to keep any profits left over.

**Collectibles**—Can be an example of hard assets, or sometimes rare objects held by investors with the hope of future profit. Items such as antiques, art, baseball cards and Goofy Glasses may be fun to collect, but it is often difficult to collect profits because of the limited number of buyers and the lack of an organized trading market for most collectibles.

**Commercial Paper**—Short-term IOUs issued by corporations, banks and other borrowers. These are normally only backed by the good name of the borrower; in other words, there is no collateral. Money Market Mutual Funds often deal in commercial paper because it can yield a reasonably safe and profitable return.

**Common Stock**—Shares of ownership in a public corporation. Holders of common stock are allowed to vote on candidates for the board of directors, attend stockholder meetings, and if all things go well, benefit from the good fortune of the corporation through higher stock prices and dividends.

**Commodities Fund**—A Mutual Fund which instead of being in stocks and bonds plays the commodities market. Buying futures contracts in such things as hog bellies (bacon), corn, coffee, wheat and precious metals. This is a very high-risk fund for those who like to gamble on the uncertain future.

**Commodities Market**—The chance to gamble on the future prices and supplies of certain commodities such as pork bellies (bacon), soybeans, sugar and coffee. This is an extremely risky way to invest; in fact more than 90 percent of commodities investors lose more money than their original investment.

**Compound Interest**—The interest earned not just on the principal but also on the interest already earned. Interest can be compounded daily, weekly, monthly or annually. The most profitable is daily compounding because each day there is new interest added to earn even more interest.

**Consumer Price Index**—Referred to as the CPI, this is the government's measure of inflation and the way it affects the average American consumer based on the price of each item in a hypothetical but statistical market-basket. Also known as the cost-of-living index, it is the inflation figure most people use as a benchmark to see how much less a dollar will buy.

**Convertibles**—Bonds and sometimes preferred stock, paying a fixed rate of interest or dividends, that can be converted or exchanged for a set number of regular common stock shares in the same company. It is a chance for a corporation to borrow money at a lower rate than it would have to pay if issuing an ordinary corporate bond.

**Covered Option**—Someone who already owns stock can sell a covered option, accepting a premium in return for the promise to sell the stock at an agreed-upon price by a specified date. This is considered a conservative move in option circles because the option seller gets to pocket the premium no matter what happens. If the option is exercised, the stock has to be surrendered, but the most the stockholder has to lose is the future growth of the stock.

**Company Sponsored Savings Plan 401(k)**—A combination tax-sheltered investment plan and salary reduction plan offered by an employer. As of this writing, generally an employee can funnel up to $7,000 of his or her salary into the plan and escape current taxes on that amount of income, beyond which the income generated by the 401(k) is protected from taxes until withdrawal. Many companies also match part of the employee's contribution, though only 6 percent of the contribution may be matched by as much as 50 cents.

**Coupon**—In bonds it represents the interest the issuer promises to pay the holder. The term *coupon* comes from the fast-disappearing brand of Bearer Bonds with detachable coupons that were clipped and exchanged for the interest payment on the due date. Now with registered bonds there is no clipping; it is all done with electronic transfers.

**Custodial Account**—An account for a child set up by the parents through a bank or brokerage house. While this has been a topic of possible change in Congress, as of this writing the assets of a custodial account are taxed at the minor's tax rate not that of the parents. But the minor cannot make any transactions without approval of the account trustee. The rules are strict in that while a parent can use the money for room and board outside the home for the child's education, the money in a custodial account cannot be used to pay for things which would normally be expected of a parent such as clothes, food or shelter. But this is considered a good tax shelter as the law allows one to give each child up to $10,000 a year ($20,000 a couple) without having to face federal gift taxes.

**Debt Security**—A loan note, bond or commercial paper that represents the money being borrowed. It specifies the repayment date as well as the amount of interest to be paid.

**Default**—What happens when a borrower fails to meet the repayment provisions of any loan. Often in the case of default the collateral is seized and sold in order to cover the balance of the loan. If there is no collateral, the lender may make claims against other assets of the borrower in order to recover the principal.

**Demand Payment**—When a loan has no set date for repayment, the lender can demand its payment at any time. Failure to meet a demand payment can be considered defaulting on the loan.

**Discount Bond**—A bond which is selling below its face (or redemption) value. A deep discount bond is one selling for more than 20 percent below its face value. The difference between the current selling price and the face value is designed to bring the bond's lower guaranteed interest rate more in line with the currently offered higher interest rates.

**Discount Broker**—One who will execute buy-and-sell orders for securities at a much lower commission rate than charged by full service (or full commission) brokers. Discount brokers neither offer advice nor give sales pitches. The savings can be as much as 70 percent less than a full service broker.

**Discounted Certificate of Deposit**—One designed for those who want to have a specific amount of money by a specific date. The bank will tell you how much you would have to put into a CD now in order to have the specified amount of money later. If you needed $10,000 in 3 years and the offered interest rate was 10 percent, then the discounted CD would cost $7,375.46 today. In 3 years it would be worth the full $10,000.

**Discount Rate**—The interest rate the Federal Reserve charges when loaning member banks money. This provides continuity to interest rates as banks set the rate they charge slightly above the discount rate.

**Dividend**—In relationship to stocks, the earnings of a corporation which are passed along to shareholders. The amount per share is determined by the board of directors and is normally paid quarterly. In relationship to Mutual Funds, quarterly dividends are paid out of the income received from the fund's investments.

**Dividend Reinvestment Plan**—Dividends are automatically reinvested in more shares of the same company. This is often done at a discount stock price without the burden of brokerage commissions.

**Dollar-Cost-Averaging**—Buying small amounts of a particular stock at regular intervals no matter whether the stock is going up or down. You buy some at higher prices and some at lower prices which means you average your purchase cost.

**Dow Jones Industrial Average**—A daily index of stock activity published by the Dow Jones Company, which takes the price of one share of each of 30 Blue Chip stocks, primarily industrial, adds them up and divides the figure according to a special formula. The Dow, as it is called, indicates whether the prices of stocks in general on the New York Stock Exchange go up or down.

**Due-on-sale Clause**—Means that a buyer cannot assume (or take over) an existing mortgage on a house. When the house is sold, the mortgage must be paid off in full.

**Earnings-per-share**—The amount of profit a corporation allocates to each share of common stocks. A corporation with a $20 million dollar profit and 2 million outstanding shares of common stock, would have an earnings-per-share of $10.

**Equity**—For the homeowner it is the difference between the balance due on the mortgage and the amount the house would be worth if sold.

**Equity REIT**—A real-estate investment trust which owns the real estate in which it invests. Those who hold stock in equity REITs earn income from rents received on the property and take part in the profit when the real estate is sold.

**Eurodollars**—U.S. dollars held in branches of American banks outside the United States, often for the purpose of handling international business transactions.

**Family Fund**—A group of separate Mutual Funds under one parent fund. The family is often made up of Money Market Mutual Funds, Bond Funds, Income Funds, Growth Funds and Balanced Funds. The advantage for the investor is the ease of switching among the various types of funds to satisfy current and changing investment strategies.

**Fannie Mae**—The nickname for the **Federal National Mortgage Association,** which buys and sells government-guaranteed mortgages to and from banks and other financial institutions. Federally chartered, Fannie Mae issues several different types of securities for sale; most are backed by the full faith and credit of the federal government; others are backed by the government agencies involved.

**Federal Deposit Insurance Corporation (FDIC)**—A quasi-government agency which guarantees deposits in member banks, up to $100,000 per account (though IRAs are separately insured for up to $100,000). (Not all banks are members of the FDIC and their deposits will not have the backing of the U.S. Treasury.) The

FDIC also performs the function of finding new owners for failing banks or making loans to facilitate mergers. The purpose is to avoid dipping into the insurance pool to pay off depositors.

**Federal Home Loan Bank Securities**—Notes and bonds issued to raise money to be lent to savings and loans, cooperative banks and other mortgage lenders.

**Federal Home Loan Mortgage Corporation**—See **Freddie Mac.**

**Federal National Mortgage Association**—See **Fannie Mae.**

**Federal Reserve Board**—The governing body of the central bank of the United States known as the Federal Reserve System. The "Fed" has the job of controlling the money supply as well as being the chief regulator of the nation's banking system.

**Federal Savings and Loan Insurance Corporation (FSLIC)**—A quasi-government agency that insures deposits (up to $100,000 per account) in member savings institutions. Like its cousin the FDIC, FSLIC also protects depositors by finding new owners for failing savings and loan institutions or providing loans to facilitate mergers.

**First-Time Investor**—Just wanted to see if you were paying attention; why of course a First-Time Investor is someone just getting started in the world of investments, who has not yet tried all the exciting possibilities.

**Fitch's**—An investment service that rates corporate bonds and commercial paper and also publishes investor information.

**Fixed Rate Annuity**—An insurance policy which guarantees a fixed lifetime income. The annuity accumulates interest tax free throughout the deferral period. When the fixed payments are received, the interest earned is taxed.

**Floating Stop Order**—A variation of a stop order, which is an instruction to your broker to sell a stock if and when it reaches a certain price. Most often this is to protect your investment when the stock is on the decline. With a floating stop order you instruct your broker to raise the stop price as the stock rises, and you have a better chance of realizing more gain.

**Foreclosure**—The legal process instigated by the lender when mortgage payments on real estate are not met. This can lead to the seizure of the property (such as a home), which can then be sold by the lender to pay off the debt leaving nothing for the borrower.

**Freddie Mac**—The nickname for the **Federal Home Loan Mortgage Corporation,** a federally chartered agency that provides more money for mortgage lending as well as selling high yielding, federally guaranteed securities to investors. Freddie Mac does this by buying up home mortgages from commercial lenders and repackaging them into new securities to be sold on the open market. This is known as the secondary mortgage market.

**Future Deposits**—Subsequent investments in Money Market Mutual Funds after you have satisfied the minimum opening investment. These minimum future deposits are often much lower than the initial deposit.

**Futures Market**—A commodities exchange where futures contracts are bought and sold. The aim is to buy contracts for the future delivery of commodities and then sell them at a profit before the commodities must be delivered. Speculators can deal in anything from hog bellies and wheat to financial futures such as Treasury Bonds and foreign currency. A true gambler's paradise because 90 percent of the traders lose all of their money, but those who win can win a windfall.

**Geographic Funds**—Mutual Funds that invest only in companies located in a certain area of the country. These funds are especially helpful for investors who want to keep their money near home or in industries or corporations that are easier to watch and with which they are familiar.

**Ginnie Mae**—The nickname for the **Government National Mortgage Association,** which sells securities to finance only those mortgages insured by the Federal Housing Administration (FHA) or the Veterans Administration (VA). These securities receive the complete backing of the U.S. Treasury.

**Ginnie Mae Fund**—A mutual fund that deals in Ginnie Mae securities.

**Government Issues**—Government obligations and debt securities such as Treasury bonds, bills, notes, savings bonds and other securities issued by U.S. Government agencies, which the federal government has pledged to repay.

**Government National Mortgage Association**—See **Ginnie Mae.**

**Graduated Payment Mortgage**—Known as GPMs or Jeeps, these feature lower monthly payments in the beginning, which increase over several years to a leveling-off point. This is to provide upwardly mobile buyers the opportunity to buy a home with a mortgage they might not be able to afford if the payments started off at the high level. The concept is based on the belief that as these buyers advance in their careers their income will rise to keep up with the increasing payments.

**Greenmailer**—Someone attempting to take over another company

who accepts a payment from the target company in exchange for
the promise to end the takeover bid. The payment is often a premium offered for the block of stock the takeover artist bought up
in his or her acquisition attempt.

**Gross National Product**—The government's broadest measure of
the nation's economy. The GNP measures the output of all the
goods and services in America, every time produced, sold and
consumed, whether it is a product or a service. It is the indicator
of whether or not the economy is in a recession or if inflation is
out of line. The GNP gives an investor a chance to see if any
given investment is in line with the movements of the rest of the
economy.

**Growth Fund**—A Mutual Fund whose goal is capital appreciation
over the long haul instead of generating income. This is a riskier
fund than an Income Fund because it invests in more volatile
growth stocks which are known for their rapid and extreme fluctuations.

**Hedge Fund**—A Mutual Fund that plays the market by using sophisticated risky techniques such as borrowing against stocks in
the fund's portfolio in order to buy more shares. This kind of fund
also becomes involved in a complicated maneuver called *selling
short,* which is a sell-high-before-you-buy-low move; in other
words the fund legally sells shares it doesn't own, betting that the
price of the stock will fall before it must buy the shares to cover
the sale. Hedge funds are high risk.

**House Account**—One handled by an executive of a brokerage firm
at the main office. In most cases the sales representative does not
receive commissions on these transactions even if it is his or her
account.

**Income Fund**—A Mutual Fund that invests in high-yielding stocks,
bonds and utilities that generate cash income without jeopard-
izing capital. These are for people looking for an income from the
fund instead of growth.

**Index Fund**—A Mutual Fund that picks a certain stock market exchange index and buys some of all of the stocks listed on that
particular index. An example is the Dow Jones 30 industrials.
These Index Funds typically match the performance of the stock
market as a whole.

**Index of Industrial Production**—A government economic indicator
that measures how much manufacturers are producing. This index is quite sensitive to economic downturns.

**Index of Leading Economic Indicators**—The government's economic crystal ball which contains 12 components which forecast ups and downs in the business cycle. A classic interpretation says if the LEI (leading economic indicators) is down, overall, for 3 straight months the economy is headed for a recession.

**Individual Retirement Account**—Called an IRA, it is someone's personally managed retirement account providing a tax shelter for a portion of annual earnings. If you have no other pension or retirement plan, deposits may be tax deductible up to $2,000 a year ($4,000 for a working couple, or $2,250 for a couple with only one working spouse). Interest is allowed to accumulate and compound tax deferred until withdrawal (beginning as early as age 59½). Early withdrawal means substantial penalties including immediate taxation. IRA investments are up to the individual with only a few restrictions.

**Inflation**—The increase in the price of goods and services that decreases the buying power of the dollars in your possession. Supply and demand is the main factor in inflation: when there is too much money chasing too few goods, the prices are forced higher.

**Inside (Insider) Information**—When someone involved in the overall decisions of a company trades on specific nonpublic information that can only come from his or her position at the top. Insider information is sometimes given to a friend so that he too can benefit, all of which is illegal and unethical.

**Interest**—The price that is paid for the use or rental of money.

**Interest-bearing Checking Accounts**—Checking accounts which earn interest on the balance until checks clear. These are referred to as NOW or Super-NOW accounts.

**Investment**—The use of money to earn even more money through property or some other possession acquired for future income or benefit.

**IRA**—See **Individual Retirement Account.**

**IRA Tie-in Account**—A combination of an IRA and a low-interest taxable account at the same institution. This is a bank or savings and loan come-on to attract investors; it has also attracted the attention of the IRS, which could disallow the IRA tax deduction depending on the type of tie-in.

**Issue**—Stocks or bonds sold by corporations or governments (local, state, federal or federal agencies) either directly, through an underwriter or through an exchange.

**Junk Bond**—Lower quality bonds, often considered below investment grade. Because of the very high risk of default these junk bonds can mean extremely high yields.

**Junk Bond Fund**—A Mutual Fund which deals in highly speculative, lower quality bonds known for their high yield.

**Keogh Plan**—A tax-deferred retirement account for self-employed individuals or those who have an income-producing business outside their regular employment. As of this writing a qualified individual can set aside up to $30,000 a year or 25 percent of the net self-employment income, whichever is smaller. Like an IRA this contribution is deducted from the top of gross income for tax-reporting purposes. Interest earned remains tax free until it is withdrawn.

**Leverage/Leveraging**—Using other people's money to generate earnings or gains for yourself. A perfect example of leverage is a mortgage, where a homebuyer gives a lender a down payment while the lender pays the seller for the home. The lender earns interest from the loan, while the borrower hopes the home increases in value way beyond the size of the mortgage. The overall yield is multiplied percentage-wise when compared with the amount of money put on the line. Leverage is also created by using borrowed money to buy stocks.

**Limit Order**—An order to buy or sell a specified number of shares at a specified or better price. There is a chance the market could move too fast and your order may be processed after the stock has fallen below that price. In that case, there is no transaction of your order.

**Liquidity**—Holdings or investments which can be converted quickly into cash. Checking and Money Market type accounts are considered highly liquid, while savings accounts are considered slightly less liquid because in many cases you present your passbook during banking hours in order to make a withdrawal. Stocks are even less so, but much more liquid than real estate.

**Load**—A sales charge or commission charged when buying shares of some Mutual Funds. This sales charge can run as high as 8½ percent for some funds. A charge for withdrawing shares from some funds is called a back load or back-end load. A fund that does not charge a commission at all is called a No-load Fund.

**Long-term debt**—One that must be repaid in a year or more with interest being paid periodically.

**Long-term Growth Fund**—A middle-of-the-road risk Mutual Fund that emphasizes stocks in companies that have both potential for long term growth and a good track record.

**Long-term paper**—See **Long-term Debt**.

**Margin**—The amount of money left on deposit with a broker when buying stock on credit, usually 50 percent or more of the value of the stock. Margin Accounts are established with brokers as a leveraging device, a chance to realize a larger percentage gain compared with the amount of your personal cash actually put into the investment.

**Margin Call**—When a stock purchased on margin falls, the broker can be forced to demand that more money or additional securities be added to the account in order to maintain the margin minimum.

**Mark Down**—Instead of a commission in over-the-counter transactions, the broker earns a profit on the transaction. The mark down is the difference between the quoted price and the amount received from the dealer when you sell off an OTC security. The amount is supposed to be kept at no more than 5 percent.

**Mark Up**—The profit between the price a dealer pays for an OTC security and what you pay when you purchase that security. The amount is supposed to be kept at no more than 5 percent.

**Market Cycle**—The ups and downs of the stock market in general. An up market is called a Bull market, while a market on the skids or in the doldrums is called a Bear market.

**Market Makers**—Dealer-brokers who create their own inventories of securities in the hopes of finding customers willing to buy those securities at a higher price later on. Market makers are registered with the National Association of Securities Dealers (NASD) and buffer the possible wild swings in price.

**Market Price**—The most recently reported selling price of a security on an exchange.

**Market Share Trends**—A company's percentage of sales in a particular industry in relationship to other companies in the same business.

**Marketable Treasury Securities**—Government IOUs sold either directly by the Treasury or through the secondary markets.

**Maturity**—The date when a note, bond or CD comes of age and the principal becomes due and payable to the holder of the note.

**Maturity Risk**—The chance taken with investments that take a long time to reach maturity, thus missing the opportunity to respond quickly to higher interest and missing even higher yields.

**Monetary Policy**—Decisions made by the Federal Reserve Board regarding the money supply. Should the economy be expanding too rapidly, increasing the threat of inflation, the policy may be one of restricting the money supply, called *tight money*. This is accomplished by withdrawing money from the economy through the issue of more government securities, raising the requirement on the amount a bank must keep in reserve and possibly raising the discount rate (the amount the Fed charges banks to borrow money). This in effect makes it more expensive to borrow money and slows business expansion and consumer purchases. In order to make the economy grow more rapidly, the Fed can do just the reverse, thereby adding more money to the system.

**Money Market Deposit Account (MMDA)**—A restricted checking account which earns market sensitive interest rates. The number of checks drawn each month is restricted, though unlimited trnasfers may be carried out at an automatic teller machine. The minimum daily balance is determined by each institution in accordance with federal regulations.

**Money Market Mutual Funds**—Mutual Funds that invest strictly in highly liquid money instruments such as commercial paper, bankers' acceptance notes, repurchase agreements, certificates of deposit and government securities. Most offer more liberal checking privileges than Money Market Deposit Accounts (handled through bankers) and pay Money Market rates of interest.

**Money Fund**—See **Money Market Mutual Funds.**

**Money Supply**—The amount of cash circulating in the economy, as well as money in checking and savings accounts. Too much money in the supply in relation to the output of goods can cause inflation while deflating interest rates. The money supply is controlled by the Federal Reserve Board which measures it as M-1, M-2, or M-3. (See Chapter 4 for a complete breakdown.)

**Moody's**—An investment service that rates bonds, municipal issues, commercial paper and preferred stocks in order to provide investors with an indication of potential risk.

**Mortgage**—A leveraged loan most often used to buy real estate such as your home or commercial or rental property. Until the debt is repaid the house or property itself is used as collateral to protect the lender in case the buyer defaults on the repayment.

**Mortgage Real Estate Investment Trust (REIT)**—Stockholders lend capital to real estate buyers and builders. Some mortgage REITs borrow from banks and relend the money at higher interest rates, a riskier form of REIT because of the volatility of interest rates.

**Multi-Funds**—Very conservative funds that invest only in other Mutual Funds.

**Municipal Bond**—Bonds issued by state or local governments to raise money for special projects such as school, water or sewage projects. Interest payments are usually exempt from federal income taxes.

**Municipal Bond Fund**—One that deals only in municipal bonds; since each bond can cost $25,000, a Mutual Fund allows more individuals to invest smaller amounts of money in a diversified portfolio with less risk.

**Municipal Bond Unit Trust**—Offered through brokerage houses, these Unit Trusts often hold a portfolio of 20 or more municipal bond issues. The trust makes the investment in municipals more affordable for the average investor because each unit costs only $1,000.

**Mutual Funds**—Pools of money from shareholders that are professionally managed and invested in stocks, bonds, money market securities, options or commodity futures, depending on the particular Mutual Fund's philosophy. The main advantage over and above the shared low cost of professional management is the risk insurance provided by diversification.

**Naked Option**—An option is the right to buy or sell 100 shares of a security at a fixed price by a specified date. If you own the stock it is called a covered option; when you don't own the security, it is called a naked option. If the naked option is called, you would have to buy the stock to cover the action and deliver it to the new owner at a possibly excessive price. See **Option and Covered Option.**

**National Association of Securities Dealers (NASD)**—The regulatory body for the over-the-counter market, a nonprofit organization sponsored by the Securities and Exchange Commission as well as the Investment Bankers Conference.

**National Quotation Bureau**—The organization that publishes the Pink Sheet, bid and ask quotes for over-the-counter stocks and the Yellow Sheet for bond quotes.

**NASDAQ**—The computerized quotation system of the National Association of Security Dealers for trading over-the-counter stocks. This does not list all OTC securities, only the largest and most actively traded.

**Nellie Mae**—The **New England Education Loan Marketing Corporation,** which backs student loans in the Northeast.

**Net Asset Value (NAV)**—The price quoted for open-ended Mutual Funds. It is the daily total value of the investments held by a Mutual Fund, divided by the number of outstanding shares. If the investments do well, the net asset value or price of each share goes up accordingly. Of course the opposite is also true.

**Net Price Basis**—Some over-the-counter transactions take place on a net price basis, so that instead of a commission, the broker earns a profit from selling the stock for more than it was purchased.

**New Issue**—A stock or bond being offered to the public for the first time. The offering is regulated by the Securities and Exchange Commission. New Issues are not limited to new or private companies about to go public but are offered also by companies already publicly listed. In the case of the latter, it is often an additional stock or bond issue. The new issues of new companies are considered a risky investment because the issue price is set by the company and may not reflect market interest in the issue.

**No-Load**—A Mutual Fund that does not charge its shareholders a sales fee or commission. In newspaper listings the designation NL in the offer price column means it is a no-load fund.

**Nominal Rate**—The stated rate of interest on a money instrument without any compounding figured in.

**NOW Account**—An interest-bearing checking account with a top interest rate of 5½ percent by law. NOW stands for Negotiable Order of Withdrawal which is a negotiable withdrawal slip offered by a bank or savings and loan in the form of a check.

**Odd Lot**—A round lot is 100 shares; an amount which does not round off to 100 is called an odd lot. People who trade in odd lots often pay a higher commission or price per share (as much as ⅛ of a point more per share) than those trading in round lots.

**Open-End Mutual Fund**—One that issues new shares to meet investor demand without affecting the net asset value. This is because it increases the fund's pool of investment money without affecting the supply and demand for the shares.

**Options**—The right to buy or sell round lots of stock at a specified price before a specified deadline. If the deadline passes without the exercise of that right, the option expires and the option buyer forfeits a premium paid for the option. A Call option is the right to buy, while the right to sell is called a Put option.

**Option Funds**—Mutual Funds that either buy or sell options in order to increase the value of fund shares.

**Over-the-Counter Market (OTC)**—The largest computerized electronic and telephonic national market for those securities not regularly traded on an organized exchange. It is overseen by the National Association of Securities Dealers.

**Passbook Account**—The traditional savings account offered by banks and savings and loans institutions symbolized by the little book used to record transactions. Many institutions are doing away with the passbooks and replacing them with monthly computerized statements, but the savings theory remains the same: high liquidity and low interest (5½ percent).

**Pass-through Certificates**—Securities which pass along part of the principal with each monthly interest check so that before the maturity date all of the principal has been repaid. Ginnie Maes, Fannie Maes and Freddie Macs are examples of pass-throughs.

**P/E**—See **Price-Earnings Ratio.**

**Penny Stock**—Inexpensive stocks traded over-the-counter; while they usually cost more than a penny, most sell for less than $1 a share. Though after the initial public offering they may increase to $10 or more, they quickly resettle at a lower price. Penny stocks are highly volatile because they are issued by companies without much of a profit or revenue history.

**Performance Fund**—A Mutual Fund that goes for capital growth instead of income by investing in rapidly growing companies which often do not pay dividends. There is a higher than normal risk with Performance Funds, but that can be balanced by a higher than average return on invested capital.

**Pink Sheet**—The daily published bid and asked prices of thousands of over-the-counter stocks. Compiled by the National Quotation Bureau, the Pink Sheets are delivered to brokers and dealers each day and cover many stocks not carried in daily OTC newspaper listings.

**Points**—Charged by almost all mortgage lenders, these points are considered processing fees, though they do increase the overall yield to the lender. One point equals 1 percent of the total loan; on a $50,000 mortgage that would mean $500. A mortgage can cost between 1 and 4 points. While this may seem like an interest payment, it is only considered the cost of doing business by the IRS; therefore, points are not tax deductible.

**Portfolio**—The combined holdings of all of your investments, including stocks, bonds, real estate or any liquid assets.

**Preferred Stock**—Shares in a corporation that pay a set dividend often three times more than common stock. Some consider it risk insurance because preferred stock has a claim on a corporation's assets before common stock. Unlike common stock, preferred stock does not rise as rapidly in good times, nor do its owners have voting rights.

**Prepayment Penalty**—A fee paid to a lender when a mortgage is repaid before a preset date. In the past, prepayment clauses assessed the penalty if a house was sold before the expiration of the mortgage; now if there is such a clause, it is usually limited to only 2 to 5 years.

**Price-Earnings Ratio**—The **P/E** is a listing that tells you how much "price" you have to pay for $1 of corporate earning power. The P/E is determined by dividing the current market price of 1 share of the stock by the company's per share earnings. For example, a company whose stock selling for $40 earned $2 a share has a P/E of 20. That simply means it is selling for 20 times earnings and appears to be on its way to growth. The higher the P/E, the higher the risk because low P/E stocks tend to be either low-growth or mature companies.

**Prime Interest Rate**—The rate banks charge their biggest and most creditworthy commercial customers on unsecured loans. For the rest of us the movement of the Prime is an indicator of which way consumer rates may go.

**Prime Rate**—See **Prime Interest Rate**.

**Principal**—In banking: the balance due on a loan, not counting the interest. In investments: the basic amount invested, not counting the earnings.

**Private Mortgage Guarantee Insurance (PMI)**—A charge often added to a mortgage payment when there is a very low down payment; it protects the lender against the costs of default and foreclosure.

**Producer Price Index (PPI)**—Formerly called the wholesale price index, it is a monthly government inflation indicator. The PPI measures the price changes of goods that are finished, completely processed and ready for sale to the ultimate user, retailer or consumer. It is considered a long view of inflation and gives consumers a feel for the pinch they may feel on the retail level in several weeks' time.

**Prospectus**—A document written by lawyers for bankers and seemingly designed to confuse buyers, but it can give investors all the pertinent facts, figures and history of a company. Securities and Exchange Commission rules say a prospectus must be presented to a prospective buyer before purchase or investment.

**Proxy**—A shareholder's written designation of someone else to vote on behalf of the shareholder at a stockholder's meeting. Normally a proxy pertains to the election of the Board of Directors or various other proposals put before the shareholders for their approval.

**Put Options**—A contract granting the right to sell a certain number of shares of a stock at a specified price before a specified deadline. Someone who expects the stock to fall buys a Put, paying someone to buy that stock at the set price by the exercise date. This can provide a cushion against falling prices while you hold on to the stock until the price hits what you consider bottom or the strike price. The person who sells the Put is betting that the stock won't drop that much and that he won't be forced to purchase the stock. If you don't exercise the option, the put seller loses nothing and keeps the premium.

**Real Estate Investment Trust (REIT)**—see **Mortgage Real Estate Investment Trust.**

**Recession**—When the nation's economy as a whole slows down; characterized by, among other things, at least two quarterly declines of the gross national product, an increase in unemployment, slowdown of the production of goods and services as well as a drop in the stock market.

**Recovery**—When the business cycle begins to climb out of a recession or depression; economic activity has picked up and the GNP has shown an increase for at least two consecutive quarters leading to increased production of goods and services, lower unemployment, economic expansion and a rising stock market.

**Renegotiable Rate Mortgage (RRM)**—A hybrid fixed/adjustable-rate mortgage. Payments are set up as they are for the traditional 30-year mortgage, but at the end of 3 to 5 years the interest rate is renegotiated with a guarantee of renewal and no balloon payment (a final payment substantially larger than the previous installments).

**Representative Ask Price**—In over-the-counter listings on NASDAQ it is the lowest price a seller was willing to accept for that day, not the fixed or final price received on most transactions.

**Representative Bid Price**—In over-the-counter listings on NASDAQ it is the highest price a buyer was willing to pay on that day, not the fixed or final price paid on most transactions.

**Repurchase Agreements (REPOS)**—A type of short-term investment favored by Money Market Mutual Funds, whereby the fund loans money to a bank overnight and the bank agrees to buy back the loan the next business day.

**Revenue Notes**—Municipal bonds that are paid off by the income earned from the completed projects. Several examples include bonds to build toll bridges, toll roads and stadiums that provide public service and generate revenue.

**Reverse Split**—When a corporation believes its stock is too low to interest new investors, it reduces the number of outstanding shares in order to raise the price of each outstanding share. For example, a firm with 5 million outstanding shares selling for $10 performs a reverse 1 for 5 split; the firm will end up with 1 million shares selling for $50.

**Risk**—The measurable possibility of losing money.

**Rollover**—Funds moved from one investment into another. For instance when a 6-month CD matures, the principal plus interest could be automatically rolled-over into a new CD with a new maturity date.

**Rollover Mortgage (ROM)**—Payments are set up much like a traditional 30-year fixed-rate mortgage, except at the end of 3 to 5 years, the loan has to be refinanced or the balance must be paid off.

**Sallie Mae**—The **Student Loan Marketing Association,** a quasi-government corporation that is publicly traded and guarantees student loans it has purchased on the secondary market from the original financial institution. Sallie Mae also provides financing to state student loan agencies. All of this is accomplished through the sale of short-term and medium-term notes.

**Savings and Loans**—Federally- or state-chartered financial institutions that receive the bulk of their deposits from consumers and most of their income from home mortgages.

**Securities and Exchange Commission (SEC)**—A federal agency to protect the public from malpractice in the securities markets.

**Sector Fund**—See **Single Industry Funds.**

**Self-Directed IRA**—An individual retirement account that can be actively managed by the individual who directs a brokerage house to carry out the investment decisions.

**Sentiment Indicators**—Different measures of the moods of investors. For example, while many may think good times are coming when the general mood of investors is bullish, many technical analysts will see the situation as just the opposite, that the market is ready to fall. When most investors are bearish, technical analysts often believe the market is about to jump.

**Share**—A unit of stock or unit of ownership in a corporation.

**Shared-Appreciation Mortgage (SAM)**—A lower-interest-rate mortgage where the lender gets to share in the eventual profits when you sell or refinance a home. One problem is that some SAMs contain language allowing the lender to demand its share before you may want to sell or refinance.

**Short Sale**—Selling stock you don't own, with a plan to buy it back at a lower price before it must be delivered to the buyer. This is accomplished by borrowing stock from a broker. It is a sell high and then buy low philosophy.

**Short-Term CD**—A certificate of deposit with a maturity date of under 1 year.

**Short-Term Debt**—A loan or obligation which must be paid off within 1 year.

**Short-Term Paper**—An investment with a maturity of less than 1 year and as short as overnight.

**Simple Interest**—Based only on the original principal. The interest earned is not allowed to be added to the principal to earn even more money as in compound interest.

**Single Industry Funds**—Mutual Funds that invest only in companies in one industry.

**Sonny Mae**—The **State of New York Mortgage Agency,** which sells securities to back home mortgages in New York State.

**Specialist**—The broker's broker on the floor of the exchange. As a floor member of the exchange, it is the specialist's job to maintain an orderly market in specific securities by buying up and selling off securities to counteract temporary imbalances in supply and demand and to prevent the whipsaw of wide swings in stock prices.

**Specialty Funds**—Mutual Funds that concentrate on a single industry. An example might be a fund that deals only in the herbicide end of the chemical industry.

**Split**—Increasing the number of outstanding shares in a corporation by dividing existing shares. With a 2-for-1 split an individual stockholder would end up with twice as many shares, but each would initially be worth only half as much as the original. For example, a corporation with 1 million outstanding shares selling for $50 each would end up with 2 million shares selling for $25. Corporations often call for stock splits in order to expand their stock base to make the price more attractive to investors.

**Standard and Poors Corporation**—Provides a wide range of investment services including the rating of bonds (corporate and municipal), stocks (common and preferred) and commercial paper.

**Standard and Poors Index**—Commonly known as the Standard and Poors 500 (or S&P 500), it is a daily measure of the movement of the stock market based on the averages of 500 widely held common stocks.

**Stock**—A share or piece of a company. When you own stock, you become a part owner and get to enjoy the company's good fortunes through rising stock value, or its failures through falling stock value. Stock is issued to raise capital.

**Stock Exchange**—The organized marketplaces where stocks and bonds are traded for customers by exchange members acting as both brokers and dealers. These include the New York Stock Exchange, the American Stock Exchange and regional stock exchanges.

**Stock Market**—The generic name for the stock exchanges.

**Stock Split**—See **Split**.

**Stop Order**—Instructions left with your broker to sell a stock when it reaches a certain price. This is often done to protect against a loss when the stock is falling.

**Street Name**—Stock which is held in the broker's name or someone else appointed by the legal owner or customer.

**Strike Price**—The exercise price or dollar-per-share price in options at which a Call Option buyer can purchase the stock or a Put Option buyer can sell the stock.

**Strips**—A Zero Coupon type certificate that is created by brokerage houses who strip U.S. Government notes or bonds into their two primary parts, the interest coupon and the principal of the bond or note itself. The certificate representing the interest is sold as a short- or medium-term Zero Coupon Security. The certificate representing the principal then becomes a long-term Zero Coupon Security. Each brokerage house has its own pet name, including Salomon Brother's CATS or Merrill Lynch's TIGRS (pronounced tigers).

**Super-NOW Account**—An interest-bearing checking account that offers a higher interest rate than a normal NOW account. The Super-NOW often requires a much higher minimum balance than a NOW but less than a Money Market Deposit Account. Unlike an MMDA, a Super-NOW offers unlimited check writing.

**Takeover**—Either a friendly acquisition and merger or an unfriendly bid to gain controlling interest of a corporation. A hostile takeover, which is designed to replace the current management, is often attempted through a tender offer of paying shareholders a premium over the market price of the stock.

**Target Company**—A corporation chosen as a takeover possibility.

**Tape**—Also known as the **ticker tape**, it is the running service which reports the transactions on major stock exchanges, including prices and volume of transactions. Many brokerage houses display the tape on a running electronic sign for all to see.

**Tax-Free Money Market Fund**—One which invests only in bonds exempt from federal taxation.

**Tax Shelter**—An investment that protects its income from current taxes; while it might reduce tax liability it is not a way to avoid taxes altogether because eventually taxes will be paid on the gains.

**Tender Offer**—In a takekover bid it is an offer to buy shares of a corporation, usually at a premium above market price.

**Term Life Insurance**—Basic life insurance protection written for a specific period that pays only upon death. Because a policy holder is only paying for protection in the event of death, it is cheaper than whole life insurance, which is a forced saving plan that builds in cash value.

**Ticker**—See **Tape**.

**TIGRS**—See **Strips**.

**Tip**—Information passed along from one person to another on the possibility of up or down action of a stock. An inside tip gives information about certain corporate moves that may affect the price of the stock and comes from an insider who knows this information before it is public knowledge. Insider information is strictly illegal to pass along or act upon.

**Trading Pattern**—The long-range measure which shows the up and down direction of a security.

**Treasury Bills (T-Bills)**—Debt obligations of the U.S. government, backed by the full faith and credit of the federal government. T-Bills are short term securities with maturities of 1 year or less sold through the Federal Reserve with a minimum face value of $10,000.

**Treasury Bonds**—Long-term debt obligations of the U.S. government, backed by the full faith and credit of the federal government. Treasury Bonds have maturities of 10 years or longer and are sold through the Federal Reserve with a $1,000 minimum.

**Treasury Note**—Medium-maturity debt obligations of the U.S. government, backed by the full faith and credit of the federal government. Treasury Notes have maturities ranging from 1 to 10 years and are sold through the Federal Reserve in denominations ranging from $1,000 to more than $1,000,000.

**Uncovered Option**—See **Naked Option**.

**Underwriter**—An investment banker or brokerage house who agrees to purchase a new issue of stocks or bonds from a company and resell the issue to investors, thereby making a profit between the primary distribution price and the public offering price.

**Uniform Gift to Minors Act**—A law that sets forth rules for the distribution and administration of custodial accounts for children. (See **Custodial Account**)

**Unit Investment Trust**—An investment vehicle that buys a fixed portfolio of bonds, mortgage-backed securities or preferred stocks for their income-producing capabilities and holds on to those investments until they mature, at which time unit holders recover the principal. Units in the trust are sold through brokerage houses and usually cost a minimum of $1,000 each.

**U.S. Government Agency Issues**—Securities such as Ginnie Maes, Fannie Maes or Freddie Macs issued by agencies of the U.S. Government. While these have high credit ratings, they are not considered to be backed by the full faith and credit of the government.

**U.S. Savings Bonds (series EE)**—The U.S. Government bond most widely available to the average consumer. Sold with face values ranging from $25 to $10,000, these bonds are sold at discount and offer both variable market-tied interest rates and a guaranteed minimum of 7.5 percent. Savings Bonds are often offered through payroll deduction plans at work.

**Universal Life Insurance**—A combination of a term life insurance and a tax-deferred savings account, earning Money Market rates of interest.

**Variable Market-tied Rates**—Interest rates that are based on the movements of the Money Markets, often pegged to one certain rate such as T-Bills.

**Venture Capital Funds**—Mutual Funds that provide money for corporations in their infancy in exchange for a percent of the common stocks and a share of the actual profits. These are considered somewhat risky but provide an above-average potential for return.

**Volatility**—The measure of the rapid and extreme fluctuations of a stock, bond or commodity.

**Warrant**—A fancy investment-type come-on by a stock-issuing corporation that authorizes the investor to buy a share or shares of common stock of the corporation at a set price during a specified period of time.

**Whipsaw**—The volatile movements of the market. Someone is whipsawed when he or she gets caught up by the volatility and loses by buying just before prices fall, or sells just before they jump.

**Yankee Dollars**—CDs held in a foreign bank though purchased through that bank's branches in the United States.

**Yield**—The return on an investment, also referred to as the income received from investments.

**Yield Rates**—The return on investments expressed as a percentage. Yield rates on stocks are determined by dividing the present indicated annual dividend by the market price of a single share.

**Zero Coupon Bonds**—Sold at deep discount and do not offer periodic interest payments; instead the interest is distributed when the bond matures.

**Zero Coupon CDs**—Certificates of Deposit sold at discount that pay no interest until maturity. These are usually sold through brokerage houses for a commission.

# Bibliography

The best way to better your fiscal condition is to continue to exercise your mind as well as your wallet. There are many wonderful books to assist you now that you have a basic knowledge of the world of investing; obviously we cannot include them all. To help, we have compiled a short list of some of the books we would recommend as further reading.

Bashinsky, Sloan. *Home Buyers: Lambs to Slaughter?* Hillsborough, North Carolina: Menasha Ridge Press, 1984. Distributed by Simon & Schuster, this is an easy-to-read guide to buying the home you want at the right price. These suggestions could save you countless dollars and countless heartaches.

Bashinsky, Sloan. *Selling Your Home $weet Home.* Hillsborough, North Carolina: Menasha Ridge Press, 1984. Distributed by Simon & Schuster, this is a survival guide for selling your home. A companion book to *Home Buyers: Lambs to Slaughter?* and just as informative.

Crittenden, Alan. *The Almanac of Investments.* Novato, California: Crittenden Books, 1984. An in-depth look at the performances of 80 top investments.

Donoghue, William E., and Thomas Tilling. *William E. Donoghue's Complete Money Market Guide.* New York: Harper & Row, 1981; New York: Bantam, 1982. This remains the benchmark book on Money Market Mutual Funds. The book is credited with popularizing the funds. While some of the figures may be dated, the basic information remains solid.

Donoghue, William E., and Thomas Tilling. *William E. Donoghue's No-Load Mutual Fund Guide.* New York: Harper & Row 1983; New York: Bantam, 1984. This book contains extremely helpful information on how to use Mutual Funds for low-risk, high-yield investing while avoiding fees and commissions.

Donoghue, William E. *William E. Donoghue's Guide to Finding Money To Invest.* New York: Harper & Row, 1985. As the title suggests, this book helps the reader better understand how to build a lifetime savings and investment program with existing, but hidden, cash reserves.

Egan, Jack. *Your Complete Guide to IRAs and Keoghs.* New York: Harper & Row, 1982. While the laws continue to change on tax-deferred retirement accounts, the basic information in this book remains sound. It was the first book devoted exclusively to these accounts and remains the benchmark.

German, Don and Joan. *The Only Money Book For The Middle Class.* New York: William Morrow and Company, Inc., 1983. A highly readable and informative book on all aspects of money management based on their philosophy, "Economics of Enough."

Jacobs, Sheldon. *The Handbook For No-Load Investors.* Hastings-on-Hudson, N.Y.: No-Load Fund Investor, Inc., 1985. A one-stop book for investors interested in no-load funds, it contains facts, strategies and timing techniques, including a number of funds for IRAs and Keogh plans.

Krefetz, Gerald. *How To Read and Profit from Financial News.* New York: Ticknor & Fields, 1984. Once you understand the basics of investing, this book will take you deeper into understanding how to use the wealth of information at your fingertips for personal gain.

Porter, Sylvia. *Sylvia Porter's New Money Book for the 80's*. New York: Doubleday, 1979. With 1200 pages of in-depth information, it is not one that can be read from cover to cover, but it is an indispensable resource.

Tobias, Andrew. *The Invisible Bankers*. New York: Linden Press, 1982. If you really want the inside scoop on the insurance industry, this is a highly readable exposé.

Schwab, Charles. *How To Be Your Own Stockbroker*. New York: Macmillan, 1984. This is from the man who built the largest discount brokerage firm in the nation. It has excellent follow-up information for the person who doesn't want to deal with a broker.

Weinstein, Grace W., *The Lifetime Book of Money Management*. New York: New American Library, 1983. An all-purpose book for personal financial planning, an excellent addition to any consumer's personal financial library.

# Index

# About the Authors

BOB MADIGAN is a host of NBC's Talknet, America's highest rated talk-radio network. His nationally broadcast financial talk show can be heard on more than 300 radio stations. Also, Bob Madigan's daily financial feature, "The Money Memo," on NBC's Young Adult Network, The Source, is distributed to more than 135 radio stations nationally and worldwide via the Armed Forces Radio and Television Service.

As an NBC News correspondent Bob Madigan covered a variety of news stories around the world, from Washington to Moscow, reporting on events such as the accident at Three Mile Island, the return of the American hostages from Iran, The Royal Wedding in the United Kingdom, the changing economic scene in the Soviet Union, presidential campaigns, political conventions, and elections.

Bob holds an Overseas Press Club Award, the Janus Award from the Mortgage Bankers Association, The National Association of Realtors Award, the International Radio Festival Award, an Armstrong Award, Freedom Foundation Award, an Ohio State Award, a Deadline Club Award from Sigma Delta Chi, a Headliners Club Award, the Roy T. Howard Award for Journalism, the San Fransisco State Journalism Award, the International Billboard Award, and two Golden Mikes from the Radio Television News Association of Southern California.

LAWRENCE KASOFF has been the director of "The Money Memo" on The Source, NBC radio's Young Adult Network, since its inception. In that capacity he is responsible for the continuing direction of this daily feature as well as long-form financial programs on The Source Report. His other directorial, production, and engineering responsibilities include pre- and post-show production as well as the live on-air operation of the NBC Television and Radio Networks. Larry has been involved with the creative, directorial, and production ends of such programs as NBC Nightly News; The Today Show; Another World; Democratic and Republican National Convention coverage; presidential primaries and elections; the Rose, Fiesta, and Orange Bowl games; the Grammy and Emmy awards programs, and space-flight coverage.

Lawrence Kasoff's numerous awards include The National Association of Realtors Award, an Armstrong Award, a Deadline Club Award from Sigma Delta Chi, an Ohio State Award, the International Radio Festival Gold Award, a Headliners Club Award, and the Gabriel, Freedom Foundation, and Clarion awards.